PRAISE FOR *ZCONOMY*

"*Zconomy* is the guide that leaders need to engage this new generation of consumers and employees, and transform the future of their own enterprise."

—Erik Anderson, executive chairman of Topgolf Entertainment Group and founder of WestRiver Group

"*Zconomy* is a must-read guide from the most authoritative voices on generational studies of our time. It is insightful, comprehensive, and uses real-world practical applications to provide invaluable guidance in navigating this generation of disruptors."

—Andrea Brimmer, Chief Marketing and PR Officer of Ally Financial

"Dr. Denise Villa and Jason Dorsey deliver a rare combination of research, insights, strategies, and practical knowledge that any executive can immediately use to understand Gen Z, unlock its potential, and shape the future of their business."

—William Cunningham, PhD, member of the boards of directors of Southwest Airlines and Lincoln Financial, and former chancellor of the University of Texas System

"*Zconomy* delivers the stories, insights, and actions that leaders of every generation can use to bravely lead Gen Z in a post-pandemic world."

—Alison Levine, *New York Times* bestselling author of *On the Edge: Leadership Lessons from Mount Everest and Other Extreme Environments*

"Well researched, entertaining, and packed with practical tools and advice, *Zconomy* should be your go-to guide for unlocking the huge potential of Gen Z."

—Andy Sieg, president of Merrill Lynch Wealth Management

"*Zconomy* is a must-read. Dr. Villa and Dorsey deliver much-needed strategies, missing data, and insights for executives, business leaders, and board members who need to understand how to engage with Gen Z."

—Martin Taylor, managing director of
Vista Equity Partners and president of OneVista

"Listen to Denise and Jason! As someone on the front lines of entertainment and culture, I highly recommend *Zconomy*. Every creator, leader, and parent should read this book."

—Kenan Thompson, longest-tenured
cast member of *Saturday Night Live*

"Jason's work with our team has had a profound impact on how we communicate with our consumers and manage our multigenerational workforce."

—Steven Williams, CEO of PepsiCo Foods North America

"*Zconomy* is exactly what CEOs, board members, and innovators need to read to strengthen their future with Gen Z. It provides a clear and valuable road map of how to connect and build employee engagement and customer loyalty."

—Betsy Atkins, member of the boards of directors
of Volvo Car AB, Wynn Resorts, and Oyo

"*Zconomy* delivers the step-by-step solutions leaders need to understand Gen Z and take action right away."

—Steve Cannon, CEO of AMB Sports + Entertainment
(owners of the Atlanta Falcons) and former
president and CEO of Mercedes-Benz USA

ZCONOMY

ZCONOMY

How Gen Z Will Change the Future of Business—and What to Do About It

JASON DORSEY AND **DENISE VILLA, PhD**

HARPER
BUSINESS

An Imprint of HarperCollinsPublishers

HarperCollins books may be purchased for educational, business, or sales promotional use. For information, please email the Special Markets Department at SPsales@harpercollins.com.

FIRST EDITION

Art by JBOY/Shutterstock, Inc.

Library of Congress Cataloging-in-Publication Data

Names: Dorsey, Jason R. (Jason Ryan), author. | Villa, Denise, author.
Title: Zconomy: how Gen Z will change the future of business-and what to do about it / Jason Dorsey and Denise Villa, PhD.
Description: First edition. | New York, NY: HarperBusiness, [2020]
Identifiers: LCCN 2020004002 (print) | LCCN 2020004003 (ebook) | ISBN 9780062970299 (hardcover) | ISBN 9780062970305 (ebook)
Subjects: LCSH: Young consumers. | Generation Z. | Organizational change. | Intergenerational relations—Economic aspects.
Classification: LCC HF5415.332.Y66 D67 2020 (print) | LCC HF5415.332.Y66 (ebook) | DDC 339.4/70842—dc23
LC record available at https://lccn.loc.gov/2020004002
LC ebook record available at https://lccn.loc.gov/2020004003

20 21 22 23 24 LSC 10 9 8 7 6 5 4 3 2 1

I dedicate this book to my grandfather Murry Ulin, who taught me about life, history, a good story, and bridging generations. I am grateful for him and am inspired by his memory every day.

—Jason

I dedicate this book to our daughter, Rya. She brings me more joy than I ever thought was possible. Her strength, warmth, and zest for life make me want to be a better human. I love you more than all the stars in the sky.

—Denise

Each new generation brings changes to humanity.
Let's embrace the change and be part of the story.

—DENISE VILLA, PhD

CONTENTS

ZCONOMY

GEN Z IS HERE

Jack remembers exactly when he saw the pineapple cake ad.

It appeared in his Instagram feed as he was scrolling. The video was of a young woman showing how to bake a cake "that looked exactly like a pineapple." Jack clicked on the ad and watched the video on YouTube. He said it was *so cool* that he immediately binge-watched more videos of the cake maker on his phone.

After watching more than fifty videos, Jack tried to bake his first cake. He failed. Then he tried his second cake. He failed. Then his third cake. He failed. And he kept trying over and over and over. And kept failing and failing and failing.

Finally, after two months of trying to bake a cake that looked right, he made one that he thought was good enough to post on Instagram. As he recalls with a huge smile, "It was the first photo I ever posted on Instagram that got over one hundred likes!" His friends commented, "OMG!" and "Howd u learn that?"

Jack loved the artistic side of baking and trying new ways to decorate the cakes. He began baking two cakes *every weekend* and then posting them in photos and videos over the next week. One by one people would follow him on Instagram and leave comments. "Hello from Brazil!" and "Great cake—Barcelona!" The cake decorator, whose *two hundred videos* he had now watched to learn how to bake, followed him and started featuring his cakes.

When asked why he chose baking cakes over other hobbies or activities, Jack says, "I tried sports, but I wasn't any good at it and, worse, you fail in front of an entire audience filled with people. Baking cakes you just fail in your kitchen. I kept failing and failing but just kept going."

His favorite baking experience so far: "I got to bake a cake for my teachers' wedding and bake the cake for a gender reveal. It was cool because, if you think about it, cakes are a part of all these great life events—weddings, birthdays, and more. And now I get to be a part of those events. I was the only one who knew the baby's gender, so I made the outside of the cake pink and blue, and the inside was all blue."

Jack has now watched about one thousand videos on YouTube on how to bake and decorate cakes.

His advice to older generations: "I would tell adults that didn't grow up with YouTube that they think in order to do something you have to take classes. My grandfather told me to take baking classes to get good at baking, but they have to realize that the way our generation learns is so different.

"Now in math class you just go on YouTube to learn the math lesson. And older generations think social media is a bad thing, and, yes, there is a downside, but they have to realize it can also be a good thing. The way we learn is changing, and YouTube, Snapchat, and Instagram are the new ways that we're learning how to do new things and finding what we like to do."

Jack says, "I could be making cakes, but it would be nothing if I didn't post it on social media because, what would I do, bring photos to school? Instead, I just post the photos or videos and get feedback instantly from people all over the world. On Instagram it shows me that many of my followers are from Europe. People in Europe know my cakes."

Eighteen months after he baked his first cake, companies reached out to Jack via his social media accounts to see if he would like to promote their products. He plans to go to college and then work toward getting a show on the Food Network. He says right now he has had to slow down a bit and only make one cake per weekend, because, as he says, "Now that I'm older I don't have the same amount of time I did when I was a kid."

Jack is fifteen. He started baking cakes when he was twelve, because of a YouTube video advertisement. He has more than eleven thousand Instagram followers on @JackedUpCakes.

Jack is in Generation Z.

And Gen Z is about to reshape the future of business, forever.

Jack is one of the thousands of members of Gen Z who have helped us shape this book and will help you to understand their generation in a new and different way.

He and members of his generation from around the world will show you how they are changing everything from how to recruit employees and help them thrive within your company to unexpected strategies for marketing, selling, and driving new consumer experiences that Gen Z loves.

Our team of PhD researchers and generational consultants interviewed members of Gen Z in person and via video around the world, tagged along as they shopped in stores alone and in groups (usually while group Snapchatting in both scenarios), and watched Gen Z as they watched their favorite YouTubers show them how to do everything from putting on makeup to playing Fortnite to studying on "Study with Me."

Our research, consulting, and keynote-speaking firm, The Center for Generational Kinetics (CGK), has led more than sixty-five quantitative and qualitative research studies across the United States and around the world. These studies have been fielded across North America as well as Western Europe, India, the Philippines, and Australia. Our quantitative research studies generally represent at least one thousand individual participants and often many more. While the data in this book is largely from our US studies, we have chosen to focus on insights that we see are also most applicable around the world, based on our work speaking and consulting from Singapore and Chile to India and Paris, and for numerous global organizations each year.

All of our interactions with Gen Z have led to a key conclusion: the ways in which leaders typically recruited, managed, and marketed to older generations will not work with Gen Z.

But don't panic. Gen Z *wants* to work. They are *looking* for brands to love. They want and expect to add value as employees and share products and services that they are passionate about. It's just that Gen Z's expectations around *how* they connect with brands and potential employers look nothing like those of previous generations. The communication strategies and platforms have changed. Their hopes in what an employer can offer them have changed. They are open to what you have to say, as long as you are open to hearing them, too.

Many leaders know they need to adapt to Gen Z, but they feel paralyzed. They don't know how or what to change, or where to even start. This book gives you the tools to do just that, starting wherever you are right now.

At CGK, companies around the world hire us to answer their Gen Z questions, such as:

Who is Gen Z?

What works to market and sell to them now—and get them to tell their friends?

What do we need to do to recruit, retain, and engage them as employees?

How will Gen Z change the future of our business?

Our team is constantly leading studies to understand Gen Z and uncover what leaders must know and do to prepare for this new, exciting generation. We've led studies on four continents, in multiple languages, and looked at everything from how Gen Z views brands, marketing, and customer loyalty to job seeking, recruiting, motivation, and retirement—all the way to how they view the world around them and *other generations*. We've led deep dives to uncover new truths about

Gen Z and shopping, banking, spending, saving, driving, investing, communicating, managing, trusting, influencing, and so much more.

For the last four years, we've also led our annual State of Gen Z Study (StateofGenZ.com). This in-depth study looks at Gen Z and the hidden behavioral drivers that are the "why" behind their perspectives, actions, beliefs, motivations, fears, and dreams.

After leading dozens of studies exploring Gen Z in comparison to other generations, one finding stands out above the rest: Gen Z's expectations are so different because *they are so different* from other generations. They are the first to lead fully digital lives. They are being raised by parents affected by past events such as 9/11 and the Great Recession, as well as contemporary realities from the COVID-19 pandemic to online gaming, Brexit, and presidential politics.

They are connected to the world, and one another, across continents and across town using technology that for them has *always* been available. They have strong and vocal opinions about social issues from student loan debt and gun control to equality and climate change. And for the first time in history, digital media has given a generation this young the power to instantly bolster (or derail) global brands, become activists, and influence how companies do business—sometimes with a single tweet, post, or cell phone video.

We've seen it firsthand and likely so have you. The world watched as sixteen-year-old climate activist Greta Thunberg addressed the UN Climate Action Summit in September 2019, urging leaders to do more to reduce CO_2 emissions. We've witnessed gun control advocates Emma González and David Hogg, along with their Marjory Stoneman Douglas High School peers, organize the March for Our Lives protest in 2018 and advocate for safer gun laws.

As Christina, age twenty-one, says, "We are definitely a generation *and a movement*. We use our voices a lot, we exercise our ability to speak about what is wrong, and what we like, and our opinions."

We've listened to Gen Z as they talk about skipping the mall to go thrifting at "G-Dub" (Goodwill). We've seen their intense focus as they watch their favorite esports player on YouTube and Twitch. We've watched as they get incredibly immersed playing Fortnite for hours and hours (and hours), and then take forty-six photos to post one great photo of their limited-edition shoes on their public Instagram account, but not their Finsta account (which is used only for their closest friends).

We've also listened intently as Gen Z talks about the impact of COVID-19 and being quarantined at home instead of going to school or work. We've documented the anxiety they feel from constant social media pressure, and their insecurities about work, money, the environment, and the future.

Kate, age sixteen, says, "I think a lot of people in the older generations call people my age weak and say if we don't get a participation trophy we will break out in tears. I don't think that's true. My dad especially makes fun of participation trophies and things like that. But I think, 'Your generation is the one who gave them to us.'"

We've also heard loud and clear from Gen Z that they are not Millennials 2.0.

Chris, age twenty-two, says, "I look at my mom's generation and my grandmother's generation and see that they have no clue what our generation has going on. My mom and my grandma, they'll be like 'your generation is off the chain, just crazy.' We do stuff that they have no clue about.

"I know each generation can be different, and I know that is one thing I can say about ours. It's different because of how we grew up and the stuff that we experienced."

Chris is not alone, as 79% of Gen Z told us during our 2019 State of Gen Z Study that they do not feel other generations understand their generation well.

Gen Z is also older than most people think, with the oldest members already up to age twenty-four in 2020. This large, diverse, connected-from-birth generation is soon to be the fastest growing generation in the workforce—likely including your own workplace.

Gen Z is already the most important generation of consumer trend-setters, and they are determined to have an effect on your business. This book will show you what you need to know to understand them, market to them, employ them, and grow as they do.

To write this book, we led original studies of Gen Zers ages thirteen to twenty-four, compared them with Millennials and Gen Xers (and even Boomers), and interviewed individual members of Gen Z as young as age nine. What we uncovered was startling, even the differences between today's nine-year-old and nineteen-year-old, because of technology's rapid change.

To understand just how different their worldview is even from Millennials, let us give you two quick examples:

1. Gen Z does not remember 9/11. That's a *huge* difference and worth repeating: Gen Z does not remember 9/11. They learned about it in history class, from a parent recalling the experience, or on a YouTube video. As a result, Gen Z can't recall the feeling of fear and uncertainty that came as this event was unfolding—and which made it the defining moment of the Millennial generation, especially in the United States. This generational difference is even more pronounced when we interview Gen Zers outside the United States because they learned about 9/11 not only in history class but also through a different, geographically localized lens.

2. Gen Z has come of age with the COVID-19 pandemic creating fear, uncertainty, vulnerability, and confusion. The pandemic has caused massive disruption in schools, work, travel, politics, family, and much more. While the long-term implications of the COVID-19 pandemic remain to be seen, it is already clear that this is the defining moment of the generation thus far.

As Chloe, age fourteen, shares, "I saw that lots of people my age at camp were wearing Lululemon shorts. They looked really cool. So, I saved up and bought a pair for $40. They were okay but not great. And then I went on Amazon and realized I could buy almost the exact same shorts but for only $15. So, I started buying those instead to save money."

Who are these young adults?! We're going to answer that and much more in the chapters ahead.

The Gen Z Opportunity

Sharing the insights in this book—and what they mean to you and your business—is our passion.

We are generational researchers, consultants, and speakers—true generation geeks—in pursuit of research-based insights and strategies into Gen Z *and each generation* as they change business, communities, and our world. We get fired up studying Gen Z, whether through the lens of an employer, marketer, family member, or neighbor—and then taking the opposite approach to dive in and understand Gen Z's perspective.

Zconomy is the best of what we've uncovered in our original research and consulting to understand Gen Z. But Gen Z is still emerging, so we're paying close attention in our work with leaders and organizations around the world. Any book we write about a generation is only a snapshot, a moment in time, because generations continue to grow and adapt—especially Gen Z given their current age and life stage. Gen Z is right now hitting their mass entry into adulthood, and already they've provided us with a trove of insights, unforgettable stories, and unexpected strategies.

Gen Z's impact on the world is already immense, but they're just getting started. To bring Gen Z to life we're going to go on a journey that reveals what is shaping them, how they're going to reshape business and the future, and how you can make the most of this generation's talent, influence, energy, and potential.

Whether you're marketing a new banking app, athletic pants, car, or milkshake, or looking to recruit the next generation of employees in your restaurant, accounting firm, tech startup, or Fortune 500 company, we've discovered that what has worked to engage previous generations will not work with Gen Z. Leaders can see this as a challenge, or an opportunity. Choose to hear and understand Gen Z, and evolve with them, or cling to the status quo and hope the storm will pass. (Spoiler: it won't—this is the new normal, and you *can* adapt to unlock the tremendous potential of this generation.)

You'll see our firsthand data, experiences, stories, and perspectives directly from diverse members of Gen Z, including those around the world, and gain new strategies for unlocking the potential of Gen Z as your employees and customers.

We're going to look at how Gen Z's access to cheap, mobile technology shapes what is often the most important relationship Gen Z has with an organization, whether they are a potential employee or customer or a current employee or customer. *Communication is the glue between every generation*, but the technology expectations and tech dependence that Gen Z brings with them will dramatically shift business going forward in a post-pandemic world.

We'll also explore the drivers behind Gen Z's behaviors. These are the "why" behind Gen Z's views about money, education, spending, work, careers, and much more. These drivers shape the generation's view of the world and the decision-making process that influences every one of their actions and interactions.

Last, we will take our new, shared understanding of Gen Z and put it into action in two areas critical for organizations and leaders: Gen Z as your customers and Gen Z as your employees.

We'll uncover what most influences Gen Z as customers, how Gen Z thinks about shopping and spending, and where retail, digital, and mobile converge. We'll also look at how Gen Z will reshape the marketplace, starting with their current spending patterns and looking ahead at the bigger-ticket items that they will increasingly influence as they age up. We'll look at how to improve a brand's trust and awareness with Gen Z, and why this is so important, even if you're not trying to sell to them.

Gen Z is a powerful force in the marketplace, and their opinions as consumers often transfer over into what they're looking for in an employer.

In Gen Z as employees, we'll look at what the research—and the generation—says they want in an employer, career, and work experience. We'll focus on the most high-value challenges that employers are asking CGK to solve: how to recruit, retain, train, and motivate Gen Z as they go from career starters through talent development to managers and leaders themselves. Even if you are not hiring today, understanding these fundamentals to engaging Gen Z as adults will arm you with a long-term strategy for connecting with a generation that will have an exponential influence on how we all work, shop, market, and communicate with one another.

Most of all, we hope this book will give you a sense of inspiration, appreciation, and your own aha moments about Gen Z. This generation has so much to offer leaders if you are open to what they bring to the world.

A Deep Dive into Gen Z

Before we take a deep dive into Gen Z we want to share more about our work and how we came to write this book. CGK is based in Austin, Texas. We founded the research, consulting, and keynote-speaking firm with one mission: to separate generational myth from truth so leaders can drive measurable results.

We wanted to uncover if there was truth to the clickbait headlines overwhelming social media—Millennials are going broke because of avocado toast(!) or Baby Boomers always carry a checkbook(!) or Gen X is the forgotten generation—by providing the *missing* data and insights into emerging trends and practical solutions that leaders need, and fast. This has never been more important, as we have five generations of consumers, employees, and influencers, which creates all kinds of new challenges as well as opportunities for leaders. Increasingly every leader will feel the pressure of needing to work and bridge generations and likely be evaluated on that, too.

Luckily, your timing for entering into the Gen Z conversation is perfect.

While Gen Z will continue to grow and evolve, they are now at the stage where their workplace, digital, consumer, and other behaviors are increasingly measurable and explainable. This is an important time for us as researchers, speakers, and behaviorists, and for you as a leader. We not only want to be able to study what Gen Z is doing but also uncover the "why" behind their actions and then determine how leaders of every generation can adapt.

In the workplace, we can finally measure what attracts Gen Z to a job because they've been able to look for jobs for several years. We can explore what gets them to accept a job (or not—or accept a job and then not actually show up), and what keeps them at a job and engaged in their work over a longer period of time.

We can see how Gen Z shops for everything from clothes to credit cards; reacts to different marketing messages and channels, whether a YouTube influencer or Super Bowl ad; and views money, spending, and even financial planning, such as saving for retirement.

As researchers, we don't always like the answers that we uncover—that is part of leading good research—but we always strive to uncover accurate answers. The more we lead Gen Z research for clients, lead focus groups for brands, and analyze our global Gen Z studies, the more we are inspired and optimistic about what this generation brings to the world and how leaders can make the most of this generation's energy and innovation. This fuels our writing and speaking.

Candidly, we did not know what we would find when we started studying Gen Z. We just knew there was a lack of national and global data exploring different generations, particularly the much-hyped yet little understood younger generations that represent the future but were already a challenge for leaders in the present.

Denise's Story

Jason and I bring *very* different backgrounds to leading research, consulting, and speaking about generations and solving generational challenges. I'm a first-generation college student from a large Hispanic family. I have fifty-two first cousins.

I grew up in a household where Spanish was the primary language between my parents, yet they spoke English to my brother and me. It was one of many experiences where I felt I was bridging cultures, speaking English on one hand yet having a strong Hispanic heritage and culture all around me. We did not have much "spending" money, but from my perspective as a kid we never went without. While I may have always thought Spam was "real" meat and that security bars on windows were an architectural feature, it didn't occur to me that my life was that different from others. I was fiercely loved and always felt safe. My mom, Elida, was amazing at stretching a dollar, and we made it work. She never once complained about the long hours she worked each day, but instead shared every day how grateful she was—and how I should be, too.

Attending college at the University of Texas (UT) at Austin, I unexpectedly found my calling: helping young people overcome challenges. I will never forget the day when I was given a six-week assignment to teach a young man who was blind, deaf, and mute how to bowl. He was preparing for the upcoming Special Olympics and it was my responsibility to teach him how to walk up to the bowling lane, aim, and launch the ball. His excitement for learning a skill that so many of us take for granted changed my life. I graduated from UT Austin and became a middle school science teacher in the inner city. I spent twelve years in education, working in some schools known for being "tough" but whose students' background was basically the same as mine. I loved every minute of it—even the inevitable tough times.

After eight years of teaching, I earned my master's degree and became a middle and high school administrator in large schools serving a diverse and challenging population. It meant early mornings, late nights, endless teacher and parent meetings (and an occasional local news conference in our parking lot), but the work was extremely inspiring. I believed in my students. I love helping young people. That is my passion.

While serving as a school administrator, I continued my studies and eventually received my PhD. Getting my PhD while helping so many young people combined research with the frontline experience of trying to understand and change behaviors. I did not realize at the time that this combination would lead to me finding my next calling.

Ten years ago, Jason and I were talking about the lack of accurate data and actionable research that existed around Millennials and younger generations. He was speaking at companies all over the world, and they would talk about the generational challenges with such conviction, yet when he asked to see their data, it almost never matched the story that was being told by the leadership.

Hearing this same conversation across industries from retail and restaurants to automotive, technology, aerospace, software, and financial services made it clear that Jason had stumbled onto the real problem: a lack of current, accurate data and research insights into these emerging generations that leaders, managers, marketers, and decision makers could count on. Even parents wanted to know what was true about these emerging generations.

Every leader Jason met seemed to have an entertaining story about "the Millennial" who asked for a promotion after a week of employment or wouldn't work on their birthday. Yet that same employer might have *thousands* of hardworking Millennials who were not talked about, yet they showed up every day, worked hard, were proud of their job (and their employer), but never made headlines. While these negative stories made for entertaining banter on social media and in management meetings, they did not represent the whole generation or provide insight into the complexity within *every* generation.

The Millennials, often labeled as lazy and allegedly "not working," were actually the largest generation in the workforce. At the same time, Gen Xers were not being talked about enough—they still aren't—and we saw them as the glue within the workforce. In fact, Gen Xers, not Millennials, are the tech-savvy generation—they were there when hardware and software came together. They also survived the '80s and were there when MTV launched and actually played music videos.

Seeing the constant disconnect between generational perception and reality, I suggested to Jason that I knew how we could solve this challenge. We could start a research center specifically focused on uncovering not just the actions that each generation were taking but diving deep into the "why" behind the actions, perspectives, and mindsets so we could uncover how to understand and *influence* future actions. Together we founded CGK, and we now serve over a hundred clients around the world each year. I'm the CEO and responsible for all of our research. We've now led more than sixty-five studies covering everything from banking and financial services to automotive, travel, apparel, technology, and even baked goods.

Jason's Story

As Denise shared, we have different backgrounds and came to focus on solving generational challenges through a *very* different lens and pathway. This combination of background, ethnicity, education, generation (she's Gen X and I'm Millennial), academia, and geography enabled us to look at and approach solving generational problems differently. It's also why we make such a great team.

I grew up in a rural area, never felt like I fit in, and left high school to start college early. At age eighteen, I was a junior in college when I was inspired to write a book and help my own generation, the Millennials, by sharing what I learned the hard way about how to get mentors and internships and create job opportunities.

I wrote and self-published the book. I ended up sleeping on the floor of a garage apartment. My parents cut me off. My friends thought I was throwing my life away. I was $50,000 in debt and sharing my garage apartment with five thousand freshly printed books—but no furniture. I had no idea what I was getting into. I just had a desire to help my generation. I slept on that floor for two years while living on free samples at the neighborhood grocery store and large quantities of ramen noodles.

Initially no one bought the book. But I persisted in talking about the message and things I was learning the hard way. I was soon invited to speak, which led to people hearing about and buying the book, which led to more speaking and media. The book I wrote at age eighteen went on to sell over one hundred thousand copies, and I began speaking around the world. I (finally!) moved out of the garage apartment. After speaking at several hundred events, I wrote more books, ended up on TV shows from *Today* and *The View* to *20/20* and *The Early Show*.

In 2007 my career changed after I was on *60 Minutes* talking about

Millennials, this new generation—*my own generation*—and how they were creating a massive challenge, frustration, and hidden opportunity for employers and businesses. I'd already spoken to three hundred thousand members of my own generation and countless more of their employers, brand leaders, and influencers, so I had a pretty candid frontline view.

Corporations then started asking me to speak about Millennials as employees, customers, and trendsetters. I quickly realized that this was not a Millennial conversation, but a *generational* conversation. We needed to be talking about *every* generation, not just one. It wasn't about Millennials in a vacuum, but how to solve challenges across multiple generations to unlock the potential in each one. What was missing was accurate data and research to understand, approach, and solve these challenges with very practical solutions.

I remember talking with Dr. Villa, who shared my interest in generational research, particularly younger generations, and the gap I kept seeing between perception and data-driven reality. I knew this was a problem that could be solved with great, original research. She saw the same vision, but through the lens of a PhD. Together, we founded CGK, and it has been like riding a rocket ship ever since. In fact, we are so aligned about bridging generations, we are married—and we have a Gen Z daughter!

Let's Not Make That Mistake Again

The biggest difference between what we noticed with Millennials' emergence fifteen-plus years ago and what we see with Gen Z's real-time emergence is that today's leaders don't want to get caught off guard like so many did with Millennials' entry as employees and customers.

There was a distinct feeling among many executives as little as ten years ago that Millennials would "grow out of it" (whatever that means) and be just like every other generation of employees or consumers. Clearly, that did not happen. The results have wreaked havoc on businesses around the world.

Gen Z represents the same massive change, challenge, and opportunity that Millennials once did, but the *big* difference is that executives now are ready to act. They don't want to get caught flat-footed again. There is a realization that Gen Z is *already* twenty-four years old, they are *already* driving change as employees and consumers, and the sooner managers, leaders, innovators, and marketers can uncover the truth about this generation—and what it means to them and their organization—the sooner they can act to unlock Gen Z's potential. Doing so now creates the type of rare, defensible competitive advantage that is extremely hard to find. We call this a defensible difference.™

For apparel companies, this means changing in ways that deeply connect with Gen Z to earn their trust and loyalty. For banks and financial services, it means creating a dialogue with Gen Z early on, so they open accounts, refer friends, and start saving for retirement at the front end of their career. And for employers, from global technology companies to an entire low-tech construction industry, adapting to Gen Z means getting applicants when competitors can't and keeping Gen Z employees when others are struggling with increasing turnover.

At the same time, we'll be closely studying how COVID-19 affects younger and older members of Gen Z differently. While school-aged members of Gen Z saw their lives transformed through remote learning and social distancing that kept them from seeing their peers for months, Gen Z seniors in high school missed major milestones like prom and graduation. However, the oldest members of Gen Z experienced the pandemic at a pivotal time in their emergence into adulthood. Many lost their jobs or were sent home from college. They saw their independence and increasing autonomy collide with the new reality of uncertainty about the present and future.

Gen Z was also deeply touched by the racial justice protests of 2020. To see our latest research on how the events of 2020 have affected Gen Z, visit GenHQ.com.

The challenge is accessing accurate Gen Z research and strategies that bring to light the data, humanity, reality, and hidden drivers behind this generation's behaviors and mindsets. This is where CGK's passion and research led to us writing this book and the insights we're going to share with you.

PART I

THE MAKING OF GEN Z

1 WELCOME TO THE NEW NORMAL

"We are a generation of choice. This means that we choose the businesses just as much as they choose us."

—Bradley, twenty

Gen Z is already putting legacy companies out of business.

Visit many indoor malls in cities large and small and see the empty spaces for yourself. While Millennials may have started the decline, Gen Z is finishing it. At the same time, the generation is driving dramatic growth for many brands and businesses. Gen Z's definition of normal is not getting into a car to go shopping, but 1-click purchases on Amazon—or ordering by voice without a single click!—and having their purchase delivered on the same day for free.

Gen Z has always been able to use Lyft and other on-demand transportation options. Throw in the rise of new vehicle prices along with insurance, and we can see why this generation is not in a rush to get a driver's license. Other generations couldn't wait to get the freedom—and responsibility—that goes with getting a driver's license, but many in Gen Z wait months or even years beyond the minimum age when they could get their license.

The same goes for using services such as Airbnb, which even Gen Z's parents think is now a normal way to stay when traveling. Gen Z has come of age not only skipping a checkbook, or even recognizing why a checking account is called a *checking* account, but they've also been fortunate to have Venmo or the Cash App to send money to friends, split the bill at a restaurant, and get paid for side gigs from babysitting to a freelance photo shoot booked through Instagram messages.

Gen Z is already driving something remarkable for their age: change. And they are driving this new version of "normal" at an ever-younger age. We remember one Gen Z event in particular. It happened in our own home.

We walked into our kitchen after work and heard our then six-year-old daughter, Rya, asking, "*Alexa*, what is twelve plus thirteen?" "*Alexa*, how do you spell rainbow?"

We'll never forget it.

We stood there looking at each other thinking, "Wow. Our daughter is using Alexa to do her homework." Rya was *six years old*. At that defining parental moment we knew how we responded would have an impact. Jason's response: he couldn't have been prouder. However, Denise is a former teacher. Alexa is now unplugged from 4 to 6 p.m.

Rya relies on Alexa daily. She asks Alexa about the weather, to set her alarm, tell her a joke, solve a trivia question, and—whenever we are not within earshot—help her with all manner of homework.

Rya will never remember a time before she could speak to a connected device and have it respond with the correct answer or action—all without learning how to type, spell(!), or look up from her homework.

To Rya, you will *always* have been able to speak to the devices that surround you, see who is at your door through your Ring doorbell, and interact with your phone by saying, "Hey, Siri." And this is only a fraction of the change this generation will consider *normal and expected as they become employees and consumers.*

Born after 1996, Gen Z brings an entirely new definition of normal to technology, information, and the world. They think the 1990s are vintage. They think binge-watching shows on Netflix is normal (and so is sharing your password). They also see social media as a resource for news, personal branding, entertainment, community, education, dating, and so much more than just memes or clever GIFs.

Shehan, age sixteen, shares how his Spanish teacher uses Snapchat to remind students to do their homework. "Last year when I was a sophomore my Spanish teacher had a Snapchat account. She'd post almost every time we had a quiz, exam, or had to read a chapter for a book. She'd post pictures to the class, like, 'Hey, don't forget there is a test tomorrow.' Little reminders so that whenever you're just looking through your feed, it shows up and you're like, 'Oh yeah, I forgot to study.'

"It's her form of communicating to all of her students while being herself, I guess. Because she knows that we won't check actual school announcements. She knows that we're always on our phones and we'll check Snapchat enough to see what she has to say. I'd probably not have failed, but I'd have a lower grade if it weren't for her giving reminders and whatnot on Snapchat."

Gen Z has *always* been able to connect online and learn online, has *always* had to deal with the grim reality of cyberbullying, and has *always* been able to dream about a potential career as an "online influencer." We'll dive much deeper into Gen Z's complicated relationship with technology and what it means to your business in future chapters.

The Future Is in Gen Z's Hand (or Digital Wallet)

Gen Z will influence the future of business in a *massive* way and eventually reshape business entirely. Anyone who studies trends, consumers, and employees knows that the youngest emerging adult generation is often the driver of the biggest change. In fact, we see that Gen Z is the generation that is driving trends from the youngest up to the oldest. Want to see what Baby Boomers will eventually do with technology? Watch what Gen Z is doing now.

One thing we are already seeing in our research: what worked to attract, keep, and motivate Millennials as employees and customers does not work as well—if at all—with Gen Z.

This could not happen at a more challenging time for many leaders. Why the urgency?

Because within *two years* Gen Z will be the fastest growing generation in the workforce. They'll also become the most important generation of consumers and trendsetters. Their economic power and influence are only going to grow with each passing day.

Adding to the urgency: Baby Boomers are retiring and moving into a "less is more" mindset. These same Baby Boomers, Gen Z's *grandparents*, were often viewed as reliable employees and customers, the backbone of many longstanding businesses. As these Baby Boomers transition into a new life stage there is only one group on the horizon to fill the gap as workers and consumers: Gen Z.

In fact, Gen Z is expected to be the beneficiary of a massive wealth transfer from older generations to the youngest, which could exceed twenty to thirty trillion dollars. How would a generational change of that magnitude affect your industry, businesses, or community? Or even your own family?

Financial services firms, banks, robo-advisors, and every other business that depended on retaining Baby Boomers and their assets are already scrambling to keep the money that they will be moving to other generations. That is only compounded with Gen Z likely not expecting to seek face-to-face conversations in order to save, manage, and invest their money, because unlike even Millennials, Gen Z has never had to go to a physical bank branch to do their day-to-day banking.

Gen Z expects the future of finance to be mobile, intuitive, easy-to-use, and, most important, extremely personalized to them and their needs—the same thing they expect at work and throughout their life. How will this level of personalization expand to other areas outside of banking?

Already, brands are struggling with Gen Z. The urgency is only going to grow.

It's Not Too Early

Have you ever watched esports?

These massive multiplayer video games enable people to play alongside and compete with individuals and teams around the world. Esports are so popular that videos of top players and teams playing generate *billions of minutes* of video streaming *each month*. That is billions of minutes of people watching *other people* play a video game—and often it's just a *recording* of them playing the video game; they're not watching it live.

Even if you haven't heard of esports, contests are selling out entire professional football arenas in minutes. As one parent says, "I don't understand how teens can just *watch* other people play video games online. Why not just play them yourself?" Yet this is no fad. The largest esports competition has over thirty-four million dollars in prize money—*and it's all crowdfunded by fans through the purchase of "battle passes" online.*

This is just the beginning as leaders, including those leading traditional brands, rush to sponsor teams, players, and games. Esports team "franchises" can sell for more than twenty million dollars.

You are not alone if you haven't heard of esports. It's often been referred to in the media as the "most popular sport nobody knows about." But esports' ability to fly under the radar is a signal that Gen Z is changing business in ways many companies are simply not seeing. Gen Z is already revolutionizing marketing in a massive way because of where the generation focuses their *attention*. Whether that is esports, Snapchat, YouTube, Fortnite, or TikTok, they are focusing intently on platforms and interests that too many brands are not yet fully embracing—and some executives don't even understand. Failure to bridge the generational divide will be perilous, yet the leaders who adapt will have a tremendous advantage they can build on for years.

The trends that Gen Z is already embracing as preteens, teens, and college-aged consumers are only going to accelerate. Boards of directors are asking their companies if they have a Gen Z strategy, CMOs are hiring Gen Z consultants, meeting planners are hiring Gen Z speakers, and leaders are recognizing that their own experience with Gen Z family members does not provide a good representation of the overall generation. Even B2B sales will be affected, as Gen Z becomes both the frontline salesperson of the company and the first line of screening for many B2B purchases over the next five years.

On the employer side, Gen Z is already changing how companies must recruit, pay employees, and offer scheduling options via messenger platforms. Gen Z believes employers should try to make the world a better place, solicit and offer feedback quickly and frequently, and be transparent in their diversity initiatives and social causes.

Gen Z is here *now*, and they are the proxy for what will become *the norm* for other generations over time. Adapting now is the key so you and your organization can build on the foundation and momentum for years.

The tidal wave of Gen Z has already begun affecting industries from retail and restaurants to employee recruiting. Taking a look at those industries it is easy to see that the risk of adapting too early to Gen Z has already passed.

Waiting until Gen Z hits their late twenties and then adapting to them is too late. You'll be left behind in the way Millennials left behind so many retailers, restaurants, brands, and employers—many of whom have yet to catch up or are now on the fast track to irrelevance. And you certainly don't want your organization to end up in a Gen Z news feed for the wrong reason. As Taylor, age sixteen, shares, "Social media is usually the way that I find out people die. They're not dying because of social media, but I know that they died because of social media."

At the same time, when you adapt to this new generation you can immediately grow with their hyperconnectedness as they exert more influence every day—from their IRL (in real life) connections as well as those they don't know but influence digitally. In fact, *now is the exact right moment* in Gen Z's life stage to understand and respond to this huge, new, global generation, so you can be informed and take the right actions to fuel your own growth for decades to come.

Are You Ready to Engage?

In 2017, sixteen-year-old Carter Wilkinson dispatched this tweet to fast-food giant Wendy's:

"Yo @Wendys how many retweets for a year of free chicken nuggets?" Their answer? Eighteen million.

Carter rose to the challenge. And meanwhile, Wendy's got thinking. They engaged their ad agency to get creative with Carter's request, and the #NuggsforCarter campaign was born. The movement quickly made international news and caught the attention of celebrities like Ellen DeGeneres, whose 2014 Oscars selfie held the record for most retweets of all time. Ellen welcomed Carter as a guest on her show and sparked a playful rivalry to keep her top spot as retweet queen. Meanwhile, brands like Google, Amazon, Apple, and Microsoft joined in to retweet #NuggsforCarter.

Carter didn't reach eighteen million retweets, but Wendy's made the call when he broke Ellen's record. He got the nuggs at 3.4 million retweets.

Carter decided pretty quickly that he wanted his media blitz to go beyond the nuggets. Raised in Reno, Nevada, with three siblings, Carter took the opportunity to sell #NuggsforCarter T-shirts with all proceeds going to the Dave Thomas Foundation for Adoption—a nonprofit created by Wendy's founder Dave Thomas that supports kids in the US foster system. The inspiration: Carter's family. Carter's little sister was born severely premature and his mom was diagnosed with Stage III breast cancer two weeks after his sister's birth.

He explains, "Whenever I'm sad or feeling ungrateful, I think back to when I was a kid. I remember when my parents would have to drive to UCSF every other weekend to receive treatments. I remember families bringing us dinners trying to support us in any way they could. I remember seeing my sister so prematurely born that she was on the brink of death.

"Then I remind myself how lucky I am. How lucky I am to have my mom today. How lucky I am to have a healthy sister who is above average in growth. As well as how lucky I am to have so many loving people in my life. I am so blessed to have an opportunity to use my voice to support something I believe in."

Carter says he "hit the family jackpot" and wants to help foster kids find their forever home. He also has a fundraising page for Pinocchio's

Moms on the Run, a local organization in Reno that provides support services to women with breast cancer and their families.

This craze started when a bored teenager decided to have some fun tweeting at his favorite fast-food chain. And it turned into a phenomenon when Wendy's engaged Carter in a conversation he started, on the platform of his choice, in a public forum. It was standard practice for Wendy's, as they've built a reputation for being one of the wittiest and most highly engaged fast-food brands on Twitter. It's a defensible difference™ among their competitors. Marketing analysts at the Ayzenberg Group calculated that #NuggsforCarter scored Wendy's $6.7 million in earned media value. Their cost? $1,960.05 if Carter eats nuggets every day, for every meal, all year. And their $100,000 donation to the Dave Thomas Foundation.

Carter and his Gen Z peers have come of age with social media as their default communication tool. They're very effective and usually way more comfortable on these platforms than the PR teams who are paid top dollar to respond on behalf of brands. Gen Z is used to starting the social media conversation and has the benefit of a generally limited downside, whereas brands must constantly track social media and risk even more downsides if they don't respond in the right way (and fast).

Gen Z has a gift for leveraging online platforms to create public-facing conversations that drive change. These conversations are not always as lighthearted as #NuggsforCarter. They're just as often criticisms, and just because Gen Z is taking a position against a company doesn't mean it's the right position or that they will get their intended outcome. But the fact that Gen Z will openly challenge legacy brands—and as teenagers(!)—that have hundreds of millions of dollars to spend in marketing and PR budgets shows that the generation's desire to be heard is real and only getting started.

In our view, Gen Z will continue to exert this external and highly public influence on brands, businesses, and leaders, for better or worse. As a leader, it's important for you to know one thing is certain: there will only be *more* pressure on brands and brand leaders to listen to Gen Z.

Getting it right now and actively listening can avoid so many of the pitfalls that have befallen brands that did not take the time to listen to this generation or shrugged them off as simply young, inexperienced, and uninformed.

The irony is that Gen Z has already proven to be a tremendously powerful force on business and business strategies *without even being a customer or employee,* but rather by being vocal about a company through social media.

Odyssey is a platform for Gen Z content creators to share their opinions on topics as diverse as shopping and food to student life and political activism. With 12 million unique visitors each month, over 128,000 content creators to date, and over 1 million original content pieces, Odyssey is particularly tuned in to the ways in which Gen Z wants to engage with brands.

Odyssey's president, Brent Blonkvist, and his team conducted a 2019 study of two hundred brand and agency advertising buyers, asking them to share their biggest struggles. "Eighty-seven percent of respondents," Blonkvist shares, "said they know they need to target this generation, but they don't know how to engage them. That can seem alarming when you consider there are so many tools brands can use to target this generation, like Facebook, Twitter, and YouTube." Blonkvist continues, "But the problem is that just targeting this demographic doesn't engage them—and if you don't truly engage them, you're not driving loyalty. If you're not driving loyalty, you don't have a long-term customer. This generation has grown up on the Internet. They understand how to manage ads; they understand how to block them or just blow by them and not even notice that they're there."

Gen Z engagement requires going well beyond one-dimensional ads. Brands need to listen to what the generation is saying and become part of their conversations.

The reality is that now a fourteen-year-old ninth grader can start a hashtag about almost anything and a twenty-two-year-old can film a video call to action—and both can collide and amplify each other exponentially online, without ever actually knowing or even meeting. (And if you are unsure how to use hashtags, well that is a completely different conversation and one you want to have very quickly.)

Gen Z has proven they can have unprecedented influence on businesses and organizations at a younger age than previous generations, and this external impact—created without being an employee or a customer—represents only the beginning of the connectedness and influence we believe this generation will drive.

A Path to the Answers

At CGK, we are excited that Gen Z is now emerging and can be accurately studied across geographies around the world. To truly understand a generation requires both quality and original research as well as quantity of research. Gen Z research is still very limited because of their youth, but our quest to lead research into the generation every day is already unearthing a trove of insights and unexpected findings. These discoveries can inform and drive understanding, strategy, and practical solutions to help leaders effectively connect with Gen Z at every point in the customer and employee life cycle.

The rise of Gen Z calls into question the future of work, life, consumerism, and the planet. Some of the questions our research addresses include:

- How will a generation that appears to have a more informed and conservative perspective of money think differently about saving, investing, and spending? What will this mean to your business?

- How will this generation navigate a world overflowing with endless information at their fingertips? Will they find a way to wield this to their advantage and drive gains important to them, or will it be overwhelming, taken for granted, and underutilized?

- How will a generation that is so immersed in a digital world adapt their social skills to enter the face-to-face workforce and society—or will they expect the world to adapt to them? How will this shape your hiring, management, or sales process?

- How will being raised by Generation X and older Millennials—not Baby Boomers—affect this generation's values, priorities, voting, and what they bring into adulthood? Will they choose to take care of their parents or choose a different path?

- How will COVID-19 and its aftermath affect the generation when it comes to work, money, education, and their thinking about the future?

The more we study Gen Z, the more excited we are to uncover and tell the generation's story, to bring them to life, not from the vantage point of a single or small sample group of Gen Z, but by looking at Gen Z across the United States *and the world* via data, stories, quotes, and frontline strategies we've uncovered that work for leaders.

Gen Z is heralding a "new normal" across industries and around the world. Are you ready to make the most of it?

2 REDEFINING THE TERM "GENERATION"

"Sure. I know all about 9/11. I learned it in history class."

—Gen Zer

From Jason . . .

I remember exactly where I was when I heard something was happening in New York City on September 11, 2001. I was in Los Angeles to film a TV show that had come out of my work writing books and speaking. I was sitting on the couch in my hotel next to my dad. We turned on the TV. The images were shocking. I'll never forget the fear and confusion I felt.

I have deep connections to New York City. My family is from there and I went to a year of college in New York. Many friends still lived in the city. And beyond my personal connections, seeing something like this happen at all was devastating. I remember sitting on that couch, crying. But my dad was completely emotionless. His face showed no hint of what he was thinking.

Thirty minutes later my grandfather called. He was my hero. He had grown up in Brooklyn. He was about seventy-nine years old at the time. I will never forget what he said: "Sonny boy, we are going to be okay. I promise you. *We are going to be okay*. This happened to us before and we got through it and we will get through this again. I promise you. *We will be okay.*"

Years later, I finally got my dad to open up about what he was thinking that morning in 2001. Our conversation allowed me to put the generational pieces together.

When my grandfather said "this happened to us before" he was referring to Pearl Harbor. My dad, who was born in 1952, shared that he was worried I would soon be drafted. What happened on 9/11 brought back his experience of showing up to the draft board for Vietnam.

For me, 9/11 was the defining generational moment of emerging adulthood. It was the turning point for my generation in the United States and forever changed my generation in many other countries, too. For us Millennials, it was our "Where were you when . . . ?" moment.

Looking back at that experience as a generational researcher, I can see why we each reacted to the exact same event in such different ways. We were all experiencing the same event, but *completely differently* through our own generational lens and life stage.

Every detail about our time and place growing up in the world affected our reaction to 9/11: our age, our prior experience with war, terrorism, political upheaval, where we'd lived, even how we learned to deal with the unknown—the context we each brought to the situation shaped how we responded to it.

This one experience has helped me put the concept of generations in perspective better than any other. And it is a key marker in my work teaching new ways to lead across generations. The reason: the same event can create different responses for each generation experiencing it—and for good reason. For Gen Z, we suspect COVID-19 will be a generation-defining moment.

Generations Don't Fit into a Tidy Box

At CGK, we believe that generations are *not a box* that each of us fit neatly inside based on our birth year alone.

Generations don't work that way.

In our view, we've found that each generation is a framework and set of insights that offer powerful clues on *where to start* to quickly connect with and influence people of different ages. This helps people work, market, build trust, and influence those older, younger, and even in the same generation as themselves.

We view a generation as a "segment of a geographically linked population that experienced similar social, technological, and cultural events at roughly the same time in their maturation leading to increased predictability by scenario." Those are a lot of fancy words to say that a generation is a group of people born about the same time and raised in about the same place.

GENERATION NAME	APPROXIMATE BIRTH YEARS
Generation Z (aka iGen)	1996 to 2012
Millennials (aka Gen Y)	1977 to 1995
Generation X	1965 to 1976
Baby Boomers	1946 to 1964
Traditionalists (aka Silent Gen)	1945 and earlier

Note that "cuspers" are people born on the edges of a generation. They tend to have characteristics of both the generation before and after. Sometimes there is a clear delineation between one generation and another, such as 9/11 for Gen Z in the United States. In other periods, there is no generation-defining moment, but rather a transitional period. For example, the transition from Gen X to Millennials means that the generations could start or end anywhere between 1977 and 1981 depending on factors such as geography, affluence, and age of parents.

Every generation has its own powerful indicators—not rigid definitions—of how its members may experience and respond in a given situation, whether shopping for a car or evaluating a job posting. Those indicators are influenced by the "about the same time" and "about the same place" aspects that link a generation within a geography. While my dad was likely not alone in worrying about me being drafted after 9/11, many of his peers born in the 1950s had different reactions. They did not all fit in the same box, but they did have a larger shared context of their upbringing that offers insights into where their response might lead.

The key that is too often overlooked, and that we always seek to make a point of in our work with leaders, is that geography plays a huge role in shaping generations. Within the same generation, we will see differences between rural and urban members, and we'll definitely see differences between Gen Z in different parts of the world. A seventeen-year-old growing up in rural Arkansas might have had a driver's license for two years already in order to help on the family farm or drive to school or work, while a teenager in New York City might not feel the need to get their driver's license unless they move out of the city. Interestingly, trends tend to originate in urban areas due to diversity and population density and then ripple out to rural areas (music, for example). In our extensive work outside the United States, we always regionalize each generation to make sure it accurately represents the part of the world we're studying or speaking to.

In addition to the timing and geography that shape every generation, there are also generation-defining moments. These are the events or occurrences that take place at a critical phase of a generation's emergence—usually as children or teenagers—that forever alter their worldview. This can range from war or terrorism to political upheaval, a natural disaster, technology breakthroughs such as landing on the moon, or the spread of COVID-19.

For Baby Boomers in the United States, generation-defining moments might be the JFK assassination, the civil rights movement, Sputnik and nuclear bomb drills, color TV, the Beatles, and so much more.

For Generation X in the United States, those experiences could range from the end of the Vietnam War, Watergate, and the Iran-Contra affair to the oil embargo, the massive rise of the divorce rate, the AIDS epidemic, the *Challenger* explosion, being a latchkey kid, Walkmans, Atari, and the launch of MTV in 1981 (where the first music video was "Video Killed the Radio Star").

Millennials emerged in the late 1980s and 1990s to the rapid introduction of the personal computer, the Internet, cell phones, email, going from "analog to digital," the rapid adoption of social media, introduction of smartphones, legalization of gay marriage, the first mass-casualty school shooting (Columbine in 1999), the launch of Amazon, ecommerce, Y2K, student loan debt, 9/11, and the Great Recession.

Recognizing the defining moments that shape a generation helps us to understand the generation's points of view, priorities, values, and behaviors. It's also important to note that how a trend or event affects an individual varies based on their age at the time of the event (were you five years old or fifteen?), geography, socioeconomic situation, culture, gender, and much more.

For example, if you were a Millennial born in 1985, then the Columbine tragedy happened while you were in high school. Your response to—and fear, emotion, and feeling about—the school shooting being replayed over and over on the news would be different from the Millennial born in 1990 who would have been in elementary school and probably not remember the Columbine tragedy as a contemporary event. They would (unfortunately) remember other school shootings that occurred later. Columbine would have also affected you differently if you'd experienced it through the lens of being a homeschooled third grader in rural Virginia, an eighth grader in New York City, or a high school student in one of Columbine's neighboring towns.

The better we understand the framework that shapes a generation, the better we can connect with and influence each of them. That clarity also makes it much easier to bridge different age groups in a variety of situations, from employee recruiting, motivation, and retention to marketing, sales, and customer experience.

The Powerful Events That Shape Gen Z

Gen Z was born from about 1996 through approximately 2010 to 2012ish. As generational researchers and speakers, we don't know when a generation ends until well after the fact, similar to recognizing when a recession is over. Unless there is a clear and profound generation-defining moment—such as 9/11 in the United States, Brexit in the United Kingdom, the Boxing Day Tsunami in Southeast Asia, or COVID-19 worldwide—generational ending dates are best analyzed by looking back instead of guessing ahead of time. Then, there is always flexibility among cuspers, who were born on the edge of two generations and often relate to aspects of both depending on their upbringing.

We do know that Gen Z starts after 1996 in the United States because, as we mentioned, they do not remember the most defining event of the previous generation: September 11, 2001. As we continue to study this emerging generation, it seems certain that COVID-19 will be the generation-defining moment that draws the line between Gen Z and the generation that follows them.

One consistent through line in our Gen Z research is the speed and impact of cheap mobile technology on the generation. While this is still not universal in all parts of the world, it has created a connection among Gen Z that empowers them and supercharges their impact on businesses.

Our 2019 State of Gen Z Study revealed these truths about the generation's relationship with technology:

- 95% of Gen Z use or access social media at least once a week.
- 74% of Gen Z are dependent on technology to *entertain themselves*.

Gen Z watches events unfold on the other side of the world in real time directly from their phone or tablet, without being limited by location or time zone. They engage in conversations with strangers who may not speak their own language but they know from playing esports online. They are connected to their mobile phones so deeply that we see Gen Z in different parts of the world respond similarly to our survey questions about technology, music, apparel, travel, sports, money, and the future of the Internet—even though their languages and customs might be different.

Gen Z has an unprecedented dependence on technology, and from a very young age: 31% of Gen Z feel uncomfortable being away from their phone for thirty minutes or *less*! And 14% say they cannot spend any amount of time away from their phones. Looking further, 26% of Gen Z boys and 33% of Gen Z girls are on their phones *ten or more hours per day.* And 65% of Gen Z are on their smartphones after midnight at least a few times a week. Of these, 29% say they are on their phones after midnight *every night*!

According to research by Common Sense Media, 89% of thirteen- to seventeen-year-olds had their own smartphones in 2018—a huge increase from 2012, when 41% of teens in that same age group had a smartphone.

Technology has had a profound impact on Gen Z—from interactive toys for newborns to the ubiquitous iPad that has programmed Gen Z kids to think every screen is a touch screen as they try to swipe up on their parents' TV. Media platforms, from apps to videos, now teach kids everything from foreign languages and math skills to makeup styles and potty training.

Gen Z is frequently compared to Millennials in terms of technology exposure, adoption, normalization, and trendsetting. This is an important comparison because it shows just how *different* Gen Z actually is when it comes to technology and their *integration* with it.

Gen Z, not Millennials, is truly the connected-first generation, and more deeply and natively due to the rise of Internet-connected devices at the right time in Gen Z's youth. Gen Z has come of age with everything from Alexa answering their trivia questions to never having to carry cash thanks to Venmo's introduction while they were preteens and teens to following their favorite YouTubers going to college, while streaming music on Spotify.

Gen Z is not living the same experience as Millennials when it comes to technology—their digital native upbringing is unlike any other we have seen (in person or via Twitch!).

Connecting with a Highly Connected Generation

Gen Z's ubiquitous access to *inexpensive* mobile technology is, without doubt, this generation's biggest defining trend. Their immersion in technology since birth has profoundly shaped their worldview; expectations for communication at school, with brands, and with friends and family; how they shop and buy; how they prefer to communicate, collaborate, and work as a team; and where they go for information, answers, dating, healthcare, jobs, and news.

At the same time, Gen Z modeled their parents, who were constantly staring at their own screens, whether on a family trip or at the dinner table, which made looking at a screen normal anywhere, anytime— and even within a close group.

Our daughter, Rya, is seven years old. She does not remember a time before she could look at the person she was talking to on the phone. When she was younger, she thought the phone was broken if she couldn't see you. She once tried to use the phone at a hotel, but when she put the handset to her ear, she heard something that scared her and that she had never heard before . . . a dial tone! Technology that was commonplace for older generations baffles Gen Z. YouTube channels dedicated to this phenomenon are enormously popular (search YouTube for "kids react to old computers" for a laugh).

Rya has never woken up early to watch a marathon of Saturday-morning cartoons, because in her view of the world, cartoons or any show are always available on demand, even on an airplane. In fact, she doesn't like TV, only Netflix.

We remember receiving a notification on our phones that Rya had changed her Netflix settings so she could watch any show she wanted. That kid! Fortunately for us, Netflix sent us a message, which led to a heart-to-heart conversation—and face-to-face no less—which was an unforeseen hurdle in Rya's quest to watch PG-13 shows at age seven.

While geography plays a huge role in shaping generations, the consistency of inexpensive mobile technology leads us to believe that Gen Z will be the most *globally consistent* generation of employees and consumers, but we won't know for sure for a few more years. However, the early signs of mobile technology's effects do point to this. From our initial work, we're seeing that a ten-year-old in the United States might have more in common with a fifteen-year-old in London or India than a fifty-year-old in their own country.

Gen Z already has a huge influence on the world as consumers, and they're quickly making their mark as employees as well. Like all generations before them, they don't fit in a tidy box, but we can identify the key events, trends, and influences that most shape this generation—and there is much more beyond technology. The clues to connecting with Gen Z are all around us and them.

As foreign as their TikTok-dancing, esports-watching, and Snapchat-messaging ways may seem to some of us, we can bridge the gaps between Gen Z and older generations by taking the time to understand the lens through which Gen Z sees the world. We don't have to agree with it, nor do they need to agree with our worldview, but taking the time to understand their viewpoint creates the foundation and space to effectively connect with and influence them.

In the next chapter we'll take a deeper look at the biggest influences on Gen Z, beyond their tech dependence, that have shaped this generation to date.

3
THE EVENTS THAT
SHAPED GEN Z

"Obama being elected was big for me because I've never seen an African American president. For anyone growing up who has aspirations of one day being president, it's about having somebody in front of you who can give you the hope that you can get there."

—Chris, twenty-two

The night Barack Obama was elected president of the United States in 2008, Josh was eleven years old.

"I remember exactly the moment when I saw on TV, 'Barack Obama will be the first black president.' I turned around and looked at my dad. My dad's not a super-emotional person but I could see that he was emotional in his eyes, and I remember looking at him and saying, 'So he did it?' And he looked at me and said, 'Yeah, he really did.'

"I turned back to the news and it had started showing people celebrating in different cities. I remember that moment exactly. The next time I turned to look at my dad he was calling my grandma to ask if she was watching the news.

"I remember thinking that my grandma grew up under Jim Crow laws and this just meant so much to us culturally. It's not as though prejudice has completely disappeared, but there was something powerful in that generational moment. It's a testament of how far we've come in such a short amount of time."

Gen Z has *always* known the United States to have an African American president, who was elected *twice*. They've witnessed gay marriage go from protests and rallies to the law of the land. They've also seen firsthand footage of school shootings as well as domestic terrorism at venues from concerts to nightclubs and the rapid spread of COVID-19. All this while they've also had to contend with an onslaught of news about climate change and the rise of "fake news."

Imagine seeing all of that as a teenager with unfiltered social media streams—and while having to maintain a "Snapstreak," work a part-time job to help support your family, take an AP class, watch your siblings, apply for college, and leave home for the first time.

Add into the mix the Great Recession that deeply affected Gen Z's parents, nasty political discourse dividing close friends and family, and student loan debt ballooning out of control. It's no wonder Gen Z feels that they are different from previous generations and growing up in a time other generations may not fully relate to.

It is also no surprise that Gen Z reports feeling significant anxiety and stress but not feeling able to talk about it. Ixchel, age twenty-two, a first-generation college student, shares, "A few months back I saw that a couple of people I went to high school with are now Instagram and YouTube famous. They're getting paid just for making videos doing what they're passionate about. I see other people who used to be absolutely nothing, used to have a nine-to-five job, and now they're making so much money on social media just for having so many followers. And I got to thinking, 'Oh, my. I need to figure out what I am going to do.'

"Seeing those posts brought fear, and I thought to myself, 'I'm still at school. I'm still following the steps. This is how you do it. This is how you become successful.' But look at this guy—I went to high school with him and he decided to not even go to college and dedicate himself to uploading videos. He's made it to the eyes of society because he's 'known,' and he gets paid really well. And I'm still on this track."

So many members of Gen Z relate to Ixchel's stress and emerging definition of "making it," yet the idea of being "YouTube famous," or even having the option to make a living from social media, didn't exist a decade ago. And it's just one of the infinite ways in which Gen Z's world looks so different from that of the Millennials who came of age in the 1990s and early 2000s.

While we're *all* experiencing the huge cultural shifts brought on by on-demand everything, inexpensive mobile technology, and divisive political climates (among many other things), this is the *only* world Gen Z knows. And despite the stress, Gen Z is making the most of it. They don't need time to acclimate. They have already mastered the technology that older generations are still working to understand or consistently blame. Gen Z embraces progress around numerous issues, such as seeing diversity and inclusion as a pillar of their generation.

This chapter takes a deep dive into the generation-defining moments that have shaped Gen Z so far. While these experiences unite Gen Z as a generation, individual responses may vary. Still, these are powerful clues that teach us, as members of other generations, how to connect with this generation.

Parenting: The Great Recession and Student Loan Debt

> "Student loans were a given when we were applying to college. Everyone filled out their FAFSA application like it was required homework. Now, my husband and I are still paying off our loans, twenty years after graduating college, and juggling the added pressure to save for retirement *and* save for our preteen's college education. Which do we prioritize?"
>
> —Parent of a Gen Zer

When we asked a group of teenage girls during a CGK focus group whether their parents talk to them about money, a chorus of voices instantly and unanimously said, "Yes! ALL the time!" Every girl in the room affirmed that their parents frequently talk with them about all kinds of financial topics, ranging from debt to budgeting.

> 66% of Gen Z are worried about accumulating or not being able to pay off student loan debt, and 79% are worried about their future overall, according to our 2019 State of Gen Z Study.

One participant shares: "We were required to take a personal finance class in high school and so that really taught me. We have parents that talk about saving, so I knew a lot about it already, but we did visual activities where you actually see the money that you saved can grow with compound interest and everything. That made me want to save early. I'd rather start now."

Gen Z did not experience the Great Recession while in the workforce, *but their parents did*—and watching the struggle many of their parents faced was painful, emotional, and raw, and affected their views of work, money, self-reliance, and the struggle to financially support a family.

The harsh reality of working—or trying to get a job—during the Great Recession was directly modeled and talked about with Gen Z at a formative age. Gen Z witnessed many of their parents' mounting debt and frustration to provide for their family. Whether this stress was shared intentionally and explicitly with the family over a meal or unintentionally through phone calls and adult-to-adult conversations that were overheard, the feeling was palpable.

Even for those Gen Xers and Millennials who were not raising kids during the Great Recession, as many Millennials in particular delayed both marriage and kids, the lessons of the Great Recession stuck and were eventually passed on to their kids. The experience was compounded by wage stagnation, the rising cost of rent and home ownership, and the all-too-real perception of a growing wealth divide.

For many Millennial parents, their financial situation was made even more challenging through record-setting student loan debt. As of September 2019, fifteen million Millennials ages twenty-five to thirty-four had a collective outstanding student loan debt of over $500 billion. Many of Gen Z's parents carry that debt with them to this day, and it has shaped how they parent and how they talk with their kids about work, spending, and money.

The unexpected outcome of the Great Recession and skyrocketing student loan debt might actually help Gen Z avoid similar pitfalls in their own lives. Our research suggests that it will. We discovered that 86% of high school–aged Gen Z kids say they plan to go to college, yet half of those are only willing to take on $10,000 or less in student loan debt. In fact, 27% say they are not willing to take on any of this debt at all. Gen Z's fiscal awareness and practicality, arising from observing their parents' and Millennials' struggles, probably hasn't been as prevalent among previous generations at this age since those affected by the Great Depression.

New Values and Social Activism

> "You are failing us. But the young people are starting to understand your betrayal. The eyes of all future generations are upon you. . . . Right here, right now is where we draw the line. The world is waking up. And change is coming, whether you like it or not."
>
> —Environmental activist Greta Thunberg at the 2019 UN Climate Action Summit

Gen Z has come of age in an incredibly intense time of publicly voiced social values colliding across generations, news outlets, street protests, and social media.

Such collisions of social values are driven in part by younger generations expecting or wanting something different from previous generations. This intense, emotional conversation is playing out 24/7, 365 on Gen Z's social media, endless cable news segments, and clickbait headlines across the web.

Gen Z has come of age at the precise time that numerous groups have publicly stated they are no longer willing to accept the status quo when it comes to issues such as racial justice, diversity, inclusion, gender pay gaps, gun legislation, environmental responsibility, and so much more.

Some in Gen Z have supported these campaigns for new norms and the expectations they want to bring with their generation as they enter adulthood.

These public outcries have given birth to highly charged movements ranging from Black Lives Matter and #MeToo to support of gay marriage and equal rights for LGBTQ+. Most surprising but important for other generations to recognize, though, is that Gen Z activists are passionately promoting what they define as the new status quo, which is the only one they've ever known.

Many young members of Gen Z never knew a time before NFL players kneeled in protest during the national anthem; the US women's national soccer team publicly demanded a pay raise; or women revealed the history of sexual harassment, abuse, and sexism they have faced. Many in Gen Z do not remember a time before climate change was considered one of *the* issues of their generation. And they will never forget the summer that was defined by COVID-19 and racial justice rallies.

The support from Gen Z appears particularly strong when it comes to diversity and inclusion. It's important for other generations to recognize that Gen Z is the most racially and ethnically diverse generation in modern US history—and they expect diversity and inclusion everywhere. According to the Pew Research Center, 48% of Gen Zers in the United States are non-white, compared with 39% of Millennials, 30% of Gen Xers, and 18% of Boomers.

Our research shows that Gen Z expects more when it comes to diversity and inclusion from employers. They expect to see women and minorities at the highest level of a company and the opportunity to "bring their whole selves to work." While this is different from what some leaders are accustomed to, it's not completely different from the type of social change and transparency that Millennials brought into the workforce and continue to carry forward—or even the change that Gen Xers and Baby Boomers brought with them in their emergence.

Perhaps some of this diversity is in the form of diversity of thought. Our 2016 State of Gen Z Study found that Gen Z does not believe Americans are tolerant of people with views and values different from their own, but they should be. The question was: Do you think

Americans *should be* tolerant toward other Americans with opposite beliefs from themselves in areas such as politics, gay rights, religion, and family values? 65% said yes. When asked: Do you think Americans *are* tolerant toward other Americans with opposite beliefs from themselves in areas such as politics, gay rights, religion, and family values? 26% said yes.

The biggest difference between Millennials and Gen Zers is that Gen Z has been able to actively engage in initiatives and movements they believe in from a young age due to social media. This ability to engage without actually showing up to a street protest or leading a walkout has led to much higher online engagements with a movement (like, share, comment, etc.)—all without leaving home. At the same time, this intensity has led to universities trying to help the generation learn how to disagree in a civilized, constructive manner. Some colleges, including American University in Washington, DC, Carleton College in Minnesota, and Wake Forest University in North Carolina, have added civil discourse programs to their curriculum to help Gen Z learn how to debate, disagree, and dialogue with those who have different backgrounds, values, and opinions.

School Shootings and Domestic Terrorism

"In a little over six minutes, seventeen of our friends were taken from us, fifteen more were injured, and everyone, absolutely everyone in the Douglas community was forever altered."

—Emma González at the 2018 March for Our Lives rally to end gun violence

As much as Gen Z is known for being the "tech-everything" generation, they are unfortunately also known for coming of age during a time of awful mass-casualty school shootings. The first mass-casualty shooting, at Columbine High School in Colorado (1999), was a Millennial experience, but Gen Z has grown up in the face of multiple instances of mass-casualty shootings such as Sandy Hook Elementary School in Connecticut, Marjory Stoneman Douglas High School in Florida, and Santa Fe High School in Texas, among many others. These school shootings will have long-term effects on Gen Z, the results of which will be seen for decades. For Gen Z, gun violence and terror in the classroom and other public places has become all too normal.

The response, however, to the shooting at Marjory Stoneman Douglas High School has inspired many in Gen Z to be more active or at least more vocal about issues such as school safety. Gen Z's natural comfort with social media was an immediate, intense, and amplified outlet to share their fears, sadness, anger, frustration, and perspective. These intense social media engagements, along with rallying from actual Gen Z school survivors such as David Hogg, led to a tremendous amount of online coverage and social media engagement.

Gen Z may or may not end up being more politically involved than previous generations, but those who want to be politically active have the opportunity with social media, and it allows them to be activists at school, on the bus, on the subway, and even from their own home. They don't have to show up at an event to be heard and to see the response.

Gen Z also has come of age during an era when domestic terrorism, beyond 9/11, is on the rise—from the bombing at the Boston Marathon to the shooting in an Orlando nightclub to the mass shooting at a music festival in Las Vegas—not to mention disturbing events from around the world that can be viewed in real time without ever leaving home.

Education and Learning

Gen Z views technology as their lifeline for learning, but how they use their various digital devices differs from how previous generations use these very same tools.

As one Gen Zer tells us, "I use my computer to do just schoolwork. My phone, I just use it to talk to my friends and see what's going on. If my teachers told me to do something for class, then I would use my computer to find the information or the answers. Otherwise, I don't really touch it."

Gen Z has come of age with more outlets for learning than any previous generation in history. Long gone are the days when knowledge was locked away and only accessible in textbooks updated every few years. Long gone are the days when only wealthy private schools or urban education centers could offer students sophisticated learning options. Now, almost all members of Gen Z can watch history on their phone as it's being made, whether that is a SpaceX launch and successful booster landing, tweets about social change from teenagers on the other side of the world, or asking Google Home the answer to a geography question.

Information is more democratized and accessible than ever before. Does that mean access is equal and all information is accurate? Absolutely not. However, in many parts of the world inexpensive smartphones have brought information, connection, innovation, and learning to individuals, families, and communities, which was not possible only twenty years ago.

One learning trend we are particularly focused on is search by voice. Right now, the youngest members of Gen Z have come of age relying on search by voice—in fact, often before they could even type! Gen Z can ask Alexa or Siri a question and get instant access to the information they need without typing a single letter. We believe search by voice will be a *major* trend for learning, engaging, and accessing information when it comes to the workplace and for Gen Z as consumers.

The combination of mobile, search by voice, tablets, and adaptive software and its integration into schools will inevitably put new demands on workplaces, too, to provide sophisticated learning and collaboration tools as Gen Z enters the workforce. We'll explore this more later in this book.

YouTube, Content Creation, and Netflix

When it comes to all-important content consumption, Gen Z primarily wants to be entertained, learn, and engage through a mobile screen. The trend is quickly moving away from linear TV (or skipping it entirely) and focused on YouTube, Netflix, and TikTok.

Gen Z spends *a lot of time* on YouTube—or as they tend to call it in our Gen Z discussion roundtables, "Google-Tube." Gen Z uses You-Tube to search for information, answers, and entertainment in the way other generations use the Google search bar. Gen Z types what they are seeking to learn or answer directly into YouTube rather than Google. For many Gen Zers, YouTube is essentially their starting screen for accessing information on the web. According to a 2018 We are Flint study, 96% of Internet users ages eighteen to twenty-four access YouTube. The typical viewing session is forty minutes, a 50% average yearly increase. YouTube is now the world's second largest search engine.

Our 2019 national study revealed that 97% of Gen Z use a video streaming service at least once a week, with 85% of them accessing YouTube. Gen Z watches YouTube to learn how to do things, like put on makeup, learn a new dance, or get new strategies to beat a video game. But they don't just watch influencers for entertainment and how-tos—they also *purchase* from YouTube influencers. We'll share much more about purchasing in Part II on brands and Gen Z.

YouTube entertains Gen Z in the same way TV once did for previous generations. They enjoy a variety of videos, including watching influencers doing pranks, playing online games, or just sharing their daily thoughts and antics in a vlog. Gen Z wants to watch the lives of other people who are like them or who they want to be like. It's similar to reality TV, but with a more homemade production feel that makes what they're viewing seem even more real.

How, when, why, and where Gen Z consumes content, and especially where they create their own content, reveal much about the generation and how brands will need to engage them, corporations will need to train them, and content providers will need to adapt to them.

Gen Z rarely has to watch two minutes of toilet paper commercials in order to catch their favorite entertainment show (a big annoyance is when YouTube does not allow them to skip an ad!). They've always been able to fast forward, pause, skip, and rate each video, too. This generation has not had to be home by 6 p.m. to view their favorite TV program or hope that their favorite song randomly gets played on the radio. Nope. Gen Z has been liberated from consuming content on the advertiser's, network's, or programmer's schedules. Instead, they access content on their own terms. Many in Gen Z cannot even remember a time when people had to wait for a Netflix DVD to arrive by mail. For Gen Z, almost everything is on demand all the time, free or inexpensive, and "recommended" based on past streaming usage and ratings.

Talk about a change from the days of Boomers, when there were only three channels and those channels stopped broadcasting late at night. Or when Gen X witnessed the rise of premium (i.e., expensive) cable networks. Gen X was also there to be the "remote control" for their Boomer parents who said, "Get up and change the channel for me." Millennials came of age with dramatically more viewing options, and they saw content go from being cord-based to being cordless. Millennials also were at the forefront of movies on demand and during the early days of YouTube.

All this streaming at no or low cost has made Gen Z the consummate content consumer, *but* they expect this content to be recommended to them individually, on any device they choose, and with limited or no commercials, *especially* if they pay any type of subscription fee.

On the flip side, Gen Zers have also become content creators—unlike most members of previous generations. Many in Gen Z, particularly those who are teenagers now, never knew a time before they could film videos with their phone. The result is that Gen Z has gone from digital audience member to digital content creator anywhere, anytime. This has led to stardom for YouTubers who attract larger audiences than many traditional celebrities and the emergence of celebrities who are discovered on YouTube, such as Justin Bieber was. One YouTuber, Ryan, earned $22 million in 2018 by uploading videos of himself opening and playing with toys on his YouTube channel, Ryan's World. He is seven years old.

While some YouTubers can make money as content creators, Gen Zers expect that most of the content they consume will be—or at least should be—free. This creates a challenge for traditional cable and TV providers even while it has created a new opportunity for Gen Z to get deeply engaged in online content topics as diverse as they are. Gen Z's hunger for diversity, esoteric topics, and personalization will bring significant changes to the workforce and to brands that want to appeal to them.

Mental Health and Physical Wellness

Alongside the swirl of technology that has influenced Gen Z's emergence is a highly public conversation around mental health and physical well-being. Our studies reveal that mental health issues are top of mind for many of Gen Z as they go through the difficult life stages of preadolescence and adolescence and emerge into adulthood. These challenges are compounded by the nonstop photos, videos, and posts by other people their own age, including friends and classmates, showing how great their life is *supposed* to be. In our studies on social media, we have consistently seen that social media can lower self-worth for many in Gen Z and adds to the anxiety, insecurity, and emotional stress of the already difficult teenage years.

According to our research, 42% of Gen Z say social media affects how they feel about themselves and 42% also say social media affects how other people see them. A total of 39% of Gen Z say it affects their self-esteem, 37% say it affects their happiness, and 55% of Gen Z have been worried or stressed about something someone posted about them online. And overall, 46% of Gen Z think that technology in general is bad for their mental health.

Outside research supports our findings. A 2019 report published in the *Journal of Abnormal Psychology* notes that adolescents and young adults experienced a more than 50% increase in serious psychological distress in the late 2010s compared to people in this age group ten years ago. The study cites use of digital media, including social media and involvement in cyberbullying, to be a top source of stress among these age groups.

As we like to explain to older generations, Gen Z tells us social media is like the stress of the eighth-grade cafeteria popularity fish-bowl but 24/7 and with people being even meaner because they can hide behind a keyboard and an anonymous profile. This is particularly true when it comes to cyberbullying, which is an issue many in Gen Z have faced since a very young age. Forms of subtle (and not so subtle) exclusion are used on social media all the time. Not being tagged in a photo is considered a snub, as is someone not liking a post or video. For some Gen Zers, it's possible to know if someone is really your friend by whether or not they like or comment on your social media posts. Gen Z is continually stressed about how to deal with social media and its implications as they grow up. In our 2019 national study, 61% of Gen Z shared with us that they think schools or colleges should teach them how to better manage their online reputation.

When it comes to talking about mental health issues, traditional methods of intervention—like hotlines and in-person visits to professionals—don't appeal to Gen Z. Some organizations are adapting accordingly by offering methods of support more suited to Gen Z preferences, such as texting. This is a trend we believe will continue as Gen Z emerges, especially within the workforce.

At the same time, Gen Z is wild for fitness trackers, monitors, and wellness-connected devices. These range from the Fitbit and Apple Watch to health trackers on phones and even Internet-connected fitness equipment. Gen Z has come of age never knowing a time when every step couldn't be tracked, every calorie counted, every meal logged, and every progress or setback charted directly on your phone. This may be a strong positive for many members of Gen Z—as one teen tells us, "I wear a Fitbit because I'm always moving around, and I like to compete with my brother and my mom for who can get the most steps." But step and calorie counting can lead to stress for others in Gen Z in terms of body image, eating disorders, and more. No surprise then that this generation has been credited with pushing back against unrealistic, highly airbrushed images of women in ads. One company that has responded to Gen Z is Aerie, a brand making undergarments for women of all shapes and sizes—as their website puts it, "for every girl."

A World of Change

Each of the trends we've explored in this chapter is part of the larger story about Gen Z that will continue to unfold for decades. Each trend has hit Gen Z at a particularly formative time in their emergence, sometimes as teenagers and sometimes as children who never had to wait for dial-up Internet or buy an entire music album rather than instantly download a song. Gen Z will likely always remember where they were when COVID-19 disrupted their schooling and daily life.

In the next chapter, we'll dive deep into Gen Z's technology experience and see how this sets Gen Z's expectations, behavioral drivers, and norms as employees, customers, and trendsetters.

4 LIFE THROUGH A 6.1-INCH SCREEN

"I use my phone everywhere I go. It's always either in my hand or in my pocket. My schoolwork is on there, my social media stuff is on there, my notes are on there. I just use it in every aspect of my life."

—Christina, twenty-one

It's Monday morning. Isabella, a twenty-year-old junior at Temple University, wakes to her iPhone alarm set to 8:30 a.m., an hour before her first class of the day.

She silences her alarm and jumps on her Google Classroom app to check assignments. Good news: her professor posted a video of the lecture she'd missed last week. Isabella makes a mental note to watch it while on the bus across campus.

Back at her phone's home screen, she launches Snapchat and checks the six Snapstreaks she has going that connect her with a mix of her high school friends; summer camp bunkmates; coworkers at the cat café; and cousins who live in Boston, Sacramento, and Stockholm. She snaps a selfie, layers on a cat-nose filter, and dispatches it to each streak. Her Snapchat score bumps up to 233,617.

Next, Isabella remembers she's finished with class by noon, so she checks TaskRabbit for any gigs she can pick up. Putting together IKEA furniture is her superpower, and she discovered last summer that this is a popular category on the app. A few taps and she's booked to assemble a desk and storage cubbies at 4 p.m. for $40. Score! Funds for going out on Friday are covered.

Speaking of going out, Isabella has been meaning to learn how to master the smoky eye shadow look. She taps "smoky eyes" into YouTube's search bar and watches four videos, then jumps to Amazon to order the eye pencil two of the makeup artists recommended.

Ack, *another* Amazon order. She gets nervous she's already maxed out her shopping budget for the month, so she opens her banking app, jumps to her checking account balance, and breathes easy. She'd forgotten about the $100 she made selling her old iPad on Facebook Marketplace. Venmo deposited the money into her account last night. Cash flow is looking good.

Thinking of money reminds Isabella that she *really* needs to figure out an internship for this summer. She pulls up LinkedIn and taps "graphic design intern" into the Jobs search bar. Dozens of results appear, but she's overwhelmed and worried she doesn't have a strong enough portfolio to qualify for any of them. So she jumps to Fiverr, the online marketplace for freelancers, and searches for design jobs. Perfect timing: a group of Wharton MBAs is looking for someone to design a logo for their event planning startup. She puts in a bid to design ten logo options for $20. She'd be making pennies per hour, but it's just what her portfolio needs. Isabella sends in the bid with fingers crossed.

Before she can close Fiverr a text buzzes in:

"Hi, love! Let me know if you're coming home this weekend for Grandpa's birthday. 😊*"*

Mom. She'll reply later.

Isabella's eyes jump to the top corner of her screen for a time check: 9:13 a.m. Time to get out of bed and head to class.

Can't Stop, Won't Stop

We're all guilty of being glued to our phones. Isabella's typical Monday morning may sound a lot like yours even if you're not a member of

Gen Z or looking for makeup tips. Your brain and thumbs race from to-do lists to apps to conversation threads (or emails for those of us in that generation). You might do your banking, order groceries, make a workout playlist, and catch up on the news all before placing your feet on the floor in the morning.

This is status quo for many people living in modern society, but if you're older than Gen Z, you remember a different way of life. You may recall a time when résumés were emailed (or maybe even faxed!), paychecks were printed, and missed homework assignments were hunted down through friends. But a life run by apps is all that Gen Z knows.

Gen Z's smartphone dependence is so ubiquitous that it is shaping this generation's worldview, affecting their expectations for communication and collaboration at work, and driving their view of education. It also shapes how Gen Z wants to interact with brands, service providers, potential employers, and even customer service.

While other generations consider these technology expectations a big shift from their own ("Gen Z has such high expectations!"), it's not actually the case. Gen Z just has *different* expectations based on what they've *always* known and are accustomed to experiencing. Recognizing the power of this generation's mindset will help you as a leader adapt to and unlock the potential of Gen Z employees, customers, and trendsetters—or even understand your own children better.

When we talk about Gen Z living digital lives, how much time they spend on their smartphones is a major factor—and they are spending *a lot of time* on their phones. In fact, 55% of Gen Z are on their phone five hours or more a day. That's over *half* of a generation that spends a majority of their leisure time connected to people who are not physically present with them. Further, our 2019 national study showed that 84% of Gen Z use messaging apps at least once a week and that 45% of them include emojis most or all of the time when sending a text message. Gen Z finds that digital interactions like emojis, memes, GIFs, avatars, filters, and videos are often more comfortable to use than written words to communicate with their friends—even for sensitive conversations. This is fascinating from a generational researcher's standpoint, because different generations occasionally assign different meaning (or just confusion) to different emojis. This is particularly true when a member of Gen Z sends a message that has a string of emojis and no words—and parents have to go online to figure out what each emoji means.

Daniel, a parent in one of our focus groups, got a shock when he checked the activity usage on the family's cell phone plan. In a four-week period his wife sent 76 texts, he sent 243, and his sixteen-year-old son sent 10,184. "Let's just take out eight hours a day for sleeping," he says. "I think he does more than that, but for kicks, let's just say eight . . . that means he had to send more than twenty-two texts each hour for every single hour he was awake those four weeks. How is that even possible? I mean, how would you get anything done?"

The beginning of the school year is always a buzz of activity and excitement, but while this frenzy didn't really start until the first day of school for previous generations, it is a completely different experience for Gen Z. For example, twelve-year-old Kaitlyn spends a lot of time staying connected to her friends, but this was never more apparent than when she put her phone in her bag for her one-hour dance class. She returned to more than *seven hundred* texts from groups of friends about classroom assignments and the start of school!

SMARTPHONE USAGE:	GEN Z:
10+ hours per day	26%
5-9 hours per day	29%
1-4 hours per day	35%
< 1 hours per day	3%
Do not have or never use this device	7%

* STATE OF GEN Z 2018

Chloe's experience also points to the gender divide among Gen Z when it comes to how much time they spend living their digital life. Our studies revealed that 65% of females are on their phones five or more hours a day while only 50% of males are on their phones five or more hours a day. Gen Z females are digitally interacting much more than Gen Z males in terms of overall smartphone usage, though Gen Z males partially make up the difference in the amount of time they spend on gaming devices and platforms.

Another interesting insight about Gen Z and their smartphones is how much they use them after midnight. In our 2018 State of Gen Z Study, we found that 44% of Gen Z are on their smartphone after midnight once a week to several times a week. But even more shocking, 29% say they are on their phone after midnight *every* night.

Here is one exchange from a Gen Z focus group we led:

JORDAN: I lose time on my phone. Like I think I am spending ten minutes, but really it's like thirty.

KATY: Or like an hour. Or "just another five minutes." And then it's like, two hours later.

JACKSON: The worst is when you're trying to go to bed at night, and you know you're tired, and then you just have to be talking.

KATY: Last night I was like, "I'm going to go to bed at 11:30." But I was up till . . . 12:30 just on my phone. And there was nothing I had to be doing. I was just on it, wasting time.

This generation is always on, always connected. For a majority of Gen Z, there's rarely a moment when their phone is not within reach, and for many there are not several minutes that go by without them at least glancing at it to check for a new message or alert.

While the long-term effects of this constant connectedness require decades of study, it is already clear that the world of Gen Z is connected more than any before. A makeup "influencer" in Australia might be livestreaming new makeup tips on Facebook or YouTube during the day so a Gen Zer in America will stay up late to watch. Or they might be playing a game online with friends, but their gamer friends live in South Korea and Abu Dhabi.

Looking ahead, this new reality of 24/7 mobile connectedness brings up many questions, such as: How does this massive technology usage influence Gen Z's sleep, mental health, learning, work, relationships, etc.? These are all big areas we will be looking into in the coming years as we continue our study of Gen Z. But until we uncover those answers, it is critical for businesses to keep Gen Z's phone dependence at the forefront of everything they do to connect with and influence this generation. Whether they're looking to hire or hoping to attract and keep Gen Z as customers, companies won't get traction unless Gen Z can find them easily, quickly, and engagingly through their handheld screen.

Social Media *Is* the *Medium*

"I think it's really sad. Honestly, really common in our generation. At lot of work goes into how many 'likes' you get. It's directly linked to the fact that getting likes releases dopamine in the brain. I'm actively trying to detach from that because likes are also tied to physical attraction. For example, if I put up a picture of my dog, I won't get any likes, but if I put up a shirtless photo, it'll get 140 likes. So, I try not to get caught up in it."

—Male Gen Zer, twenty

With smartphones as their appendage, much about Gen Z's information and communication expectations can be understood through the apps they use and how they use them. Social media apps top the list and also lead to tremendous, documentable insights that leaders can use to become more knowledgeable about the generation.

Gen Z has come of age with social media as the pulse of connectivity between them and their peers, family, news, world events, entertainment, and much more. Social media is essentially the digital glue that connects Gen Z to other people and the world around them. And it's all happening through that little screen they hold in their hands.

While this has made it easy for Gen Z to stay up to date with five hundred friends on Snapchat, social media also has a clear downside. As we'd noted earlier, our national studies show that social media negatively affects everything from Gen Z self-worth and self-esteem to body image and confidence. Our 2016 national study revealed that 42% of Gen Z feel social media strongly affects how other people *see them*, and 42% of Gen Z also said social media strongly affects how they feel about themselves. Almost four in ten say social media strongly influences their self-esteem.

Despite the potential meanness and negative side of social media, Gen Z relies heavily on it. The social platforms are a massive driver of their expectations and behavior, from needing immediate feedback (How many reactions did my Instagram story get?!) to extended exposure to social norms, such as whether or not people like your hair, clothes, new tattoo, or vacation photos. Gen Z takes multiple pictures to get just the right one (sometimes more than fifty photos for one Instagram post), edits the image with filters, and then chooses the platform, set of friends to message, and perfect time of day to post. Gen Z is in effect operating as if they are in the media, which they are: social media.

For Gen Z, "prime time" isn't related to TV viewing. Instead, prime time is the best time to post an image or Story on Instagram or video to TikTok for the most likes and comments. As one member of Gen Z explains, "My friend, just like two days ago, she posted a picture and it wasn't prime time, which is when most people are on it, so she deleted it. She posted it like two hours later when she knew it would get more likes."

We also found in our 2018 Gen Z study that social media is a materially bigger deal to Gen Z females than males. Females consistently showed that social media was more important, and they were more active on it than males. This shapes everything from where they shop, when they shop, and who they shop with to what they ultimately buy—all of which can be shared on social media at every step.

Specific Platforms for Specific Tasks

Our research shows that which communication platform and technique Gen Z currently uses largely depends on the situation, whether

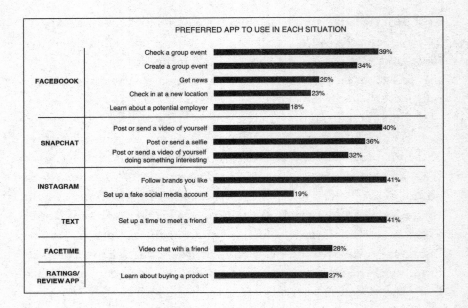

PREFERRED APP TO USE IN EACH SITUATION

that is asking a friend a question about school, setting up an invite for a party, or dealing with something that has to do with money. Gen Z expects communication to be fast, to the point, screen-based, and, when available, highly visual.

In the world of social media, a few platforms stand out as most influential for Gen Z and are most important for leaders to know when engaging this generation. Here are a few of the platforms and why they're important.

Snapchat

Gen Z loves Snapchat. You can gauge how much a person uses it by looking at someone's Snapchat score, which is *generally* based on how many times a person has sent and received snaps on the platform.

CGK RESEARCHER: What is your Snapchat score?

GEN Z1: Oh, it's really high.

CGK RESEARCHER: Like, over 70,000?

GEN Z1: Oh, it's like over 200,000, I think.

CGK RESEARCHER: It's 200,000?

GEN Z1: It's 283,000.

GEN Z2: Mine's 301,000.

CGK RESEARCHER: What is yours?

GEN Z3: 190,000.

GEN Z4: 388,000.

GEN Z5: Mine's 594,000.

GEN Z6: Mine's only 147,000.

Five hundred ninety-four *thousand*. With such intense and ongoing usage, Snapchat is the high-trust and high-engagement platform for many members of Gen Z, particularly in the United States (in other countries WhatsApp, WeChat, or Weibo might hold the mantel of most used, trusted, and engaging). Why is Snapchat usage so prevalent with Gen Z? There are many reasons, including right platform, right place, and right time in Gen Z's youth, but one of the main behavioral drivers is that Snapchat posts are seen as more "in the moment": real and candid photos and stories.

"Snap's just more informal because I can send friends just my face and they'll send theirs," explains one Gen Zer in our focus group. "We haven't talked but it feels like it, kind of. With texting, you actually have to have something to talk about. You have to take time to text it. I don't know, I just feel like it's easier because it's just a picture."

Snapchat photos are intentionally not supposed to be polished or perfect—as is the case with Instagram—but rather "Snaps" are playful, fun, and more IRL in appearance. Snap filters and customized avatars allow Gen Z to make their images unique with only a few taps or swipes on a screen and in almost no time at all.

This quick creation of unique and personality-driven images appeals to Gen Z and their highly visual generational norms. At the same time, the expectation that the photo and message doesn't have to be perfect is a relief for Gen Z in a world where many images—especially promotional ones—have been highly edited to look posed and perfect. "Snapchat's a lot less formal," explains another focus group participant. "My dad's in the military, so I've moved a lot. I have a bunch of different friends across the country on Snapchat and we stay in touch with 'streaks.' So I have emojis in front of my friends' names and every morning I take a picture of something random. It could even just be my bedsheets, and I'll say, 'good morning, streaks,' and then I'll slide and send it to all hundred of them. I do that every morning."

In a Snapstreak you can send one picture to a group of your closest (or selected) friends and in return they send you a picture back within twenty-four hours. Many Gen Zers keep these streaks going for one hundred–plus *days*. For some, it's considered rude not to send a picture in response to a streak request and can get you unfriended quickly. That is a lot of social pressure to respond quickly, no matter where you are that day.

As one mom tells us about the importance of Snapstreaks:

"This spring break our family planned a trip to Big Bend, a national park in Texas. I mentioned to my thirteen-year-old son, Ezra, that he would not have Wi-Fi in those parched, rugged mountains. The only light we'd see would be the moon and stars. His eyes immediately grew wide and he said, 'Mom, we can't—I'll lose all my streaks!' I was hesitant to cancel the trip because of this particular impending doom, to which he replied, 'Okay Mom, I can give Griffin (his BFF) the password to my account and he can keep my streaks alive.'"

Snapchat sends *only* your selected friends the photos, which removes some of the risk, anxiety, and discomfort of posting an image for all the world to see, such as what happens when you post on Instagram to all your followers who may or may not be your friends IRL.

Snapchat also appeals to Gen Z because it generated widespread adoption *after* Facebook, which means it is the *contemporary* social media platform of Gen Z. In other words, parents use Facebook; Gen Z uses Snapchat. This sense of privacy is important to teens and preteens, who often are already going through the awkward adolescent years and are looking for an outlet where they can be candid and vulnerable with their closest friends. Eventually, other generations are likely to adopt Snapchat, particularly Millennials, but for now it skews younger than others—particularly in the United States—making it a more obvious digital gathering place and platform for Gen Z and younger Millennials.

Instagram

While Snapchat is designed to be more intimate, in-the-moment, and "behind the scenes," Instagram carries an expectation of polished photos showcasing a lifestyle, experience, identity, values, or personal brand that a member of Gen Z wants broadcast to the world. As Gen Z frequently tells us, "Instagram is how you want the world to see you. Snapchat is how your world really is."

The difference is all in the preparation for creating a post. According to the many Gen Zers we interviewed, they may only take three or four photos to create and send a Snap on Snapchat. But for Instagram, they could take up to forty or fifty photos to find the one photo they will then edit with various photo-editing tools and post on Instagram.

Instagram is also the platform that spawned the phenomenon of social media influencers. As word spread of celebrities receiving huge sums of money for a single post on Instagram (Kylie Jenner supposedly earns up to $1 million per post), it only raised the bar for Gen Zers making their own posts on the platform. Even nanoinfluencers, who have very small followings, can still earn money, gifts, or access—such as to live events—by creating a single post.

Now a well-known marketing channel for both established and emerging brands, these "influencers" play an important role in shaping Gen Z's tastes for products, services, and offers. Social media influencers are the new celebrity endorsement. And unlike traditional endorsements that appear on TV, in advertisements, and other one-direction ad channels, an influencer's followers can respond directly to the influencer on the actual post—sometimes even receiving a reply from the influencer or their team—and then engage in post-driven replies with other followers. This creates a cycle where the comments and responses to the comments by others keep the post in more people's feeds, so more people see it, and that leads to even more engagement.

None of that is possible with traditional advertising, but it is the norm for Instagram, which is why brands covet high-profile influencers. They can drive awareness and excitement, but, more important, direct sales and ongoing conversation with their customers well after the post goes live.

Facebook

"Facebook is for old people, you know, like Millennials."

—Gen Zer

"I have Facebook just because of my parents, because they post pictures. My grandma just went to Europe and she's like, 'Like my post!' So, I had to like her posts not to be rude."

—Gen Zer

Where is Facebook on the list for Gen Z? That is a subject of heated debate. As a Millennial, I (Jason) remember when I first heard a member of Gen Z make statements like this about Facebook. I came of age with Facebook as the platform for connecting and sharing information, photos, videos, stories, and life events. Now it also appears to be the hub for sharing baby photos, school reunions, and any manner of mundane life updates. But for Gen Z, Facebook is "old, you know, like you." Ouch.

While Facebook definitely has a place on the list of social media that Gen Z uses, alongside Twitter, we find that Facebook is viewed by Gen Zers as lower in terms of importance, trust, and influence than other social media outlets. Making it even more out of style, Facebook is the place where Gen Z's *parents and grandparents* often hang out. Making matters even worse, it's not uncommon for Gen Z to tell us that their parents and grandparents add comments on a post as if it was a private conversation, yet everyone can read it. In fact, our 2019 national study showed that 41% of Gen Z are not on Facebook because their parents or older relatives are on it. This may change as Facebook continues to evolve and refine its offering and experience, but the likelihood of Gen Z suddenly leaving their preferred social media platform to move to the one older generations use is probably pretty low. Facebook's acquisition of Instagram was an attempt to address this issue, but we'll have to wait and see what else Facebook launches to attract a generation that has come of age with many more social media options than previous generations had (if at all).

In our discussions with Gen Z we found that Gen Z likes Facebook for keeping up with local events and creating group events of their own. Several college-aged Gen Zers mentioned starting a Facebook page for their clubs so their groups can keep track of activities and events.

A member of Gen Z shares, "I'd say Facebook is a lot more common in college. In high school I never used Facebook and I came into college and that's how you get into groups. The Spirit group has a Facebook page for recruitment, and they have a huge class of '21 page. That's how I found my roommates."

Twitter

Many older members of Gen Z *depend* on Twitter for breaking news stories. Gen Z, especially those who are politically active or passionate about social causes, will use Twitter as their go-to news source and connection hub for information and to engage around specific topics. This enables them to bypass traditional news media because they view Twitter as a real-time information source from real people who are right there as the events are unfolding—at least that is the perception.

Here is what one of our Gen Z roundtable participants said about news on Twitter:

"That's what I like about Twitter. No matter where in the world, people are livestreaming and posting videos before the regular news even knows about it. It gets popular so fast. So, I feel that's nice because people know about it before the regular news does."

Gen Z feels that the information they receive via Twitter isn't being filtered through large media conglomerates with their own agendas or advertisers trying to push a certain narrative. This doesn't, however, mean Gen Z thinks everything on Twitter is accurate; they understand that sources can be misinformed or intentionally trying to stir the pot.

But overall, they still view Twitter as a direct link to the news from a point of view that is closer to the action and more unfiltered than traditional news sources. This is particularly true of videos, which may lead to an interesting future as technology such as deepfakes (which make it appear as if someone, such as a politician, is saying something; it looks believable yet is entirely fake) infiltrate popular content. A quick search for deepfake videos will yield examples that leaders need to see and know about, as this will be a true contemporary challenge for Gen Z as they age up.

Gen Z also knows Twitter as a platform for activism, as the generation has used the platform to get brands and businesses to change policies and to amplify social cause positions. They've joined Millennials and Gen Xers to turn hashtags such as #WomensMarch, #MeToo, #BlackLivesMatter, and #LoveWins into massive social and political movements. And if you as a leader want to know what Gen Z expects, all you have to do is ask or look on Twitter and pick the trending hashtag. Their answers will appear, and if they are emotional, expect a round of answers and comments to follow.

Instant Message, Text, Video Messaging, and Live Chilling

One of the biggest differences between Gen Z and other generations when it comes to communication is that they have *always* been able to send and receive instant messages—and they do it almost exclusively through their phones. This has transformed their communication standards and preferences. They typically choose not to actually talk on a smartphone or use email and instead use a phone for instant messages (from standard IMs to WhatsApp and Facebook Messenger), text messages, video messages, and now Live Chilling (more on that in a second).

Gen Z is bringing this heightened expectation of instant, personalized communication into everything they do, from working on a team to shopping, customer service, car buying, travel, and so much more. Managers, executives, marketers, and sales professionals—and parents—must adapt to this new communication reality if they are to connect with and influence this generation. Gen Z will have come of age without needing to pick up the phone at a hotel to get a question answered or even go to the front desk. They'll just text the hotel to get their question answered—or room service delivered! (That is, if they stay in a hotel at all. They're more likely to stay at an Airbnb where their host is also a text or WhatsApp message away.)

The leaders in digital messaging and peer-to-peer instant connection include WhatsApp, which is hugely popular, especially outside the United States (and, by the way, owned by Facebook), Facebook Messenger, WeChat, and Live Chilling apps such as Houseparty, which allows for group video chat. Houseparty in particular is an example of what is seen as normal to Gen Z and will influence their expectation for workplace communication. The app allows up to eight members of Gen Z to be on one phone screen all by video. It's like a house party—with people talking over each other and everyone seeing everyone else. Whether or not the app succeeds long term, the concept of video chat will be considered a standard method of communication for Gen Z. Already, messaging has made the leap from social media and various messenger platforms into the workforce via platforms like Slack and Microsoft Teams. We expect digital collaborative spaces to continue to grow in importance as Gen Z enters the traditional workplace. They will want to not only send and receive messages instantly in a more social media–like platform, such as Slack, but also see in real time those they are working with on a team or project around the world with applications such as a video chat.

Ubiquity of the Smartphone

Gen Z's smartphone dependence will only intensify as their younger peers come of age. While teens and adults of all ages are hailing rides with strangers, applying for jobs, and ordering food through those tiny screens (also delivered by strangers), phones are becoming deeply intertwined in kids' lives as early as grade school. Everything from how they learn to how they unwind is happening through their smartphones.

Gigi is thirteen, in the middle of eighth grade, and her education is happening much differently than yours probably did. She's both learning and submitting her homework in a virtual classroom, powered by Google. She does still have a pencil somewhere in her backpack, but her primary tools of learning are an iPhone, the Internet, YouTube, and Google Classroom. In fact, she often gets reminders from her teacher via Snapchat to submit her homework.

Yes, she still goes to an actual middle school, hears bells, and shuffles between classes, but her digital experience of learning and connecting is the beginning of a massive educational change powered by new technology tools such as Google Classroom, which includes Google Docs, Google Slides, and online student communities. Schools are using other online classroom management systems as well, but Google Classroom is frequently viewed as at the forefront of changing the education experience in a major way.

Gigi explains, "Google Classroom is an online site. It's connected to the school district here in Arizona, and you have all of your classes listed out for you, and you get to click on them and they say, 'Oh, your homework assignment is blah, blah, blah.' And if you have to write something down or, you know, type something, you use Google Docs and you submit it there. I usually use my phone to check it and submit my homework."

When Gigi gets to algebra, she may experience a flipped classroom, one where all the algebra lessons are videos viewed at home or on the bus or wherever she happens to be, on her smartphone. A teacher on the video works through each problem and then a series of problems are presented, and she can tap in the answers on the smartphone and submit them. When she gets to class, her non-virtual algebra teacher may help her with a problem she is stuck on, but the majority of the teaching and practice happens away from the physical confines of the campus.

Her school is equipped with a limited Wi-Fi signal (it blocks social media, for example), but she doesn't use that one. She feels bad for the students who don't have a cell plan and have to use the school's signal: "The bad side of having to use the school's Wi-Fi is the signal's really trashy."

Beyond teacher-produced videos, much of Gigi's formal and informal education is happening via YouTube. "I am a huge fan of YouTube." On the weekend she reports watching fifty videos a day or more, depending on how much her parents limit her cell phone use. She says she's "very particular" about the videos she watches to relax. Her favorite topics? Videos on Game Theory and Film Theory.

"Basically, it's videos of people who overanalyze games and movies. It's awesome. And it's exactly what the name says, like making theories about games, and game endings, making theories about movies, and movie endings."

Gigi is critical of older people who think cell phones and new tech tools are bad for kids, but she acknowledges their concern. "They always say that we're always on our phones, but what they don't realize is that some of us are actually gathering information that we're going to use in real life because school doesn't actually tell us what we'll need to use for real life, and what real people in real life actually do. Although other times we're just literally sitting there rotting our brains."

Forward-thinking leaders are embracing Gen Z's preference for everything mobile rather than criticizing them for it. Blake Garrett is the founder and CEO of Aceable, an online platform and mobile app that offers driver's education courses. When coming up with the idea for Aceable, Garrett shared that he wanted to pair the future of mobile as a learning device with education that helps people change their lives.

"The question I asked myself," he says, "was 'Who would want to learn on mobile?'" That led him to teens. Then he dug deeper and wondered: "What is something teens need to learn outside of their K through 12 education that hasn't been done in an interesting way?"

The answer: driver's education.

"The idea was to deliver an engaging mobile experience that teens can access from wherever they are, on the devices they love to consume content on, and build a relationship with them. Then, as they continue through the life cycle of education, we can keep helping them in other areas," Garrett explains.

Garrett and his team spend a lot of time developing and updating Aceable with teens in mind. They hire high school and college interns to help them make Aceable's teaching approach connect with teens, because, as Garrett admits, "they understand that voice a heck of a lot better than me as a thirty-five-year-old guy."

Every detail of Aceable is teen-tested, from the robot avatar, Ace, who teaches the course to the in-app gamification details that make each lesson fun and competitive.

Garrett shares that since launching Aceable in 2013, he's been impressed by how determined Gen Z is to learn new skills and how they take ownership of that learning. He's observed that more than half of Aceable's Gen Z customers purchase courses using a payment method that is under their own name. And that same ratio of teens calls customer support to troubleshoot questions vs. having their parents call in for them.

One of his most memorable customer interactions was with a teen named Hannah. "She wrote in to customer support asking for a refund because the iPad she'd been using to take the course broke, and she couldn't get a new one," Garrett recalls.

"It was 2014, a time when we were getting about five new customers a day. So refunding $100 was not something we were eager to do.

"I wrote Hannah back and offered to ship an iPad to her. We had one in the office that didn't get used much, so it was worth a try. We were seven employees at the time (now we're 225) and we all worked around one table. We took a vote on who thought Hannah would send the iPad back when she was done, and we were split down the middle. Those who thought she would send it were on Team Life and those who didn't were on Team Death."

The verdict?

"Hannah shipped back the iPad with a handwritten letter thanking us for trusting her as a young adult with something so valuable. She shared that she'd nicknamed the iPad Blue (because it had a blue case) and that she would forever be thankful for her Aceable experience. We still have the iPad in our office today."

It was the perfect blend of offering Gen Z learning tools on the platforms they love to use, and then believing in the generation to follow through.

For Gen Z, what "an education" actually is is now up for debate. Learning is increasingly self-directed given their access to the world's knowledge—or, at least the knowledge that's searchable by Google, YouTube, and more. But Gen Z is certain of one thing: learning is now deeply integrated with their phones. And, frankly, so is just about everything else.

As Gen Z's younger set grows up there is no question that they will expect all communication to be able to come through those small screens. Quite simply, they won't know any other way of life.

5 MONEY, SAVING, AND SPENDING

"Carrying my credit card in my cell phone feels normal because I feel like wallets are old-school."

—Gen Zer

When fashion designer Tyler Lambert was just nineteen years old, his clothes were already being worn by Kylie Jenner and Sofia Richie. Tyler grew up in the small town of De Pere, Wisconsin, but that didn't stop him from finding a way into the fashion world. He made a habit of buying clothes at thrift stores and then transforming them into his own designs.

Tyler's flair for fashion was inspired by a grandmother who took him shopping at estate sales and a mother who was deeply immersed in her sewing hobby. Tyler's art teacher and another local artist mentored him on art history. He worked at his family's diner to earn money to buy materials. When not in school or at work, he was at his sewing machine repurposing curtains, lace doilies, denim, flannel, and other thrift store finds to create his own fashion line. Then he leveraged social media to get eyeballs on his creations.

By the time Tyler graduated from De Pere High School, he had a profitable clothing company.

Tyler left his hometown and briefly attended the Art Institute of

Chicago before dropping out to focus on his company. He now lives in Los Angeles, where he outfits celebrities and is creative director of his fashion line, LAMBERT.

Tyler may sound like a Gen Z anomaly, and in some ways, he is. Most teens don't scour estate sales and build fashion companies. But the qualities that fueled Tyler's success are prevalent throughout his generation. Many Gen Zers are frugal. They want to be financially independent. They value opportunities for unconventional learning over the glitz of attending expensive schools—much to the consternation of their parents, who might still prefer or push for a fancy school.

Even those in Gen Z whose lives look nothing like Tyler's share many of his values around money. Sixteen-year-old Alessandro shares with us:

"In my eyes, earning money is really important so I can save for the future. I'm heavily invested in learning about finance. I want to have money so I can do more things in the future and not be tied down. Right now, I save around 80% of the money I make and I invest 20%.

"I was fourteen when I first started trying to figure out ways to make money. I'd do jobs for people. I'd rake leaves or cut bushes. I used to teach chess to younger kids for money."

At age fifteen, Alessandro rode his bike to a local nursing home and asked if he could volunteer. They agreed and allowed him on to volunteer twice a week, and when he turned sixteen, Alessandro was hired as a part-time employee serving food and drinks.

When asked why he works at a nursing home, Alessandro said, "I felt a strong connection with older people in general. I love talking to them. They have tons of experience and stories, so it's cool to learn from them. I really felt like they needed someone to just talk to them.

"When I volunteered there, I used to play a game called Rummikub with Ms. Storn. She was ninety-three. Her family had left her there. She has been there for six years. She had no one to really talk to. So, as I volunteered, she'd always wait for me and play Rummikub for a good couple hours, and we'd talk.

"When I started working there, I'd always come to her, serve her, take a little bit of time in between serving food to talk to her for a little bit. We'd just keep talking."

Alessandro credits Ms. Storn for teaching him a lot about life and money.

"She said to enjoy my time now instead of thinking too far ahead in the future, and to really just be in the moment, because it flies by fast. And that's kind of how I see money; just how fast it comes and goes, and how you can lose it in the blink of an eye, or also gain it. It's hard not to always think of the future and just appreciate today. But I've got to save for the future."

Alessandro is in tenth grade and has already saved over $5,000 from the money he's earned from the nursing home. His favorite brand is Apple, because "I like how long they last." He goes on to say, "I feel like their build quality is pretty solid, and it's simple, and it works well."

He invests his money through an app in an account his parents opened for him and trades under their names, since he's too young to have his own investment account.

Tyler's and Alessandro's lives couldn't be more different, but they're prime examples of the ways in which Gen Z is taking control of their financial future. According to our 2019 national study, 70% of Gen Z over age eighteen pay at least some of their bills, with 23% supporting themselves fully and 21% paying the majority of their own bills. Some in Gen Z are driven by a desire to avoid the financial challenges that their Gen X and Millennial parents faced. From witnessing their parents struggle with job loss during the Great Recession to living through the realities of crippling student loan debt, Gen Z is eager to write a different financial future for themselves.

And the best part? They're growing up in a time when mobile technology is making it easier than ever to earn, save, invest, and spend money. Gen Z is using apps to leverage just about every part of their financial lives, whether they're banking or shopping—or, like Tyler, using social media to build brand awareness for their businesses.

Gen Z has strong opinions about spending, saving, and earning money, and before anyone can try marketing to them as potential customers or employees, it's critical to understand where their financial values and expectations lie.

Gen Z's Sources of Money

> "Even though my parents are supporting me with an allowance,
> I don't feel good about it. I don't want to be like, 'Oh, I need
> money.' I'd rather be busier and have a job and be supporting
> myself than them supporting me. My family was really open about
> finances and everything. That's where I learned to save because
> they'd talk to us about it and everything. I feel like, bad. I'd rather
> have my own thing. Yeah, 'cause of all the expenses of life."
>
> —Gen Zer

So where does Gen Z actually get their money? If the oldest is in their early twenties, are they getting their money from work, parents, or starting their own business? These questions are key to seeing what Gen Z connects with the sources of their money. Is money something that is earned through work, effort, or achievement, or is it something that is just given to you by family members or others?

In our national study of Gen Z ages fourteen to twenty-two, we looked at this question, and the answers were surprising. What we found:

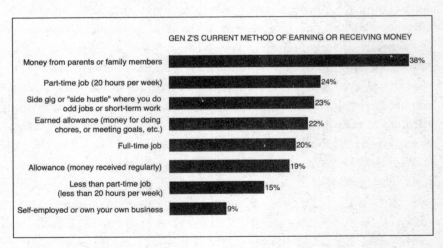

GEN Z'S CURRENT METHOD OF EARNING OR RECEIVING MONEY

Money from parents or family members	38%
Part-time job (20 hours per week)	24%
Side gig or "side hustle" where you do odd jobs or short-term work	23%
Earned allowance (money for doing chores, or meeting goals, etc.)	22%
Full-time job	20%
Allowance (money received regularly)	19%
Less than part-time job (less than 20 hours per week)	15%
Self-employed or own your own business	9%

Of course, as Gen Z continues to get older, more and more of them should earn their money from work. However, what most interests us now is how the younger members of the generation are earning their money. It was fascinating to see how many *earn* their money in some form or fashion rather than just receive it as a handout, which bodes well for the generation as they enter the workforce and have to become increasingly self-reliant.

Gen Z's eagerness to earn their own income is prevalent across the generation, although sometimes their inherent ways of communicating get the best of them. A family friend shared with us how his thirteen-year-old son, Will, started a lawn-service company by posting flyers throughout their neighborhood. For contact information, he included his email. After a month he hadn't heard from a single person. When his dad asked him if he had logged into his email to check his messages, Will said he hadn't. He hardly uses email, so it just hadn't occurred to him to check the account. When he finally did, his inbox was flooded with inquiries—but they were already a month old!

It will be interesting to see how entrepreneurial Gen Z becomes as they age up. Already, a small segment of teens and tweens are bringing in income as YouTube stars, although not as much as the hype might suggest. Research out of the University of Applied Sciences in Offenburg, Germany, notes that only the top 3% of YouTube channels receive 85% of all views, making it difficult for the average creator to earn substantial income. Our research continually shows that Gen Z wants to have stable work, be financially independent, and avoid debt after seeing the financial pains that their Millennial and Gen X parents went through. The research predicting *how* they will achieve this is split down the middle. According to data from Online Schools Center, 41% of Gen Zers in middle school and high school say they plan to start their own business. It's an impressive number, to be sure, but it also leaves more than half of Gen Z with plans to pursue traditional work. Whatever path they choose, Gen Z will find a way to financial stability—it's among their biggest goals.

Who Needs a Wallet?

"Can you Venmo me five dollars?"

I remember the look on the other person's face. What. In. The. World. Is. Venmo?

Venmo and its competitor, the Cash App, are the currency of Gen Z.

If you aren't familiar with Venmo or the Cash App, then you probably don't have—or need to pay—a Gen Z kid or grandkid. Venmo and the Cash App are mobile apps that allow you to instantly send money from your account to someone else's without a fee. This includes being able to instantly send *very* small amounts—such as a single dollar. Along with sending money, you include a short message (which could be only emojis!) about why you sent the money or anything else you choose to write to entertain yourself or the recipient.

How popular is Venmo? In a single quarter of 2019, more than twenty-four *billion* US dollars were transferred on Venmo. That is a lot of missing crinkled-up one-dollar bills in old gym shorts! In fact, Venmo now has more than forty *million* users.

As the pioneer in its space, Venmo has developed an early lead by conditioning Gen Z to not need cash. This generation has never had to struggle with dividing a dinner bill via credit cards. Instead, one person at dinner "Venmos" their friend their portion of the bill. Some restaurants like Chipotle and apps like Grubhub even offer the option to simply pay directly with Venmo, with many more retailers likely on the way.

The rapid rise and adoption of Venmo; a flurry of peer-to-peer payment services, such as Zelle, which is heavily promoted by traditional banks; and the rapidly growing Cash App have made it normal for Gen Z to not have to carry cash, ever. This is true not only for the United States but also for a variety of payment apps that are highly localized and extremely popular around the world.

At CGK, we have found from our research with a major financial client that Gen Z is less comfortable carrying cash than older generations. Gen Z is the first generation that will enter adulthood seeing cash as largely optional. In-app payments are also playing a huge role in this shift to going cashless. An app-based payment provides the convenience you feel when you order your Frappuccino at Starbucks using the Starbucks App and then show up, skip the long line to order, and celebrate with your drink being ready when you are.

The rise of mobile payments, such as Apple Pay, PayPal, Facebook

Pay, and countless others, also means that Gen Z will become less reliant on cash, coins, and certainly checkbooks (which some in Gen Z will never use, ever). Already, our 2019 national study reveals that 59% of Gen Z are using money transfer apps at least once a week, and that number jumps to 69% for members of Gen Z in the eighteen to twenty-three age group.

All of this creates a new and interesting distance between Gen Z and their view of money, as if money is something that exists as "numbers on a screen" rather than "cash in your wallet." Gen Z not carrying cash is already affecting a variety of services, such as Gen Z being unable to tip valet and baggage handlers as well as restaurants struggling to tip out their servers after a shift because not enough people paid in cash for their meal or tips. In fact, some restaurants have to have cash *delivered to the restaurant* so they can tip out their servers at the end of a shift.

The generation's digital spending habits have also opened opportunities for new tech platforms to better serve Gen Z's needs. Scott Gordon, CEO and cofounder of Kard, saw a gap when he learned that 70% of spending among Gen Z in Europe happened through digital channels, but only 10% of those transactions were completed using a payment method that was under the shopper's name. So he created Kard, a challenger bank that allows shoppers in France to open an account starting at age twelve and use it to shop worldwide. Customers under eighteen get an approval link sent to their parents, and funds get transferred to their account from their parents' bank or credit card.

"It's a way to empower Gen Z to take control of their money, and as a result, take control of their life," Gordon shares with us. He designed Kard specifically for Gen Z in two ways. First, he and his team know how impatient they are with inefficient digital platforms, so it takes only two minutes to set up an account from your phone (minus whatever time the parent takes to click the approval link!). It's also designed for Gen Z's love of social media sharing: after they make a purchase, they can choose to share the item with their online networks—or not.

Meanwhile, Larry Talley and his team are helping companies engage with Gen Z by giving them a way to pay via one of their favorite communication methods: text. His company, Everyware, partners with credit card companies and other payment processers to embed a pay-by-text option anytime a customer shops or needs to pay a bill. They can even resolve customer service issues by text.

Everyware started when Talley also saw a gap between how Gen Z prefers to handle money and the payment options available to them. "What we've found," Talley tells us, "is that it's not that Gen Z doesn't want to pay their bills. It's just an inconvenience for them to log on to a website, or mail in a check, or call a 1-800 number. They're not checking the traditional mail for bills. They don't read statements. This generation wants everything super-fast, so it's a way to give them that convenience and connect with them where they are—on their phone."

One of Everyware's biggest outreaches has been with churches and nonprofits. "Gen Z doesn't carry cash in their pockets, but if they're in church and a pastor says to text 'give' to a certain number, they're much more likely to donate," Talley said.

While the positives of going cashless appear to outweigh the negatives, like all change driven by technology, there will be challenges and unexpected side effects—and new solutions that emerge every day to combat them. Gen Z, however, will be the generation that simply expects to be able to *always* send money without opening their wallet—or even having one—and to be able to pay for things with the swipe of their phone or smartwatch, or by tapping on their favorite ordering app or using Apple Pay.

College and Debt

"I just don't want to end up in debt like the Millennials."

—Gen Z focus group participant

So what does Gen Z think about money in general?

In the United States, this is a generation that has been forever shaped by several financial events that have swept across the country: the Great Recession, student loan debt, and wage stagnation.

Many in Gen Z saw their parents or their parents' friends and neighbors struggle mightily during the Great Recession. The generation read the headlines of people losing jobs and houses, and certainly had a front-row seat to seeing many parents and adults lose their confidence. They heard about the challenge of finding jobs and saw the protests about a "living wage" and a $15 minimum wage. At the same time, they constantly talked about the crush of college student loan debt facing Millennials; this was repeated over and over as a financial anchor that many Millennials may never overcome.

Gen Z saw each of these money-related challenges and events at a formative time in their youth and adolescence. The result is a generation that has a view of money, debt, work, and their future that is different from the generation before.

This is not just limited to the United States, as a generation of young adults from Greece to Japan often say they may never be as successful as their parents or grandparents. The same is true in countries in Latin America that have struggled for external and internal reasons. In addition, the overall global recession that many countries, not just the United States, felt shaped Gen Z and their views of money, work, retirement, and more. The effects have been felt all the way to the latest volleys about Brexit.

Now that the oldest members of Gen Z have a work, saving, and spending history that can be tracked and analyzed, several trends are starting to emerge. In addition to the tracking data, our research team has led numerous studies specifically diving into Gen Z's view of money, debt, spending, and much more. The results are startling and show a distinctly new trajectory and mindset from the generation before them that leaders need to know about.

Gen Z on College

"How did you pick the college you chose to attend?"
    "It was easy. I picked the best college that accepted me *and* gave me a full scholarship."

"So you turned down four other colleges that are more
famous and prestigious than the one you chose to attend?"
"Yes. It's more important to graduate college with no debt
than to graduate from a famous school with a ton of debt."

—Gen Zer

"I would rather go to a cheaper school. If I had two options and
one was a better school but it was more expensive, I'd rather go
to the lesser school but be at the top in my class and pay less. I
know if I went to a better school I'd be more or less middle and
I feel like it's about GPA. So I'd rather have fewer loans and be
at the top of my class than have more loans and have a lower
GPA."

—Gen Zer

When it comes to college, our studies consistently show that Gen Z does want to attend college. In fact, our 2018 national study uncovered that 86% of high school–aged Gen Zers (thirteen to seventeen) plan to go to college. However, they are very nervous about taking on student loan debt in order to get their degree. They are not alone, as their parents often feel the same way. On the flip side, over 50% of all private colleges and universities are now having to discount their tuition. In 2019, 89% of freshmen received financial aid from their private college, covering nearly 60% of their tuition.

This mindset of "If I'm going to go to college, I want to graduate with as little debt as possible" appears increasingly pervasive with Gen Z, and not just for those within the generation who come from modest backgrounds. Even affluent families are concerned about the skyrocketing cost of college and the return on their education investment. As we mentioned earlier, among pre-college-aged Gen Zers (thirteen to seventeen), our national studies reveal that half of Gen Z are only willing to take on $10,000 or less in student loan debt, and 27% are not willing to take on any of this debt at all. Both Gen Z and their parents have seen the cost of college increase dramatically as well as the burden that can create on young adults for decades. Gen Z is well aware of this situation and in many cases is trying to be as fiscally pragmatic as they can to get in and get the degree they desire.

What does this mean long term? Graduating with less college debt makes it easier for Gen Z to move to another city to pursue a job or career, to save money for emergencies and retirement as they get older, and to build credit through a track record of better financial decisions and debt-to-earnings ratio. If Gen Z continues with this more practical mindset about debt, the combination of a college degree and fewer financial anchors could bode well for the generation in the long run. At the same time, if paying off the college debt they do have is a priority, this creates an ideal situation for companies to offer student loan repayment programs as both a valuable and effective recruiting and retention tool.

In our 2017 State of Gen Z Study, we asked Gen Z where they thought they were going to get the money to pay for college. Here are the top answers (note that they could choose more than one answer):

Scholarships: 54%

Work during school: 38%

My family or parents will pay: 32%

Student loans: 30%

Personal savings: 24%

The vast majority of Gen Z plans to pay for college with scholarships and by working at a job while attending college. Student loans and parents paying are the next most frequently chosen options.

Consumer Debt

We've heard the horror stories of Gen X and Millennials who were wooed by credit card brochures and blindly applied for credit, then spent and spent and spent—only to realize the consequences of late fees and APRs when it was far too late.

Gen Z knows better than to do this. After all, those debt-ridden Gen Xers and Millennials were *their parents*. If they didn't witness the stress that consumer debt brought to their families, they certainly heard the stories. And they don't want to repeat those mistakes. Our research shows that 23% of Gen Z believe that debt should be avoided at *all* costs and 29% of Gen Z believe debt should be reserved for a few select items. Meanwhile, 18% of Gen Z believe debt should be used as a last resort.

But Gen Z is not shunning credit cards completely. Early data from TransUnion shows that 7.7 million members of Gen Z who are credit eligible had a credit card in 2019. Before we can draw conclusions about this trend, we would want to review more years of usage to better understand how they are managing that credit—particularly in an economic downturn. It will also be interesting to see how credit-eligible members of Gen Z respond to being able to instantly compare rates and fees before selecting a credit card and how they ultimately pay for bigger purchases. Until we know more, it is reasonable to say that older members of Gen Z are approaching credit with caution: 36% of Gen Z ages eighteen to twenty-four told us during our 2019 State of Gen Z Study that they worry about their credit score monthly or more often.

One major change sure to hit the world of consumer debt is that Gen Z will demand more options for paying off large purchases and more transparency when it comes to securing personal credit—and they're getting it. Companies like Sezzle allow customers to break up a purchase into four payments with no fees and no interest. It's the convenience of a credit card without the risk of fees or total freedom that a credit card gives you to make purchases anywhere the card is accepted. Others, like Affirm, allow customers to choose a payment plan up front with transparency on interest rates. Again, buy now, pay later, and know exactly what you're getting into.

Fintech—apps used for banking and other financial services—is helping Gen Z with debt on the education side, too. SoFi is a company that enables student loan borrowers to refinance their loans. They've already refinanced more than $18 billion in student loans for over 250,000 students. Vault is a company that enables employers to make contributions to pay down an employee's student loan debt. Talk about a powerful recruiting strategy for a generation that wants to get out of debt.

On one hand Gen Z has access to a wide marketplace of personal loans and refinance options, and on the other hand they are trying hard to avoid debt.

Cryptocurrencies and Blockchain

We can't have a chapter on Gen Z and money without talking about cryptocurrencies and blockchain. While the awareness of Bitcoin spiked with the exponential increase in its valuation—and subsequent implosion—in 2018, the larger idea of alternative currencies has definitely caught Gen Z's attention. However, much of the cryptocurrency speculation did not occur with Gen Z. In fact, Gen Z was often too young to invest, didn't have the money to invest, or for a variety of reasons wasn't allowed to invest (thanks, Mom). The generation that most often jumped into cryptocurrencies were the Millennials, who too often thought of it as easy money, meaning it would always go up in value, or at least had less downside risk than it really did. As innocent bystanders to the crypto bubble, Gen Zers are likely to interact with money, investing, and risk in a new way. They may appreciate the utility of blockchain technologies as an alternative to traditional financial vehicles without getting caught up in the same gold rush mentality that attracted previous generations.

Retirement

"The threat of not having Social Security benefits freaks me out. It makes me have to focus that much more on working my job, not getting the Social Security benefits that our parents get and everything."

—Gen Zer

Surprising statistic: 12% of Gen Z are already saving for retirement.

That is right. In our 2017 State of Gen Z Study, 12% of the generation, ages fourteen to twenty-two, are already saving for retirement. That is a *shocking* number considering their youth. Why are they saving for retirement? For the same themes we've discussed earlier in this chapter: the Great Recession, their parents' advice, Millennial debt, and a strong need for financial security in case of the unexpected. In the United States, they also know they may not have Social Security but will rather be self-financing any retirement they hope to achieve. Even though the majority of Gen Z is not saving for retirement yet, 69% believe that doing so should be a top priority once they can.

In addition to saving for retirement, we see Gen Z coming of age at a time of overwhelming change and innovation in the financial advising, investing, and retirement space. Gen Z will remember there always having been robo-advisors, such as Wealthfront and Betterment, always having access to Health Savings Accounts (HSAs), and always having to self-fund their retirement plans because pensions are now a thing of the way past.

Robo-advisors, in particular, could bode very well for the generation as they enable Gen Z to open accounts for very little money and contribute only a small amount at a time but see their investment change over time. Robo-advisors usually have a user experience that feels more like a consumer app, so it often feels easier to use, less intimidating, and much more visually compelling. Each of these elements aligns well with Gen Z's comfort for seeing money as numbers or visuals on a screen and the desire to set up an automatic plan so "it just happens" in the background.

Gen Z clearly recognizes that government safety nets for retirement, such as Social Security in the United States, may not be there for them.

So if Gen Z does want to retire it is going to be up to them to make it happen. What is fascinating about the interest in retirement, including the action approximately one in nine Gen Z is taking, is that they are so young. There is a tremendous likelihood of reaching retirement goals if you start investing for retirement at a young age, especially as young as your twenties.

Over one third (35%) of Gen Z expect to personally start saving for retirement in their twenties. What remains to be seen is if Gen Z actually moves into investing toward retirement rather than putting money in a bank account and thinking that is investing. This is a real risk, as a recent study we led with Millennials found that their number one action to save for retirement was to put money in a savings account—which will not allow them to earn a return large enough to be able to afford to retire in the future.

The reality is that Gen Z has the mindset and years ahead to be able to limit their spending now and continue saving. If they can go from saving to investing, particularly with self-directed retirement plans offered by employers, they will have a head start on creating a financial foundation that will afford them the lifestyle they say they want.

PART II

MEET THE WORLD'S MOST INFLUENTIAL CUSTOMERS

6 WHAT GEN Z WANTS FROM A BRAND

"I'm a big athlete and soccer fan. So, I follow Nike and Adidas and big-name sports brands. I like these brands because of their marketing on social media because they post pictures that appeal to a fan base, whether they're eighty or a sixteen-year-old like me who is scrolling through Instagram."

—Shehan, Gen Zer

Did you see the viral and hotly contested Nike ad featuring former San Francisco 49ers quarterback and social justice activist Colin Kaepernick? Over a black-and-white photo, the ad displayed white text that read "Believe in something. Even if it means sacrificing everything."

The controversial ad created a media firestorm and led to an immediate drop in Nike's stock price. People were burning their Nike sneakers and cutting the Swoosh logo off their socks. Within a few weeks, however, Nike's stock price surged as much as 9.2% after it reported second quarter results. The ad had driven a large uptick in engagement by consumers, and according to Apex Marketing Group, it brought $163.5 million worth of media exposure to Nike.

Why would Nike have courted such controversy? The answer appeared clear within days: Gen Z had an overwhelmingly positive response to the ad.

Nike was playing to their future, not their past, consumer. Nike recognized that Gen Zers prioritize diversity, inclusion, and social causes when making purchasing decisions. We've seen this repeated in our research into Gen Z and brand trust.

Nike, a legacy brand, was *not* targeting older generations that already had a belief of what the brand stood for, but rather a new generation of buyers who are strongly engaged with social causes and activism. *Ad Age* said it was "a bold move in an age where marketers often talk a big game about becoming part of the cultural conversation, but often fall short by refusing to take much of a stand on anything."

Nike released the ad first on social media rather than TV because they were targeting their *future* consumers, not their current or past consumers—and it worked to drive tremendous Gen Z engagement.

Nolan, age eighteen, shares, "I think people really loved how impactful the ad was and that it was not something you'd really ever see in the past in terms of marketing strategies. People in my generation really enjoyed it because it was such a statement. Regardless even of the content the *boldness* of it spoke really well for Nike."

When market research firm YPulse polled Gen Z and Millennials on their response to the campaign, Nike scored the highest among four top competitors—often by a 20% to 30% margin—as a brand they consider to be popular, to support causes, that is often talked about, and that they will buy.

Nike knew what they were getting into when they decided to make Kaepernick the face of their new ad campaign. They knew they would lose some loyal, valuable, long-term customers, but more important, they would position themselves as a culturally relevant brand willing to push the envelope to prove they are in alignment with an incredibly important demographic of shoppers that is being bombarded with new brands every day: Gen Z.

Brent Blonkvist, president of the Gen Z–focused online platform Odyssey, shared with us that their research shows that 79% of the platform's audience believes they should leverage their buying power to support brands that care about the points of view that they do— where there's true ideological alignment.

Nike understands that Gen Z has huge spending power, and that their spending power grows *dramatically* each year as Gen Z moves further beyond spending their parents' money to entering the workforce as professionals who have their own salary to spend. Nike knows that if they want to earn Gen Z's dollars and keep them for *decades*, they need to be more than a company selling sneakers. They need to become a key part of the cultural conversations surrounding Gen Z.

Present and Consuming

Gen Z is the new "it" generation and will be for *at least a decade* or more. This generation makes up the group of diverse, hyperconnected, short–attention span influencers who are fast becoming the tastemakers across industries, brands, and digital platforms.

Gen Z is the first generation to come of age where power has significantly shifted from those creating and selling items or services to those actually buying (and recommending!) them—thanks to the rise of mobile shopping, social media, and ecommerce. Gen Z can easily create an influential bullhorn on social media that can directly affect a brand, as well as swipe, tap, and click to buy anything in seconds.

Already, Gen Z spends billions annually across digital and traditional buying experiences, and they're influencing the way products and services must position themselves to align with social causes. Gen Z's spending habits are also influencing which products and services other generations think are cool, hip, or smart to buy—especially in trend categories like apparel and personal technology. It's common knowledge that younger adult consumers, particularly of apparel, makeup, and music, are seen as essential trend drivers—that is why advertisers covet them—but this has reached a fever pitch with Gen Z because they can be their own circle of influence through social media. We see this in areas as diverse as women's razors, where brands like Billie are leveraging the power of video among Gen Z to promote body acceptance, to entire engagement platforms like UNiDAYS specifically built to connect Gen Z college students with brands.

Momentum will build as Gen Z further enters into their mid and late twenties. This is why Gen Z has already become so important for bigger-ticket industries such as automotive, insurance, real estate, technology, and travel. Gen Z is at the beginning of their spending tsunami, yet they never knew a time when you couldn't buy these products or services with just a push of a button.

Gen Z's rapid consumer emergence and trendsetting prowess are a wake-up call to brand leaders and business executives, too many of whom realized too late that Millennials were a different type of shopper, influencer, buyer, and loyalty-building customer than Gen X before them. Millennials did not respond well to traditional marketing, advertising, and sales techniques. The results for many brands were declining sales, declining stock prices, and entire brands going out of business because they never adapted to engage Millennials as long-term customers. Brand leaders have taken the tough lesson Millennials delivered to heart and are being more proactive in understanding and adapting to Gen Z—and they can't start taking action soon enough.

Gen Z offers a fresh start for driving new customer awareness, a new brand narrative, new sales experiences, brand loyalty, customer referrals, and much more. For one thing, Gen Z is creating *tremendous* amounts of consumer data as they communicate, shop, buy, share, return, refer, rate, and react. This data is housed in payment transactions, loyalty programs, social media engagement, website visits, and other platforms. This trove of data—when analyzed through a generational researcher lens—provides predictive clues to help marketers, brands, and entrepreneurs to win this generation's loyalty. Gen Z tells us exactly what they want through their actions and attitudes. We just need to listen to them.

Expectations as Consumers

So, what does Gen Z want when it comes to brand awareness, initial trial, payment, referrals, and loyalty?

In our work with brand leaders, from CEOs and CMOs to corporate boards and entrepreneurs, we find it's best to start by looking at the world through the lens of Gen Z as a consumer generation. Our research consistently points to three key qualities that attract Gen Z as shoppers: value, individualized content and ads, and social responsibility.

Make It Worth Their Money

As we've mentioned, Gen Z has come of age in the aftershocks of the Great Recession. This generation-defining period has made Gen Z more fiscally conservative and practical than their age would suggest. Gen Z really wants value for their money—whether through pricing, utility, or durability. This can look like purchasing a product that lasts a long time (even jeans!), receiving a deep discount on the purchase price on Amazon or in-store, or buying name-brand clothes for 95% off retail at thrift stores.

In fact, Gen Z tells our research team over and over that they *love* to shop at thrift stores. They share the importance of being able to buy clothes at a huge discount, the excitement of not knowing what they're going to find, the lack of pressure in shopping in a thrift store versus the mall, and the diversity of options within a single thrift store.

One member of Gen Z shares: "My friends thrift shop a lot. I have friends who cosplay, and so they love going thrift shopping for that. We had a whole weekend two weeks ago where we went thrift shopping and we got things to do a casual Sherlock cosplay. We go a lot for things like that, and then they wear it to school, too."

Thrift shopping may seem like a quintessential Gen X or Millennial hobby, but Gen Z is teaching us that the trend is not a trend at all. In the last few years alone, Gen Z showed the biggest jump in second-hand clothing purchases compared to older generations. They bought 46% more used items in 2019 than in 2017. By comparison, Millennials' purchases of secondhand items grew 37% in that time span, while Gen Xers' and Boomers' purchases grew by 18% and 15%, respectively. So while shopping for secondhand clothing is on the rise across generations, Gen Z is leading the charge.

But clearly this is for those who can't afford to shop at the local mall or on Amazon, right? Nope. One of the big surprises of our studies is seeing how much members of Gen Z who are affluent love to shop at thrift stores. They talk about how ridiculous the price of clothes has become and how thrift stores allow them to get cool clothes at a great price. They talk about the value of what they are able to buy. In short, they say almost verbatim what members of Gen Z from lower socio-economic situations say: value, value, value.

However, Gen Z's desire for *value* does not mean they will tolerate *poor quality*. They would rather opt for well-made thrift clothes or save up for a high-end pair of shoes than spend very little on cheaply made items. The world watched Forever 21, a fast-fashion clothing retailer that specifically targets teens, declare bankruptcy in late 2019 because they failed to appeal to Gen Z. The generation's response? The Internet was overrun with memes and jokes about the company's off-the-mark designs (including a line of USPS-branded clothes), cheap quality, and too-small crop tops.

When Gen Z does decide to splurge, they get behind brands that support their drive for value such as Nike, Adidas, Glossier, and Aerie.

Make It Personal *at All Times*

Gen Z has come of age seeing more product, service, and brand advertisements and content at their current age than any other generation in history. This is due to the unending time this generation spends on their phones, tablets, and larger screens as well as on viewing advertisements or promotional events everywhere from their high school walls to college cafeterias and even ads that pop up when they look for directions on Waze.

But consider this: most of Gen Z has never been wooed by advertisements in the Sunday newspaper or coupons delivered to their mailbox. Our studies show that 24% of Gen Z ages thirteen to seventeen have never even read a physical newspaper at all. Instead, they are inundated by highly customized ads tailored to each of them as individuals—ads that are sandwiched between pictures of their friends, family, and memories on social media feeds. Remember when you first started seeing targeted ads years ago? Most of us found it a bit creepy to see ads on websites or in our social media feed for something we googled only moments ago—and then those ads for shoes, travel, or a blender followed us around the web through retargeting. Now, highly individualized advertisements and content are something that Gen Z expects, making nontargeted, generic ads a complete turnoff to them.

Mary Ellen Dugan is chief marketing officer of WP Engine, the WordPress digital experience platform powering brands and agencies of all sizes. WP Engine serves 120,000 customers with more than 600,000 websites among them, and they regularly run thought leadership studies and analyze customer data to better understand how people prefer to engage with brands. WP Engine's research, led in partnership with CGK, revealed that 44% of Gen Z say they will leave a website if the company doesn't know what they are looking for *before* they get there. Dugan shares, "This generation has made the shift from *fearful* to *fearless*. Previous generations were afraid to share their personal information online. Gen Z is fearless when it comes to sharing personal data, but in return, their expectations for a personalized experience are incredibly high."

Brands also need to be careful about making sure their highly targeted ads appear within the right context. Lisa Utzschneider is CEO at Integral Ad Science, a firm that tracks and analyzes digital advertising to make sure it connects with the right audiences. Before IAS, Utzschneider held leadership roles at Yahoo!, Amazon, and Microsoft, and is an expert at helping brands avoid what IAS calls "brand risk."

"The Internet today is a lot bigger than it's ever been before," Utzschneider explains. "And while that means there's a greater opportunity to reach a wide audience, there's plenty of risk involved, too. Running your ads for a cruise on a travel website is a great idea—until they start writing about the tourism industry creating an increase of pollution in the Caribbean. Advertising is the best way to get your name out there, but there's an inherent risk in putting your company next to potentially unsavory content."

Utzschneider points out that since Gen Z has grown up in the era of targeted ads, mismatched ad placements are even more obvious.

Already, when Gen Z searched YouTube when they were younger, they were conditioned to see the latest LEGO set or Disney princess dress follow them around in ads or other relevant competitors' ads based on their web search history. Gen Z did not experience a time *before* remarketing ads shadowed them or when Amazon didn't recommend other products to add to their shopping cart.

In addition, Gen Z has been conditioned to constantly create data about themselves as they shop. This includes everything from the record they create of their past purchases (including apparel sizes by brand), recommended drinks based on their last order in the Starbucks app, and subscription services where you can send back any items you don't like for free and tell them why you didn't like the item. The result: next month, the items in their subscription box will be even more tailored to their preferences—whether it's clothing in their Stitch Fix box, dog treats in their family's BarkBox, or makeup samples in their Birchbox.

The risk of buying something and having to return it has also largely vanished. Companies today, from clothing to car dealers, will send you a shirt or deliver a car to your driveway. Take Carvana: they let you try out a car, and if you don't like it, you can send it back or request to have them pick it up from your driveway at zero cost to you. In fact, mattress companies like Casper and Tuft & Needle will refund your money if you don't like the mattress they sent in the mail—and then you just have to show that you donated it to a charity or nonprofit that will swing by your apartment or house to pick it up!

Gen Z expects the entire customer experience, from ads to checkout to returns, to be completely customized to their individual preference. If it's not, they will walk.

Make It Stand for Something

Gen Z believes brands should stand for something besides profit and should showcase the positive impact they make in the world. This expectation is already moving fast toward a new normal as the Business Roundtable, an association of nearly two hundred of the most powerful CEOs in the United States, signed a pledge in August 2019 that redefines the purpose of a corporation. Their promise states that companies should no longer just serve shareholders, but all stakeholders.

Who are those "other" stakeholders and how do these CEOs plan to serve them? Their commitment includes delivering value to customers, investing in employees, dealing fairly and ethically with suppliers, and supporting the communities in which we work. Shareholder value is only mentioned at the very end of the pledge, and within the context of being focused on the long term.

This new normal for corporations is well timed, as Gen Z has come of age *always* seeing ads for brands promoting a social position and companies donating everything from shoes (TOMS) and eyeglasses (Warby Parker) to food and water to help others in need. While this highly public alignment with social values was new and in many ways a rallying cry for Millennials, many in Gen Z *expect it*. Before they consider spending on a brand, they want to know that the brand stands for something bigger than its products.

Lisa Utzschneider at IAS sees this as a driving force in her work to help companies reach their target audience—as both consumer brands and potential employers. "Gen Z cares about your mission, and they want to see that you care as well," she shares with us. "They want to see that you value them, and that you stand for your values in the greater world. They're not afraid to call out companies."

Nike knew this when they made the bold move to align themselves with Colin Kaepernick. Although previous generations did not see Nike as a brand that stood behind social issues, Gen Z is coming of age only knowing Nike's evolved image. Meanwhile, other legacy companies that were always known for standing behind larger issues, like Patagonia, are still finding new ways to support their causes. In 2018, Patagonia made international news when they donated the entirety of their $10 million corporate tax cut to groups committed to protecting air, land, and water, and finding solutions to the climate crisis. This is on top of their 1% for the Planet giving initiative, which they have been running since 1985. The company also empowers its employees to make a difference. In 2018, Patagonia closed its stores on election day so their employees could go out and vote.

Not every brand can—or has to—be a full-time social justice or environmental warrior to show customers that they stand for something.

But if you're not already, do think about how you can make a positive impact beyond your daily work. If you're a small clothing retailer, can you donate items to a local women's shelter or run a clothing drive in your community to help others who cannot afford to buy new clothes? If you're a pet groomer, can you sponsor local adoption drives? If you're a mid-sized marketing agency, can you donate a block of hours to help a local nonprofit launch their next fundraiser? Sometimes your desire to change the world is baked right into your company mission. But if it's not, it just means you have an opportunity to get behind any cause you want. The worst thing you can do, from Gen Z's perspective, is only worry about business as usual.

View Your Brand as a Platform

In our work with executives, entrepreneurs, and corporate boards, we spend time uncovering how their brand can become a platform that will draw Gen Z. Becoming a platform—and not just a brand—involves much of what we've been discussing until now: standing for something, whether that is a mission or problem to solve, or a lifestyle your brand represents, and bringing that to life across multiple channels. It includes extending beyond a physical product or memorable name to be a conduit for content, collaboration, purpose, trust, and much deeper engagement with consumers' daily life. This means not just having a mobile-first website, but also being active on the right social media channels and providing experiences and events that amplify conversation and physical-to-digital connection.

Viewing a brand as a platform aligns the company's vision across all of its components, from manufacturing and operations to marketing and public relations. Manufacturing now has increased importance, for example, because Gen Z wants to know where and how a product was made and if it was responsibly sourced. They also want transparency in areas like food ingredients, a company's commitment to equal pay and inclusiveness, and environmental responsibility. Operations needs to align with marketing and external communications, because a viral video can create demand that breaks the supply chain; or a video that uncovers practices that run counter to a company's messaging—like footage of operations polluting a stream—can negate years of careful branding.

Transparency regarding digital privacy plays a huge role in this as well. As we stated before, Gen Z is willing to share personal data with companies, but in exchange, they want to know they can trust that company to keep their information safe.

Arlo Gilbert is the founder of Osano, a company created to help businesses be transparent about digital privacy. Osano's consumer-facing product, Privacy Monitor, weeds through the endless fine print in a company's terms and conditions and distills them down to a few digestible points consumers can understand.

Gilbert explains, "Everybody tells the same lie every single day. And it has consequences. That lie is: 'I have read and agree to the terms and conditions.' We all do it."

Hardly any of us actually reads a company's terms and conditions before clicking "yes, I agree." But the more that business leaders like Mark Zuckerberg and Jeff Bezos are put under the microscope for potentially irresponsible use of our data, the more consumers care. Gen Z, especially, cares, as they grew up making data-informed decisions. If they know they can trust a company to keep their data private, they are more likely to align themselves with that platform.

"It's the supply chain of software and services," Gilbert says. "Just like Gen Z cares about where something was manufactured, whether child labor was used, or whether it has chemicals in it, they want to know what's happening with their data. They want to know who's good and who's bad. If you're transparent about what you're doing with their data, and that you're handling it with care, it becomes a marketing opportunity for you. Because you can now say, 'You can trust us to process your credit card, or to collect your email or some health information, because we're going to do a good job with it.'"

Becoming a platform ultimately comes down to trust. Can customers—especially discerning Gen Z—trust you to do what you say you will do and be transparent about what you are already doing? Can they trust you enough to want to share your message and product with their friends? To share their personal information with you? Will they want to align themselves with you and everything you stand for?

A great Gen Z brand platform has three key elements: consistency with the channels most effective to reach their audience (e.g., Wendy's catchy Twitter persona aligning with their in-store product displays), responsiveness with data-driven tracking (e.g., measuring everything and tying it, when possible, to individual customers), and a meaningful connection with Gen Z consumers that fits their life stage and priorities.

Adapting Faster

As Gen Z's importance in the consumer world grows, they are on the front end of many important purchases, from buying (or leasing) their first car, renting their first apartment, or buying more expensive apparel for work to looking for a cool new restaurant for a dinner date made on Bumble. Regardless of the occasion, however, one thing is certain: Gen Z brings a whole new definition of "normal" to the consumer experience, and both brand and sales leaders must act now. Sometimes leaders tell us that Gen Z's expectations are simply too high, but we disagree. Gen Z just has different expectations than other generations—their own definition of normal—and they infuse this into every step of their consumer journey.

Gen Z has come of age in a time of brand and consumer transparency, connectivity, and fast trend hype and implosion (think of the rise and fall of fidget spinners and hoverboards). Gen Z has never had to wait for seasonal clothes changes in stores because they could go to American Eagle Studio, Zara.com, or HM.com and see new styles almost monthly. However, they think waiting in line for the latest phone is not unusual, especially if they serve Popsicles at the iPhone release. But waiting in line to place an order at a restaurant or check into a hotel seems like an inefficient, broken process.

The generation also knows they can walk into any retailer, find a product, take out their phone and read reviews about the product, comparison shop while still in the store, and potentially buy it through their phone only to have it delivered before they return home. While this shopping approach, called showrooming, was new for Millennials (and the bane of many retailers' existence), it is simply normal for Gen Z. In fact, if they're really interested, they can go on YouTube and watch any one of the millions of videos of people "unboxing" something they ordered, from toys to the latest smartphone. These "unboxing" videos are so popular that they've generated millions and millions of dollars for YouTubers whose sole occupation is opening packages of new toys, technology, and more.

The bottom line is that Gen Z has come of age in a time of mixed and even contradictory consumer messages. On one hand, they were raised to be thrifty with their money and practical with their spending because the economy could get tough again just as it did for the generations before them. On the other hand, Gen Z is definitely motivated and excited to shop thanks to social media and a lifetime of seeing more highly individualized ads than any other generation at their current age.

Brands of all sizes and across all industries will be tasked with recognizing this new normal and adapting if they want to benefit from the purchasing power Gen Z brings today, the dramatically greater purchasing power Gen Z brings with each passing year, and the exponentially greater *influencer* power the generation brings to almost every category through their influence on other generations by digital channels.

7 WHAT GEN Z IS BUYING

"I've probably spent $150 on makeup products because I saw them on Snapchat."

—Taylor, sixteen

The oldest members of Gen Z reached twenty-four years old in 2020. Depending on their education and career pathway this means that many have just finished their college career and started working full-time, have already been in the workforce full-time for years if they bypassed college and went straight to work, or some combination of the above (not to mention driving for Lyft or doing side gigs on Task-Rabbit).

On the younger end of the spectrum, Gen Z is also comprised of preteens and younger children who are having birthday parties at trampoline parks, playing Minecraft at the dinner table, wearing JoJo Siwa–branded *everything,* watching TV on Amazon, and likely have a cell phone or a Wi-Fi connected tablet before they get to middle school. This range of life stages within the generation plays out in their current consumer spending patterns and priorities and affects how they spend money and what products and services they choose to put their influence behind.

We've identified the top areas where Gen Z is spending today and how their buying habits are disrupting the way many retailers have been doing business for decades. But this is not cause for alarm. While many companies panic at the thought of reinventing their well-oiled practices, Gen Z's shopping preferences unlock huge potential for brands to connect with this next generation of consumers. In the pages ahead, we take a closer look at how some companies are already making huge strides with Gen Z and how their approaches can spark new ideas for others who are eager to connect with young shoppers.

Apparel

Gen Z believes what they wear is an expression of who they are and can even represent what they stand for—from social groups to social causes. While many in Gen Z are not yet in the coveted "twentysomething" demographic spending bigger dollars on fashion, they will be very, very soon. Gen Z and their apparel shopping have tremendously affected traditional malls and apparel makers. This includes a decrease in foot traffic in many conventional apparel stores as well as a desire for fast fashion, with more affordable and shorter production runs, and a rise in thrift store shopping.

Thrifting, as we mentioned, is a trend we're watching, as the generation appears to like saving money on brand-name clothing, discovering new things for themselves, and socializing with friends as a group. Thrifting has been around for decades, but its rise in popularity across socioeconomic spectrums within Gen Z is important to watch. Brands will need to know how to bridge the "thrifty" mindset through durability, pricing, or other offers—such as instant cash back through apps like Dosh—while still being "on trend." That requires a different approach and a new set of operational skills.

Apparel makers will also need to rethink their in-store experience. For example, dressing room areas need to be designed so Gen Z can take pictures of themselves trying on different outfits in great lighting and with an appealing background so they can post directly on social media. They also want to be able to interact with sales agents immediately, such as requesting a different size or color via message, rather than trying to find a salesperson every time they go into a dressing room.

Leaders in the industry should also look at their digital communication between store visits (or when there are no store visits involved), how they connect to social causes, and how they can personalize Gen Z's shopping experience at every stage of their interaction with a company—from customized ads and shopping cart suggestions to outfit recommendations from a personal shopper.

Brands like Aerie are getting it. They've carved out their defensible difference™ by shunning dated conventions of beauty and embracing body positivity every time they connect with their audience, which ranges from preteens to college-aged women. Their commitment to being #AerieREAL includes not touching up any of their models' photos. Ever. Blemishes, stretch marks, curves, and all other forms of realness are embraced in Aerie's photos. Their models also represent the full spectrum of body shapes, sizes, and colors. On social media, they tag posts with "#AerieREAL is . . ." and encourage their one-plus million followers to share their REALisms.

Gen Z notices Aerie's efforts and approves. As one college student comments on an Aerie Instagram post, "Name a more diverse and accepting clothing brand. I'll wait."

Gen Z's response to brands like Aerie is so palpable that they've contributed to putting Victoria's Secret in crisis. The lingerie frontrunner reported a 45% drop in 2018 sales and spent 2019 attempting to revamp their brand. At a time when self-acceptance, authenticity, and inclusiveness dominate the cultural conversation—especially among some of the world's most powerful shoppers, Gen Z—Victoria's Secret's thin, flawless models are becoming less relevant every day.

Cosmetics and Beauty Products

Gen Z is in prime time when it comes to influencing and being influenced by makeup trends. The really exciting moment for Gen Z is that today's makeup influencers are also members of Gen Z, such as

Kylie Jenner and her hugely successful makeup empire, Kylie Cosmetics. She's been able to drive hundreds of millions of dollars in makeup sales through her social media channels. She strikes the right chord with Gen Z in no small part because she is one herself.

In general, the cosmetics industry is ripe for continued disruption given that most industry leaders are legacy brands stuck in old marketing routines. If they don't adapt to Gen Z in all the ways this generation wants to connect, such as brand transparency, social responsibility, and creating social media–shareable buying experiences, Gen Z will be quick to move on to newer brands that *are* engaging them and their values.

Content-driven marketing will be an important factor in this effort. This generation loves how-to videos, and as younger Gen Zers begin to wear makeup they typically have no idea how to use it or what to buy. Guess where they'll go to learn? YouTube and TikTok. Forget free makeovers at the mall counter. Show Gen Z what shades go with which skin tones, how to apply eyeliner, how to apply lipstick without getting it on your teeth, how to properly care for acne using your skin toner—all through YouTube, TikTok, and social media channels. Then link to your products from the proper platform.

Makeup brands such as Glossier are clicking with Gen Z by being so much more than their products. Glossier has built its empire by offering useful content to its Gen Z–heavy audience. *Into The Gloss*, the blog from which Glossier was born, refers to itself as "a beauty experience." The blog became especially well known for its profile series Top Shelf and Top Shelf After Dark, where they sit on the bathroom floors of everyone from Kim Kardashian to models, restaurateurs, doctors, and DJs to "talk products, career, and what beauty means to women today." The blog also offers product reviews, how-tos, and fun, relatable beauty advice, such as "How to Prep Your Skin When It's a Million Degrees Out" and best practices for using glitter makeup, embracing freckles, and managing acne.

Into The Gloss and Glossier are deeply connected to their readers. Glossier takes social media comments into consideration when concocting makeup formulas, and the blog caters to Gen Z's specific makeup concerns while also empowering them to embrace their own definition of beauty.

Meanwhile, Lush, another Gen Z–approved beauty brand, goes beyond its products by weaving climate change advocacy into every part of their business. You might even call them the Patagonia of cosmetics: on September 20, 2019, Lush closed all of its stores so their employees could march in the youth-led Global Climate Strike to advocate for new climate change policies around the world. They even shut down their ecommerce site for the day.

Lush describes itself as "creating a cosmetics revolution to save the planet." Its products are vegetarian, cruelty free, and handmade. Their social media posts range from how-tos for using their products to inspiration for upcycling their cosmetics containers and behind-the-scenes footage on how their products are made.

Gaming and Consumer Technology

"I always play Fortnite with my friends, and if none of my friends are online then I just get off the game because playing with my friends is what makes it fun for me. I talk to my friends while playing. We talk about life, school, and all sorts of things. I can talk to them about all the same stuff I talk about with them in person. I've probably made friends with six or seven kids at my school through the game and made friends all around the world because I kill them or they kill me and you're like 'hey good job' and then you say 'do you want to play together' and then you just start playing together and then you can play with each other whenever you want. I've made friends in Finland and Australia and new friends in Chicago, Connecticut, California, and New York."

—Will, thirteen

Gen Z are heavy—and often *very* early—tech adopters, from smartphones to Alexa and esports. This generation *relies* on consumer technology in every aspect of their life.

Personal gaming in particular has become so popular with Gen Z that, according to a study by consumer research firm Whistle, 68% of Gen Z males say that gaming is an important part of their personal identity.

Our own research studies found that 88% of Gen Z males and 65% of Gen Z females own a gaming system, and they are spending 3.2 hours *every day* on those gaming systems (that doesn't include games they're playing on their smartphones—on which they're spending another 6.6 hours every day). A total of 70% of Gen Z gamers feel that gaming is addictive.

While playing video games has long been considered an antisocial activity, Gen Z's gaming experience is highly connected and social. Gone are the days of inserting a game cartridge into a console (if it doesn't work, blow on it and try again!) and playing against the computer, or at best, one friend sitting next to you. Gen Z is playing with their friends across town, across the country, and across continents as all of their games connect to online communities, whether it's on the PlayStation Network, Xbox Live, or other online platforms. Whistle discovered that 74% of Gen Z view gaming as a way to stay connected with their friends.

But what is Gen Z *spending* on gaming? According to a study by Nielsen, they're averaging $92 a month between subscription services, game purchases, and additional in-app purchases. That's an impressive number when you consider most of the generation is not earning a full-time income yet.

There is a huge opportunity for leaders to tap into Gen Z's love for gaming, regardless of their industry. Andrea Brimmer, chief marketing and PR officer at Ally Financial, worked with her team to create a virtual reality game around the 2018 Super Bowl. She tells us, "I felt it would be duplicitous for us to buy a Super Bowl spot while we're talking to customers about being good stewards of their money. But we wanted to take advantage of the momentum around the Super Bowl, so we created a game called the Big Save."

The app offered a way for Ally to encourage saving money without preaching to players. In order to download the Big Save app, players first had to tell Ally the biggest thing they are saving for. The brilliance is twofold: not only was Ally engaging with customers and prospective customers in a fun way, but they were collecting data on what people were saving for the most. Out of 31,224 people who played the Big Save, their top two motives were saving for a home (9,362 people) and saving for an emergency fund (8,909 people).

The game only worked when the Super Bowl was in commercials, during which players were challenged to catch money that was raining down into their phone and move it to their virtual piggy bank. After the game, Ally gave away $250,000 to players to put toward their savings goals. That's right: instead of spending millions on a Super Bowl commercial spot, Ally decided to gift money to the people who engaged with their game.

Players were a mix of all generations, but Ally was definitely catering to their younger customers, as 49% of them are Gen Z and Millennials.

In addition to gaming, consumer tech is integrated into nearly every part of Gen Z's life, from how they learn and how they relax at home to how they connect with friends and family. Another big opportunity, particularly with younger members of Gen Z, is how their connected in-home devices will affect their communication and shopping. Many Gen Zers will not remember a time before Alexa. This generation thinks email and Facebook are old, and face-to-face meetings are not the best way to collaborate. This is a trend that started to emerge with Millennials who were quite comfortable using communication and collaboration tools in the workplace even when they weren't officially supported by their employers. According to research done by the platform management company Unify Square and Osterman Research, 28% of Millennials use unapproved collaboration apps like Slack two to four times per week, and 71% use unapproved apps at least a few times per year.

This push toward digital collaboration will only intensify as Gen Z enters the workforce. Gen Z could be renamed Generation Collaboration because of their strong desire to use technology to communicate and work in groups. Other studies we led have shown that younger generations actively consider the workplace's technology when considering whether to accept a job and stay at one.

Whatever your industry, know that Gen Z's dependence on technology is at the forefront of everything they do. Use that to your advantage. How can you integrate new technology into every part of their experience connecting with you?

Entertainment

Gen Z is leading the trend of streaming virtually everything they can. They have always been able to pull up YouTube to discover new music, switch to Spotify to stream that music, and then get a playlist of exactly what they want. Netflix and YouTube conditioned the generation to see recommendations, rate entertainment, and then watch the entertainment on virtually any device, anytime. You start the show on your iPad, then move over to your mom's iPhone, and if it's really good you finish watching it on your smart TV. All the same show, all continued at exactly the same spot on every device, and your next video is recommended based on your rating of the previous one. Now Gen Z can see endless options from movies and TV shows to documentaries on Netflix, Amazon, or YouTube Premium, or go to YouTube and learn how to bake a cake, surf, dance, or watch Fail videos. TikTok took short videos to a new level. At the same time, concerts and live events recognize that Gen Z wants a more immersive, interactive live experience—from ticketing and event updates to interactions with screens from the crowd and even live virtual concerts inside of Fortnite.

Gen Z's desire to interact with entertainers gives those artists the ability to build legions of fans who "heart" or "like" their every post, from musicians like Taylor Swift, Lady Gaga, and BTS to celebrities such as Selena Gomez and The Rock. These influencers have built an entire Gen Z advertising platform through their social media followings. More and more, brands are turning to these celebrity-driven social platforms to connect with Gen Z as an alternative to traditional advertising. In the film industry, for example, this can look like celebrities such as The Rock getting separate contracts to promote the movie in addition to being paid to star in the movie. With 170-plus million Instagram followers, The Rock can garner tremendous excitement over a film by posting behind-the-scenes photos and selfie videos about working on set directly to his Instagram feed. That will spark more excitement for the film than any billboard or prime time TV commercial ever could.

Smart companies recognize that artists, whether world famous or niche, can be powerful advocates for their brand and, depending on the platform, directly drive sales from a social media post, video, or event mention. The key is to find entertainers or influencers who align with a brand's market position, have the right following that can be *measurably* engaged, and have the ability to extend the relationship over a period of time for maximum Gen Z impact. Numerous ad agencies have sprung up to specialize in these offerings; likewise, some companies have created internal specialists whose primary focus is connecting the right entertainer to the right brands for promotion. These connections can now even include featuring the celebrity as an investor or collaborator in the company itself, which has become the norm for forward-thinking celebrities and brands such as Justin Bieber (Spotify), Jessica Alba (Honest Company), Ashton Kutcher (Uber), Tyra Banks (The Muse), and Gary Vaynerchuk (Snapchat).

Diving deeper into entertainment, brands are now focusing on how to integrate directly into video games. For example, brands such as Marvel offered a skin upgrade in Fortnite for players to have an Iron Man skin. Pushing the limits of the convergence between games and entertainers, popular musician Marshmello held a "live in-game concert" on February 2, 2019, which was attended by over *ten million people*—in the Fortnite video game!

For most in Gen Z, entertainment itself is the engagement vehicle. And that engagement should be 24/7, 365 on their favorite connected device with their favorite entertainers. For example, when we work with professional sports, such as basketball teams, getting fans to the stadium early delivers big return on investment (ROI), so giving them a *compelling* reason to arrive early—such as entertainment and celebrity interactions—drives results with a generation that might otherwise not want to arrive early, or at all. The connection is then maintained with behind-the-scenes, athlete-driven content being delivered between games and seasons to keep Gen Z fans interested and on a platform they like, such as Instagram.

Food, Beverages, and Restaurants

We lead a significant amount of research in the food, beverage, and restaurant space, specifically focused on Gen Z compared to other generations. Gen Z has come of age during the food messaging wars, a time when companies heavily promote features and phrases such as non-GMO, organic, locally sourced, fewer than five ingredients, food allergy labels, and countless fad diets. They've also been able to watch cooking shows designed specifically for kids and teens (some even hosted by them), which are popular on traditional cable TV and *really* popular on YouTube. Gen Z has shown that they enjoy cooking—part of our view of them as a "throwback" generation—and many in the generation never experienced a time before calorie counts were printed on the menu alongside their hamburger (or Beyond Meat burger), Frappuccino, or Froyo at their favorite restaurant or on their favorite food ordering app.

Of all the categories we study, food, restaurants, and grocery has already experienced the biggest changes because of this generation's emergence and collision with tech innovations in this space. Gen Z has come of age being able to have food from their favorite restaurant delivered wherever they are—and often with notifications of where the food is in the process of being made and delivered! The delivery apps, from DoorDash and Uber Eats to Grubhub, offer a variety of restaurants and price points and usually twenty-four-hour delivery. While on the surface this would seem to be a boon for restaurants, it has actually had a negative impact on many restaurants' margins. The reason? When you order food online people often bypass the upsell for the appetizer special, dessert of the day, and alcohol. In addition, the restaurants often absorb some of the costs of participating in these delivery apps. Many restaurants rely on selling beer, wine, or a cocktail with your buffalo wings or pizza—yet they don't get those sales via apps. The result is that while some restaurants are selling more food overall through delivery apps, their profits are decreasing.

Also entering into the fray are hybrid options, such as groceraunts. These are the restaurants in grocery stores, such as Whole Foods, which are very popular but take people out of traditional restaurants. Also, ghost restaurants, i.e., restaurants with no physical location that only exist on apps or websites and deliver your food, are creating more choices and testing the limits of what it means to be a restaurant (or a chef-driven concept). For Gen Z, all of these options and many more are poised to give them tremendous choices for food and food delivery. Or as we like to say, Gen Z is still eating, but where they're going to eat, how they're ordering food and drinks, how they're paying, and how they're recommending are all different from other generations—with much more change on the horizon!

Adding to the change of dining options and experiences is the food truck boom that Millennials are known to have driven to massive popularity and now Gen Z comes to expect. The idea of supporting a local chef or concept, sitting outside in a place with cool lighting or that authentically represents the area—and bringing your dog if you have one—is a magnet for Gen Z (and social media posts). Some developers are now courting and including food trucks as part of the overall vision for their development, both to serve workers if an office building is present and to serve a neighborhood with multiple food options at a very low capital investment.

One underlying trend we're seeing affect what Gen Z buys now: fewer total in-store shopping occasions. Gen Z is often driving less, or being driven less, to shop—whether that is for food, alcohol, clothes, or consumer tech—and the result is fewer occasions to spontaneously buy things as they browse a retail store or wait in the checkout aisle.

So what can food, restaurant, and beverage brands do to thrive with Gen Z? We're seeing a lot of test cases and the early findings show that hitting Gen Z's hot buttons is critically important, both for initial trial and repeat visits. This includes offering food that meets diverse dietary needs and supports the local community or a bigger purpose.

Physical spaces would benefit from good music and lighting; compelling visuals—such as images of local hot spots or murals by local artists—so people will want to take pictures with the walls as a background (and not just of the food or drinks); easy access to mass transit, walkability, or parking; and any other details that show the owners truly understand their customer. In addition, savvy food brands like Wendy's and Chick-fil-A regularly reach out to Gen Z via social media to stay top of mind—including having their own "social media beef" about who has a better chicken sandwich.

On the flip side, new mall and store developers are recognizing that they must make the physical environment much more experiential if they want to win Gen Z. This includes outdoor and entertainment spaces, digital integration within stores and throughout entire properties, carefully curated stores physically near each other to attract the right mix of foot traffic, and free Wi-Fi throughout the property. In essence, Gen Z wants a place where they can comfortably shop, eat, hang out, and explore without feeling like they are stuck in the '90s—which they think of as retro!

Spending in the Future

There are many more categories where Gen Z is already driving spending trends, from school supplies to taking care of their pets (no change from older generations here—they also love their pets—but a study by research firm Packaged Facts revealed that they depend on their vet for a much wider variety of information and advice than previous generations). The industries we've mentioned so far provide a good initial representation of the ways Gen Z is spending money now.

But where will Gen Z spend their money—and much more of it—in the near future?

This is where Gen Z aging up starts to have a *much* bigger effect on the economy. Our research has identified several industries in which Gen Z will soon start to have a significant impact and over the next ten years could reshape the balance of company power within those industries. This impact will be amplified in many industries because Baby Boomers will retire over the same time frame and their spending will flatten or decrease accordingly. There is also the impending transfer of wealth: some estimates say $30 trillion could be transferred from Boomers to younger generations. Gen Z should also be earning significantly more money than they do now as they enter and advance in the professional workforce.

Here are the industries we see as having an immediate opportunity—and a small amount of runway—to act now to prepare for Gen Z's emergence.

Banking

What does Gen Z do with the money they are saving due to their more financially conservative ways? They put it in a mobile phone–based payment or banking app. They will likely be able—and expect—to do all their banking in the future without having to visit a bank, from securing a car loan to saving for retirement.

Gen Z has come of age always being able to save money using a variety of financial technology (fintech) options, from banking apps offered by traditional banks to savings apps that automatically skim your account to create an emergency fund for you—and some in Gen Z just keep much of their money in a Cash App or Venmo account. All that saving will eventually lead to credit card and auto loan offers along with a variety of other financial products. Banks and fintech are poised to significantly benefit from Gen Z's combined technology demands and savings patterns, but only if the banking leaders focus on a world-class *mobile-only* experience. This includes opening accounts, transferring money to friends and for bills, providing data visualization and analysis to show Gen Z what they are spending and what they are saving (even what they are saving compared to other people their age), and ultimately integrating with their personal financial goals.

Millennials have already shown the banking and investment world how quickly change can take hold, with their rapid uptake of solutions such as Acorns, Betterment, and Robinhood. While Millennials were introduced to these fintech solutions at a much later stage than Gen Z is in now, their popularity is only a precursor for Gen Z, who will always expect to have them as an option.

Ally Financial was thinking ahead when they launched as one of the world's first all-digital online financial services company in 2009, on the heels of the Great Recession. Andrea Brimmer recalls that everyone told them the world didn't need another bank. "We agreed that the world didn't need another bank—but the world needed a better bank. We took a huge bet that we didn't need brick and mortar."

Ally established their defensible difference™ by setting their focus on authenticity, which helped the bank build a relationship with their customers. "We aim to teach financial literacy in a fun and engaging way," Brimmer shares. "We do a lot of surprise and delight." There was the 2018 Super Bowl Big Save virtual reality game, and in 2016, Ally delighted customers with their Lucky Penny campaign.

"We created a scavenger hunt around the idea that 'a penny saved is a penny earned,'" says Brimmer, "and that Americans don't give pennies any love anymore. We put out fun penny facts, and if you found one of our Ally Lucky Pennies it was worth $1,000."

Other ways Ally has engaged with customers include confession grams, where they challenged people on Instagram to have the "money talk" with their partner, and a "Banksgiving" campaign, where they thanked customers by giving gifts to people who called their customer service line during Thanksgiving (gifts ranged from getting a person's leaves raked to $50,000 in cash).

The outcome of all of Ally's less-than-typical bank behavior? They welcome more than two hundred thousand new Millennial and Gen Z customers every year. That's nearly 65% of their annual new customer base.

When we asked Brimmer why Ally has been able to thrive with Gen Z while other banks struggle, she was able to distill it down to three key points:

1. You have to have the courage to go after a target that doesn't have much money today, but that you know will be the recipient of a huge

wealth transfer in the near future. Many companies have pressure from their board or CEO to focus on the short term and don't get to take that long-term view.

2. This generation will sniff out pretenders pretty darn fast. There is an authenticity to our brand because we do what we say we're going to do and we're out there being very real.

3. We surround ourselves with the right inputs. My kids are in Gen Z. Our agency partners are young. We listen to our customers. You have to listen, then try things that you think will resonate and see how it goes.

Brimmer and her team discovered there is a misconception that Gen Z is not interested in saving. Ally knows they're *huge* savers—saving close to 50% of everything they make—and they have a voracious appetite for learning more about financial literacy.

All banks, whether legacy brands or startups, have a great opportunity with Gen Z. They can bet on the generation's future and empower them with easy-to-use digital tools and valuable content, or not—and miss out on the huge wealth transfer that will soon be passed down to Gen Z.

On the technical side, banks will be challenged to create a seamless digital banking experience. This will include making their platforms more visual, requiring fewer clicks to get information, responding to voice questions, transferring money instantly, and being able to analyze saving and spending.

Integration with new saving and investing options will also become a priority, whether it is new payment types or payment options that don't involve a credit card, such as Sezzle or Affirm, or tools that help account holders manage their money—before they actually receive it. Much better customer service options, including artificial intelligence (AI) chatbots and answering questions about improving credit scores, will become commonplace and a minimum in order to compete and win with Gen Z bank customers.

Cars and Transportation

When it comes to cars, Gen Z could be the start of the "new normal" that disrupts the entire industry. In a national study we led, we've already found that Gen Z is the generation most willing to ride in autonomous cars. This is great timing as automakers rush to create their own version of increasingly self-driving cars and companies like Lyft, in partnership with Aptiv, were already testing self-driving cars with actual customers in Las Vegas at the time of this writing.

Already, we see Gen Z choosing not to get their driver's license right away. The *Wall Street Journal* reported that the percentage of teens getting their driver's license has dropped by nearly 20% since the 1980s. This is due to the cost of owning and driving a car in many areas, the lack of need for a car during college and in urban areas, and the prevalence of ride-sharing options, such as Uber and Lyft, in increasingly suburban and even more rural areas. In addition, mass transit has also gotten easier for many in Gen Z to navigate as it integrates with their phone for easier payment and usage.

When Gen Z does consider driving, our studies found that their expectations include wanting carmakers to offer high-quality electric cars that they perceive as better for the environment. Gen Z also thinks autonomous cars will become the norm in the not too distant future. Buying or leasing a car straight from a dealership is now one of many car-buying options for Gen Z, and they also have the opportunity to subscribe to a car leasing service with the option to switch their car out for other cars regularly (Flexdrive, Clutch, and numerous auto-brand subscription services) or buy a car at a multistory car vending machine along a highway (Carvana).

Automakers and the entire auto industry—from financing to service— have already seen tremendous change over the last ten years, led by Millennials, Tesla, dealership consolidation, the financial crisis, tech advances, and the sharing economy. But Gen Z is going to drive even more change, because the disruptors that are already shaking up the auto industry will be status quo to Gen Z. In other words, the changes are just beginning.

As researchers, speakers, and consultants, we work a lot in the automotive space and see that there is both a huge challenge and tremendous opportunity ahead depending on how automakers, auto lenders, service providers, and car dealers adapt.

The challenges Gen Z brings to automakers include how the generation shops for a car, wants to communicate with dealers, and thinks about debt and finance. Already, Gen Z has shown a strong preference for buying used cars over new and choosing sedans over SUVs. The generation sees pre-owned sedans as a better value, with room to drive more of their friends. Gen Z also prioritizes sedans' better gas mileage over that of larger vehicles and appreciates that they are easier to park in urban areas.

In terms of shopping, Gen Z will do most of their browsing on a mobile device to comparison shop and read reviews before they show up at a dealership. However, once they show up, they are still often looking at their screen regularly, which can make for a challenging conversation when the salesperson wants to make eye contact.

John Fitzpatrick is the CEO of Force Marketing, a fast-growing, tech-driven marketing firm that helps automotive groups, dealerships, and brands connect with every generation of auto buyer. One of Force's most popular tools is Drive, a platform that creates targeted, customizable videos that include car listings a viewer had recently browsed.

Force tracks every bit of data that their platforms pick up from customers, and they've noticed some startling gaps between how younger car buyers shop and how automotive brands attempt to connect with them.

The biggest opportunity Fitzpatrick and his team have noticed is with video. "Our research shows that Facebook and YouTube reach 85% and 92% of car shoppers respectively, yet less than 3% to 4% of car dealerships have an active video strategy on those platforms," Fitzpatrick explains.

"And while it may come as no surprise that younger car shoppers increase their video consumption every year, our data shows that older generations are also turning to video more often for their car-shopping needs. Between 2018 and 2019, we found that eighteen- to twenty-four-year-olds grew their rate of video consumption by 57%. But the numbers skyrocket with each age set:

twenty-five- to thirty-four-year-olds increased video ad views by 60%

thirty-five- to forty-four-year-olds by 90%

forty-five- to fifty-four-year-olds by 92%

fifty-five- to sixty-four-year-olds by 140%

sixty-five and over by 131%."

Fitzpatrick says shoppers look for videos to show them everything from how a car's audio system connects to their iPhone to what the experience of sitting inside the vehicle during forty minutes of traffic is like.

Fitzpatrick and his team also see a disconnect between how younger customers *expect* companies to use data about them and what many companies are actually doing.

"I believe data is the new oil. A lot of people will say the same, but they don't fully back that with their actions. The missing piece is that a lot of people misuse the data they have. They want to send one message to many people instead of many messages one-to-one.

"We have to flip that mindset as we think about connecting with the consumer," Fitzpatrick says. "If you don't use technology to drive personalization, to speak to folks when they want to be spoken to, how they want to be spoken to, in the cadence in which they want to be spoken to, you're absolutely missing it.

"The idea that consumers are scared by the data we have on them is gone. Now they *know* you have the data. So their expectation of proper usage of the data is higher than ever."

This is true for marketing transportation options as much as it is for anything else Gen Z is shopping for. But in the case of cars, the opportunities to stand out with video and highly personalized messaging are especially ample.

Renting and Home Buying

Gen Z saw their parents' generation face housing foreclosures and eviction due to aggressive home lending prior to the Great Recession. While 91% of Gen Z tell us that they still want to own their own home one day, it is likely they will focus on buying a home they can comfortably afford rather than stretching to buy one they cannot.

Interestingly, early data shows that Gen Z are already buying homes and generally on par with past generations. This bodes well for homebuilders who are designing entry-level products that meet Gen Z's needs as well as for home sellers who need the next generation of home buyers to sell their home. In fact, according to data from TransUnion, Gen Z home buyers doubled between 2018 and 2019—from approximately 150,000 to 319,000.

However, one area of home-buying intelligence that is ripe with Gen Z is determining whether it is better to rent an apartment (or house) or buy. There are a number of websites and other services that quickly tell Gen Z the right way to think about rent vs. a mortgage, which is making the equation easier for them as they finally enter the front end of their prime home-buying decades.

Long term, we believe Gen Z could be a boon for the real estate market, both as buyers and renters, because they appear to be more conservative with their money and more thoughtful about their debt, particularly college debt, and credit score.

When we work with real estate developers and institutional investors, we make sure to hit on the key things Gen Z wants in real estate: they want their immediate outdoors to be their living room, proximity to their desired lifestyle, and everything in the home connected to the Internet of Things (IoT), and they feel location trumps square footage until they start a family.

Smart real estate leaders are quickly adapting to these trends to be positioned to win Gen Z, while those in the student housing industry have already struggled to quickly adapt to the higher and different expectations of Gen Z compared to Millennials. In the apartment world, nice finishes are expected, as are better fitness centers, outdoor areas, and tie-ins with local businesses—but we see Gen Z, again, willing to trade down on luxury amenities and finishes if they can get a better location at a lower price through less square footage, such as micro-apartments. Major student housing companies like American Campus Communities are taking Gen Z's preferences heavily into account while investors are buying older properties and updating them to fit this new generation but at a lower price point.

The *New York Times* reported major differences in Gen Z's student housing preferences compared to Millennials. While Millennials were drawn to resort-style amenities like rooftop pools, tanning beds, and rock-climbing walls, Gen Z cares more about having as much as possible at their fingertips and getting the most bang for their buck out of their increasingly expensive college education. Gen Z much prefers amenities like Amazon lockers, shared study spaces, and meeting spots for Uber, Lyft, and food delivery drivers than recreational add-ons.

While Gen Z certainly wouldn't mind luxury housing, location with a better lifestyle at a lower price consistently wins with them over bells and whistles in the space itself. This will include smaller footprint apartments where the amenity is the proximity to restaurants, entertainment, transportation, and work—as well as space designed for freelance and gig economy work. Smaller-footprint apartments with fewer amenities yet better location lead to a lower monthly rental payment, less reliance on a car and the associated costs, and more of what Gen Z actually wants: proximity to work, life, play, and a dog park!

Purchases of homes and cars are both significantly determined by where Gen Z lives. If they choose to follow recent generations and move toward urban areas for work, lifestyle, and more, then that would make owning cars less important and more of a hassle while also making purchasing a house harder to do. But if they are able to live and work somewhere less dense or somewhere they can commute from, then purchasing cars and a home are clearly in their future.

One thing we do know about both car and home purchases is that Gen Z will want a connected home and a connected car, no doubt about it. In fact, over half (53%) of Gen Z want more household items connected to the Internet.

Gen Z will expect everything in their house to be prewired (or set up) to make the most of IoT solutions ranging from security and video cameras, such as Ring, to smart thermostats, such as Nest, and smart appliances and lighting. This expectation carries over to cars, where Gen Z will expect cars that last long and are reliable—both of which speak to the generation's emphasis on value and durability—but also have all the bells and whistles of IoT. This includes immediate and seamless integration with their phone, the ability to stream music from Spotify or Pandora, the ability to play podcasts, and a variety of sensors that help with everything from driving to navigation.

In the next five years, over one third of Gen Z expect the Internet to predict what they need and alert them before they need it.

The question for both housing and cars will be interest rates and the ability to access financing, which remains to be seen in the current environment.

Insurance and Investments

In our 2017 State of Gen Z Study, we found that 12% of Gen Z were already saving for retirement! That is a *stunning* finding given the age group we nationally surveyed was *fourteen to twenty-two*. This propensity to save or invest for the future bodes very well for this generation as well as the financial services industry, but only if the industry adapts to Gen Z's communication, technology, and financial preferences. The biggest headwind we see to Gen Z picking a traditional financial advisor is the avalanche of robo-advisors, AI chatbots designed to answer questions without a holiday, and online-only investing solutions that offer very low-cost options with easy banking integration and, importantly, the ability to open an account with a very small amount of money—and all on your smartphone.

The importance of Gen Z investing, particularly as they are already thinking about saving for their emergency account—and even retirement—provides an interesting counterbalance to Millennials, who have often postponed saving for retirement due to student loan payments and not enough income relative to their expenses. Gen Z could also be the beneficiary of the impending wealth transfer and then jump-start their retirement nest egg, but that is a big "if" as the amount and timing of the wealth transfer is hotly debated—but it will come eventually.

For financial firms offering mobile-based technology solutions that show Gen Z how their account is growing by even small, regular amounts and make it easy to refer friends, the future is very bright. Gen Z and the entire financial industry stand to benefit if Gen Z starts investing and saving for retirement now, which is particularly important given the very low likelihood of a government financial safety net or healthcare safety net for Gen Z when they are ultimately ready to retire.

Traditional investment firms will need to train their advisors to reach this generation, who are likely the age of their kids or grandkids given the median age of a financial advisor in the United States is now fifty-one. That training must be grounded in data about the generation—rather than stories about "young people today . . ."—and fully integrate technology to make the advising experience completely low friction for Gen Z. The good news for advisors is that Gen Z loves to refer their friends to products and services they trust, so building business with Gen Z now will likely lead to decades of referrals ahead.

At the same time, insurance will continue to become more important to Gen Z as they age up and have to leave their parents' insurance, whether health, dental, vision, or auto. Already, Gen Z shops online for car insurance and renter's insurance. The further they move into the workforce the more they will get offered group insurance options and, eventually, will consider life insurance options.

However, just like banking is being disrupted by fintech, the insurance industry is being upended by insurtech. Companies such as The Zebra and Policygenius have made comparing and buying auto insurance and life insurance transparent and easy, as simple as booking a place on Airbnb. New technology companies are also flooding into other areas of the insurance market, which is putting tremendous pressure on traditional insurance companies. With most insurance purchases starting with a web search, and these new insurtech companies optimized to convert those searches into leads and fast underwriting, Gen Z will only know a time when buying insurance online was fast, easy, and a great experience—not the human-to-human experience many Millennials and certainly previous generations have come to expect with an insurance pitch over lunch, at your home, or via a group plan presentation at your workplace (complete with brochures!).

Overall, financial services and insurance is one of the largest industries where we work, and the trends we're seeing with Gen Z are *very* different from Millennials—who are known for already driving tremendous change. Looking ahead, Gen Z will expect immediate policy pricing, rapid acceptance, multiple payment options and time lines, video FAQs, discounts or rewards for good behaviors (such as exercise), and instant claim filing via a mobile device—all without having to talk with a human. These trends will accelerate greatly as Gen Z continues to enter the workforce, becomes the new trend drivers for financial services and insurance, and navigates a potentially large transfer of wealth, which will exponentially increase their financial importance.

Travel, Hospitality, and Tourism

The travel industry underwent tremendous disruption when Millennials decided they were happy to sleep in a stranger's house so they could attend a festival, make all their travel plans online using one of dozens of aggregator sites, and stay at boutique hotels with funky rooms and unique menus over big brands and loyalty points. Gen Z is the beneficiary of all these changes, from Airbnb to Kayak, Localeur, and Expedia. The number of ratings and reviews about tourism lodging options has soared over the last decade, giving Gen Z a deep—highly visual—and multifaceted look at the places where they might want to stay and, once there, what they should do to experience it like a local. Localeur is a perfect example.

Localeur shows you where locals go to stay, play, eat, drink—and party. Gen Z's desire for "authentic" travel experiences along with their spending patterns will likely drive more economical travel, which works well with the options created through the sharing economy and easy mobile booking. In other words, Millennials and the sharing economy shattered traditional travel and lodging barriers, and Gen Z will get to savor the benefit of the change while they are still young! Where we see Gen Z differ is they will expect easier check-in and check-out processes and payment options—such as paying with a credit card by text message (such as Everyware)—and much deeper property integration into local events, food, drinks, meetups, and experiences.

Jewelry and Style Accessories

As Gen Z moves into their twenties, jewelry and style accessories will continue to play a key role in their personal identity and brand. So far, Gen Z appears to have a bifurcated approach to jewelry, purchasing lots of low-cost jewelry items so they can have numerous different choices—ideal for endless social media photos. At the other end are more affluent members of Gen Z, or those willing to splurge on luxury items, who do buy luxury jewelry and goods, from name-brand rings to purses. However, it is clear that the biggest jewelry purchases for Gen Z lie in their future, as both their income increases and life events such as an engagement take place.

Right now we do see two trends continuing: the first is that Gen Z will still feel comfortable buying less expensive but high-style brands, such as Kendra Scott. Her jewelry is high style but not at an overly expensive price point, making it a more responsible jewelry brand that is also not seen as cheap—a rare feat to accomplish. Gen Z could very well continue the Millennial trend of seeking out alternatives to traditionally mined diamonds, for social cause reasons and for cost efficiency, as Gen Z does appear more utilitarian in their general spending patterns thus far. Gen Z also is at an ideal age and life stage for new jewelry and accessory brands to be introduced to them via social media and influencer campaigns, which reduces the risk of having to spend heavily to open traditional format storefronts. We are seeing this now as jewelry brands are building successful engagement and interest online via social media and digital first and then moving into stores, particularly if they have a celebrity tie-in.

As Gen Z gets older, they become bigger earners and spenders on the staples they are *already* buying: clothes, technology, food, and more.

Longer term, the majority of Gen Z tells us in our research studies that they still plan to buy a house, get married, and have at least one child in the future. However, for this majority, getting married and having their first child is likely ten-plus years down the road. This is why we expect to see most of their spending in the near future focused on themselves personally through their experiences, needs, and wants rather than spending to take care of their dependents or other family members. It will be exciting to see how Gen Z navigates the consumption decade of their twenties and becomes more self-reliant spenders and marketplace influencers! You know we will be paying close attention—as they pay by Venmo, Cash App, Zelle, or any other way.

8
EARNING BRAND LOYALTY WITH GEN Z

"I rarely get my clothes from advertisements. I just see a kid wearing it at our school, and I like it, and I go buy it."

—Gen Z male, fifteen

The 2016 financial results were in, and Sprint knew they needed a new game plan. As Verizon and AT&T battled for the top spot among US cell phone carriers, Sprint was struggling to tread water. They'd ended 2016 with a net loss of $1.2 billion. Clearly business as usual was not working.

Like Nike, Sprint knew their business's future was in Gen Z's hands. Yes, they had to provide reliable cell phone service just like Nike needed to offer a decent pair of sneakers. But Sprint knew their survival required more than that. They needed to convince younger customers—a demographic that was glued to their mobile phones for up to *six hours or more per day*—that Sprint sees and understands them.

Sprint needed to let Gen Z know that they understood this generation's dreams and vibrant personality. They knew that Gen Z wants to break boundaries across every facet of their lives: personally, professionally, politically, and socially. And somehow, Sprint had to convince Gen Z that connecting their mobile phone to Sprint's network would help them achieve all of these things.

But, aside from the $1.2 billion annual loss, Sprint faced another problem: they had no clue how to make their appeal to Gen Z.

At least they were self-aware. So Sprint assembled Candy Bar, a team of Gen Z marketing experts who created the #LiveUnlimited campaign.

#LiveUnlimited spoke to Gen Z on a personal level, on the platforms where they're hanging out (social media and YouTube). To start, Candy Bar knew Gen Z was not interested in the "Can you hear me now?" guy, and certainly did not remember or care that Sprint stole him from Verizon.

But Gen Z *did* care what Instagram and YouTube influencers like Prince Royce, Lele Pons, Bradley Martyn, Rachel Cook, and Gerard Adams had to say. Don't know who most of these people are? That's okay, but when you're trying to understand and win Gen Z, it's a smart idea to hire someone who knows who these influencers are—and actually listens to them.

Sprint's #LiveUnlimited campaign brought all of these influencers together in a YouTube video that spoke nothing of data plans, 5G networks, download speeds, or roaming fees. Instead, these Gen Z role models empowered viewers to live life on their own terms.

As a Gen Z kid sits on the sofa gazing into his phone, Lele Pons, who has a combined social media reach of fifty-plus million, opens the video saying, "I want to inspire you to live life your own way." Then she pops into his living room. Another prominent influencer, Bradley Martyn, also in the room, chimes in with: "It's about pushing yourself to the next level." And so it continues, with a series of influencers offering empowering encouragement to this Gen Z kid—all of them seemingly stepping out of his phone and into his living room.

The campaign's slogan scrolls throughout the video and across every social media platform: *You only live once, but you choose to live unlimited every day.*

The campaign had each influencer blast the video across their social media platforms in the summer of 2017. The results? Well, one person on Reddit gave Sprint the thumbs-up, saying:

"This needs to be every business's focus. Instead of blaming Millennials for a business failing, realize (like T-Mobile and apparently now Sprint) that we are the future of business. The best idea is to embrace us and market toward us. That is both where the money is and will be. Smart move Sprint."

But what did it do for their bottom line? (Cue the hand-clapping emoji.)

Sprint closed out 2017 by delivering their best financial results in company history. Within one year they went from $1.2 billion in *net losses* to a *net income* of $7.4 billion.

It wouldn't be reasonable to credit Sprint's complete fiscal turnaround to this campaign alone. But it certainly contributed, and there's a lot we can take away from Sprint's approach to adapting to connect with Gen Z.

Above all, Gen Z demands much more from a brand than just a reasonably priced, reliable physical product. As Mary Ellen Dugan from WP Engine says, "Gen Z doesn't buy brands, they join brands." Following a brand for Gen Z is a personal expression of identity, often aspirational, and they expect brands to create (both digitally and in person) a consistent feeling or experience as the hallmark of the brand. The #LiveUnlimited campaign did not try to win over Gen Z with promises of great 5G coverage. That went without saying. They attracted younger customers who wanted to align themselves with a brand that empowered them to break boundaries by giving them the tools (a reliable phone plus solid coverage) to chase their dreams. To truly live life unlimited.

Before Gen Z will even consider joining a brand, they need to feel they can get behind what that brand stands for. This crosses over into everything from how a company manufactures a product, what that product will help a customer achieve, and how seriously a company takes social responsibility. Gen Z expects a brand to reflect how they live their life—or how they aspire to live their life.

Gen Zer Kate tells us, "I personally follow a lot of outdoor brands. I follow REI and Nat Geo and other brands like that. I just love the outdoors. I like the outdoor aesthetic that goes with REI and all the gear.

I look at it and think about it. I'm planning on hiking the Appalachian Trail after I graduate college, and so just thinking about that trip and getting the gear is fun.

"I follow REI on Instagram because it's kind of like a little escape. It doesn't take a lot of brain power and at school I always have to work with my brain. It's like my own mental vacation. It's nice. It's relaxing."

Kate sees the function of a brand very differently than those from other generations do. The physical product is only part of the reason she is drawn to REI, National Geographic, and other brands like them. The brands' appeal is tied to the lifestyle they reflect on social media platforms even more than the products they're selling.

Kate describes how she became an outdoors person: "It all started for me from being on my phone and watching Netflix and YouTube.

"I definitely got outdoorsy because, and I know this is going to sound weird, but I was watching the *Gilmore Girls* revival on Netflix and the character was planning to hike the Pacific Crest Trail and I didn't know what that was. So I looked it up.

"Watching that show lit a fire in me and I just got super outdoorsy.

"Since then, I've been following one hiker on YouTube mostly, and then I see other recommended videos that seem interesting. I watch her a lot because she does weekly blogs while she's hiking the trails. I watch hundreds of her videos, definitely, because each trail that she's hiked has hundreds of videos."

Connecting with Gen Z starts with paying attention to what kind of content they're consuming, where, and when. If you've read this far you understand just how much they're staring at their phones. They don't check their classroom website for homework assignments, but they get into high gear studying when their teacher reminds them about a quiz via Snapchat. They could not care less about billboard ads and likely won't ever see a commercial if it only appears on linear network TV, but a product might immediately make their wish list if they see a favorite YouTube or TikTok personality using it or if an Instagram post stirs an emotional reaction in them.

Authenticity is everything with Gen Z. They don't want to be sold to. They have created a powerful pool of influencers among their own generation and trust a peer recommendation over anything else, period.

This is all good news, because there are *so many more* opportunities to connect with young buyers than ever before. Listen to what they say they want (they told us—and they are trying to tell you, too), and connect with them where they are (yes, on their phones).

The Customer Journey, Gen Z Edition

If you've given sales and marketing any thought in your work, you're familiar with the idea of a customer journey. It's the series of steps a consumer takes before deciding to make a purchase.

The basics of the customer journey have remained relatively unchanged since the days when hunters and farmers were bartering their wares. If you want to earn a long-term customer, consumers need to be aware of what you're offering, decide it's for them, choose to buy it, choose to continue buying it, and then ideally encourage others to do the same.

How we achieve these customer milestones constantly evolves. Past generations brought awareness to brands through newspaper advertising, TV and radio ads, and even the Yellow Pages—all of which have trended dramatically down in importance or have been skipped altogether when it comes to Gen Z, *especially* the Yellow Pages. When it comes to engaging Gen Z as potential customers, the playing field looks nothing like it did even less than a decade ago. As we've helped hundreds of companies earn Gen Z as loyal customers the same themes emerge again and again, and we've codified them into this Gen Z edition of the customer journey.

Positioning: What's your story?
Every brand needs to know who they are before they can convince others to align with them. This is more critical than ever when connecting with Gen Z. Before they even consider your product, they want to know what you stand for. What is your story? What is your purpose?

What problem are you trying to solve? How do your leaders represent your company? How does your brand engage with, and view, the world?

Love Your Melon is an apparel company run by Millennial founders Zachary Quinn and Brian Keller. Launched in 2012 as a project for their entrepreneurship class at the University of St. Thomas in St. Paul, Minnesota, Love Your Melon reached $31.5 million in revenue by the end of 2017. The company's mission is to support the fight against pediatric cancer. They started with the sell-a-product, donate-a-product model that was made famous by brands like TOMS Shoes and Warby Parker: for every hat purchased, they would donate one to a child with cancer. Their model has since evolved, and now they donate 50% of their net profits to nonprofit partners that help pediatric cancer patients. Since 2012, Love Your Melon has given $6,214,565 and more than 185,000 beanies.

Gen Z understands that not every company is designed to serve such an explicit charitable purpose. And they don't expect every brand to give away 50% of their profits. But they do want to know that you are taking a stand for something, and that your leaders care about more than just your bottom line.

Engagement and Awareness: What are you offering, and why will they want it?

At this stage in the customer journey, they are at the top of your sales funnel. Your task is to convince people that your product is for them—even if they don't decide to buy it for some time.

But Gen Z has limited interest in the classic marketing strategies that work to build awareness among older generations. Again, they want nothing to do with billboards or print and TV ads. They're more influenced by their friends' recommendations, and those "friends" include online personalities whose opinions they trust yet they've never met and likely never will.

Engagement also means much more than simply putting your brand in front of Gen Z. This generation cares about value, and that applies to the content they consume. Engagement can include offering how-to videos, social media photo contests, or other activities that build relationships regardless of purchase. Warby Parker keeps engagement ongoing and fun on Instagram. In 2019 they partnered with the New York Public Library for "library trivia" games in Instagram Stories. Followers who answered any NYPL trivia questions were entered in a drawing to win a free pair of glasses.

This stage is also a first chance to connect with Gen Z's aspirations. REI engages with Gen Z every time they grab their attention with breathtaking photos from a hiking trail—often long before Gen Z will ever buy even a water bottle from REI.

Engagement and awareness also encompass online advertising, instore promos, instant couponing for initial trial, content marketing, and ratings/reviews.

It's so critical to get engagement and awareness right with Gen Z, and this is usually the stage where our clients need to make the biggest changes. We take a deeper dive into engagement and awareness throughout this chapter.

Initial Trial: When will they decide to buy *for the first time*?
This is the moment someone decides to make their first purchase with you. Gen Z tells us, again and again, that they value easy and low-risk buying experiences. Make it simple to buy and simple to return anything.

1-click payments are the norm for Gen Z. In fact, for many of them, it has always been an option in their customer journey for online items. The fewer steps necessary for them to shop and pay, the more likely they will make the all-important first purchase. For Amazon this means a 1-click button; for other companies it will mean making it easy to create an account for fast and easy checkout. In addition, Gen Z wants to be able to use a preset payment account, saved into their browser or phone, so that when they are on a new site and need to place an order, they don't have to hunt for a debit card or other payment information. Making your website easy for payment and checkout is a must for Gen Z, because if it is *work* for them to shop, select, and buy, they won't.

Retailer payment options will eventually include apps Gen Z is already using to exchange money with individuals, like Venmo and the Cash App. This goes beyond online transactions to retailers connecting with payment apps so customers can make in-store purchases. Remember, most of Gen Z is too young for a credit card (or doesn't want one), doesn't carry cash, and sometimes doesn't even have a physical wallet! Businesses would be wise to adapt and make payments—whether online or in store—as easy as possible.

Making returns simple and easy is just as critical as the buying experience. By making it easy and risk-free to return an item—the opposite of the traditional retailer approach—Gen Z feels more confidence making *initial* purchases online and buying items without having tried them before. Being able to simply return the item in the same box and get a full refund, including free shipping, lowers hassles and risk for your customers. This is true for *all* online shoppers today, but as Gen Z's consumer reach grows, easy and free returns will become the norm across the board—and companies that don't comply will feel the fallout. Consumer research by Narvar reveals that 96% of shoppers would shop with a retailer again based on a good returns experience, while 69% say they would not buy from a retailer if they had to pay for return shipping and 67% would not buy from a retailer that charges a restocking fee.

For Gen Z, easy returns, whether it's a new mattress, a car, or a pair of jeans, makes purchasing less stressful and makes all of us more confident about clicking the buy button.

Loyalty Building: What will keep them buying?

How do you get Gen Z to buy from you again? In our conversations with Gen Z, brand loyalty comes down to more than a great quality product or good service experience. Those are the basics and to be expected no matter what. For Gen Z, brand loyalty aligns with the mission of the brand, its people, and its impact—and then making it easy to buy, shop, or eat there again (and get instantly rewarded, such as through the app Dosh). Brand loyalty is especially important these days, since Gen Z consumers (and all consumers) can keep searching for cheaper options. So what keeps them coming back? What the brand stands for, how it communicates what it stands for, and how it shows its positive impact in the world. That messaging starts with your positioning, continues through engagement and awareness, and if done consistently, transparently, and through quality content, builds customer loyalty.

This loyalty will be increasingly important as more and more members of Gen Z exert their spending influence and soon will have the greatest lifetime value of any customer for a brand, product, or service. Creating brand loyalty means delivering the tangible experiences Gen Z expects consistently (e.g., value, ease of purchase, and returns) in alignment with the intangibles they feel it should also deliver (e.g., standing for something other than its product).

As Gen Z expands its spending power into a broader variety of items, making more expensive purchases, brand loyalty will matter more than ever. Even legacy brands recognize they can no longer sustain themselves, let alone grow, by focusing their attention on older generations alone. Every company, whether a startup or an incumbent, must recalibrate their offerings to create loyalty with Gen Z starting right now.

Referrals: How likely are they to encourage others to buy?

Word-of-mouth marketing, particularly driving direct referrals, is still the most influential way to drive direct sales among Gen Z. So what do brand leaders need to know to get Gen Z to talk about their brands the right way? First, recognize that Gen Z may not actually have bought or experienced your product or service. Gen Z saying "I love those new Nikes" or "This place looks awesome!" on Instagram or Snapchat can drive sales even if the Gen Zer making the statement hasn't been there or bought the shoes! Of course, the most influential direct referrals are from actual Gen Z customers to their peer groups via social media, and encouraging those referrals or recommendations is both an art and a science.

The easiest way to get Gen Z referrals is to . . . *ask them* to tell their friends if they love your product, service, or what your brand stands for or is motivated to achieve. When they do post, even if it's only an emoji, fire, or rocket ship icon, respond quickly in a way that shows them you noticed yet doesn't seem canned or corporate. For Gen Z referrals, offering a discount if they come back with their friends, a coupon for their next visit, or an immediate reward for recommending a friend can work well. The best referrals are still sparked by a great experience, but a nudge to take five seconds and message some friends via Snapchat about their experience is a great way to build referrals where Gen Z already hangs out: on digital platforms.

Another way to spark organic referrals is through the valuable content you share across digital platforms—and that others share for you. When Glossier posts a "Get Ready with Me" video with a celebrity or beauty editor, or a how-to video on shaping your eyebrows, engaged viewers who share that content are organically referring the brand at the same time. This blurs the lines between awareness, engagement, and referrals.

Think of ways your brand can be integrated into shareable content, whether it is content you create or through partnerships. Park Tool is a company that designs and manufactures bicycle repair products. They blended engagement and awareness with organic referrals by partnering with mountain biking influencer Seth Alvo of Seth's Bike Hacks. Park Tools regularly sends Seth tools for his in-home shop; they also invited Seth to tour their HQ in Minnesota, which he turned into a video. That means Park Tool's iconic blue-handle items show up in most of Seth's how-to videos, and his behind-the-scenes video at their HQ is on regular rotation among Seth's 1.6 million followers. Park Tool also has their own YouTube channel with three hundred thousand followers, with every video focused on bike repair education. Each time one of their how-to videos is shared, it's an organic referral. Brand awareness, engagement, trust, *and* loyalty need to be developed even before a product is purchased. And when it is time to buy, cyclists who have seen those videos will be drawn to Park Tool products.

Every stage of the customer journey is critical, but engagement and awareness is the step where we find companies need to make the biggest changes in their strategy and where they struggle the most. It's also where some of the biggest opportunities lie. Gen Z consumers might linger in this stage for months before deciding to purchase from a brand, and along the way, their opinion of that brand is constantly being influenced by the content Gen Z consumes. Let's take a closer look at the factors that shape Gen Z's decisions to engage with a company.

9
CUSTOMER ENGAGEMENT
AND AWARENESS

"Everything I've bought recently has been because I watch a
YouTube video and there's a suggested video. I ended up buying
face wash because I watch Jackie Aina on YouTube and she used
Dermalogica."

—Gen Zer

In 2018, Jason Cook and his marketing team were looking for new
ways to attract applicants to Baylor University. Cook had recently
joined the school as chief marketing officer, and he had a huge job on
his hands. Baylor had made national headlines in prior years for sexual assault allegations against members of its football team. Although
Baylor had since made significant improvements to enhance the safety
and security of their campus, they knew they would need to work hard
to reposition their brand and earn trust with Gen Z.

As Cook and his team were thinking through marketing strategies,
one of them noticed that a pair of YouTubers—identical twins Brooklyn and Bailey McKnight—had been mentioning Baylor in their videos. No big deal . . . except Brooklyn and Bailey happen to have six
million YouTube subscribers.

Baylor was a top-choice school for Brooklyn and Bailey, and they
had been vlogging their college search journey to their millions of

viewers. Sounds like a marketing dream, but Cook and his team didn't jump. Not yet.

"About seven months later," Cook shares with us, "Brooklyn and Bailey had been accepted to Baylor through our normal channels, and we heard they were interested in attending. So we thought about how we might be able to engage with them to help generate interest in our school."

That's how it started. But what followed was a much more dynamic partnership between Brooklyn, Bailey, and Cook's marketing team than an agreement to promote the school. The sisters agreed to help Baylor understand how to better connect with their generation.

"Higher education marketing is, in some ways, a dinosaur," Cook says. "It's marked by a sea of sameness, and it becomes hard to distinguish the institutions from one another. We knew traditional marketing techniques often pushed by higher education were not going to reach Gen Z in an authentic way. So we were excited to connect with Brooklyn and Bailey and learn what they know works to engage their peers."

Cook credits Brooklyn and Bailey with bringing two key Gen Z influences to his attention: the power of video to engage on a personal level, and the generation's interest in new experiences.

Brooklyn and Bailey vlogged about their daily antics at Baylor, bringing fans with them as they moved into their dorm room, joined a sorority, and attended their first homecoming football game. It's personal, it's experience-driven, and it's an approach Cook and his team have integrated into many other aspects of how they communicate with their students.

"On campus, we have restructured how our president communicates with our students. She is very much about experiences," Cook shares. "On our first day back to campus this year, our president gave out Popsicles on her front porch as students walked by. So instead of inviting them to come by to meet the president for coffee at the student union, the president is engaging students where they are on their own terms."

Baylor has also changed how they communicate with students in writing. They've ditched formal, long emails from the president that usually only hit inboxes once a semester. Now students hear from their school president every Thursday in the form of a five–bullet point email highlighting important news. It's more personal, it's easy to read where they are usually looking at it (on their phones), and it fosters an ongoing relationship with students.

It doesn't matter whether you're trying to recruit college applicants, hoping Gen Z will eat in your restaurant, or aiming to sell them a new kind of athletic shorts. Our research studies and those of others consistently confirm that the best way to build awareness and engagement among Gen Z is through candid and personal connections. And there are many, many ways to achieve this. Candid can mean an honest referral from a friend—and that friend can be IRL or a favorite Instagrammer. A personal approach can be a highly targeted ad that tells a potential customer you are paying attention to what they want.

As Cook and his team at Baylor discovered, any opportunity you take to integrate candor and authenticity into everything you do—from building awareness to creating a personalized customer experience—reinforces your relationship with Gen Z and turns them into loyal followers. Gen Z is happy to hear from you as long as you show up where they're looking and you aim to connect with the experiences that align with their life.

Gen Z Buying Influences

"I use Snapchat a lot for my friends to weigh in on purchases I'm considering. I went to Warby Parker once and their glasses are kind of expensive. I went into the store because I didn't want to order online, because I wanted to try them on. I tried on a bunch and snapchatted my friends. Then I took pictures of the ones my friends liked and went home and made the decision at my house. It was like a big purchase."

—Gen Z college student

In a time of seemingly unlimited product and service options, our research reveals the most important factors for attracting and keeping

Gen Z as customers. Understanding these influences enables you to design a brand, sales, and marketing strategy that works for your offering and in your key sales channels.

In our 2018 State of Gen Z Study, we found that friends and family have the biggest influence on Gen Z's purchasing decisions. Just behind personal influencers are brand platforms themselves, with Amazon, Nike, and Adidas getting the most mentions from Gen Z as brands that have influenced them to make a purchase decision. This can include Amazon's AI, which is constantly analyzing data and using that information to recommend products before we even know we need or want them. Next, a blend of social media, celebrities, and online influencers top the chart.

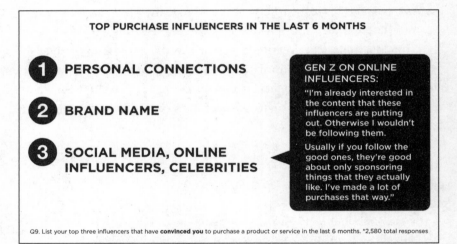

TOP PURCHASE INFLUENCERS IN THE LAST 6 MONTHS

1 PERSONAL CONNECTIONS

2 BRAND NAME

3 SOCIAL MEDIA, ONLINE INFLUENCERS, CELEBRITIES

GEN Z ON ONLINE INFLUENCERS:

"I'm already interested in the content that these influencers are putting out. Otherwise I wouldn't be following them.

Usually if you follow the good ones, they're good about only sponsoring things that they actually like. I've made a lot of purchases that way."

Q9. List your top three influencers that have **convinced you** to purchase a product or service in the last 6 months. *2,580 total responses

This is a generation looking to *others* for advice before they make a first-time purchase. The result is that companies need to get friends and family members talking about a product or service—friends if it is a purchase that is peer influenced (such as apparel and restaurants) and a parent if it's a decision about choosing a bank or an expensive consumer technology. Advertising alone doesn't work; you have to get Gen Z's community of influencers making or supporting a brand, product, or service.

Creating the online word-of-mouth conversation is best driven by leveraging technology, including ratings and reviews, social media posts and interactions, and prompts to get those who have purchased something to write a review or share their purchase experience online. At a basic level, this can include a five-star rating system for the fastest review possible and then the opportunity to add additional comments, photos, or videos. Millennials really pioneered the push for ratings and reviews, but Gen Z has now made them a *minimum* requirement for many products and services, particularly a first-time purchase. Reviews have such a huge influence on Gen Z's buying decisions that our 2019 national study revealed 70% of Gen Z have not bought something they really wanted because they read a bad rating or review about it.

When asking for a review or comment, make it easy for Gen Z to post the review—and then respond quickly to the review thanking them for sharing. This creates the quick feedback loop that a Gen Z reviewer wants. This also allows you to show them and anyone who reads the comment that you actually read it and replied with a personal touch, not with a generic template. In fact, you'll often see Gen Z respond again when you do thank them, which builds more positive momentum for their positive review or comment. In other words, when it comes to Gen Z, high-five the positive reviews and thank them for sharing their experience.

In addition to making ratings and reviews easy (and providing fast high fives), create moments that are share-worthy so Gen Z and their influencers talk about your product, service, or experience. This might include an unexpected art or visual installation in a restaurant, a hashtag that when used leads to a charitable donation, or a pop-up event on a Saturday that brings people together to support a local cause.

When sending out a product, share-worthy details might include an over-the-top delivery presentation to a list of key influencers, such as YouTubers, Instagrammers, or a group of VIP customers in your loyalty program. Also consider creative packaging that might inspire an unboxing video or props for taking photos with your product in a fun way, such as on TikTok.

Service experiences also have lots of potential for social media–worthy chatter. If you're offering tours of an apartment that is up for lease, consider making it unexpectedly fun and with special amenities. You can do a dessert bar in the kitchen (with Instagram-worthy, colorful treats) and place eye-catching notes throughout the apartment that highlight its features as potential customers walk through at their own pace ("check out this view of downtown from the living room window," "look up: the refurbished tin ceiling is a quirky complement to the mid-century modern fireplace!"). If you're renting out an Airbnb space, you can provide your customers with a map showing a "scavenger hunt to know the area like a local" complete with homemade trivia questions.

Being unexpected and visual are key with Gen Z, along with incorporating their smartphone into the experience rather than expecting them to keep it in a pocket or purse (which they wouldn't do anyway).

When it comes to the youngest members of Gen Z (twelve and under), connecting with them through their parents via online advertisements and school partnerships continues to be an effective way to create initial awareness and conversation. The reason? The parents of the youngest members of Gen Z are Gen X and older Millennials. To reach that group of Gen X and Millennial shoppers, traditional media, marketing, and digital channels are still the most effective way to influence what they recommend and buy for their kids. Short, targeted videos in their social media feed, in particular, are a good way to influence parents by providing them with content, context, and a quick "wow" insight or angle that gets them interested in learning more about a product or service for their Gen Z child.

As Gen Z gets older, their parents will remain important influences, but the generation will also gain more freedom to make their own purchases.

Mobile Is Everything

You know by now that when it comes to reaching Gen Z the one channel that rises far above the rest is mobile. Gen Z is glued to their smartphone (our studies show their anxiety, unfortunately, goes up if they are away from their phone for as few as fifteen minutes). This deep, emotional dependency on their phone has made mobile first the key channel for reaching Gen Z where they are and when they are ready to be engaged. As we'll see in the chapters ahead, Gen Z's dependence on mobile has already been carried into the workforce and marketplace as their view of "normal," so even B2B companies need to move to a mobile-first strategy if they have not already.

Mobile can present a layer of complexity for many legacy brands because their digital experience was designed for a larger screen or previous generations, so the cost and time of moving to mobile first can be significant—but it's absolutely worth the investment. Many of our clients are already surprised to see the *tremendous* amount of traffic to their website from mobile—often well over 50% of traffic for them is now via mobile—and the even greater usage of mobile within their physical stores (if they have them) along with mobile comparison shopping. Our studies show that 70% of Gen Z and Millennials price check items on their smartphone while standing in a physical store looking at that item. In fact, many of our clients now show the majority of their website traffic is from a mobile device, yet their websites are only "mobile friendly."

Friends, being mobile friendly is not enough. Now brands must be *mobile first*.

To see where you stand on mobile, we recommend assembling and observing a group of Gen Z to experience your website and digital offerings *who have never used them before*. You will be shocked with how they navigate the site. We do this for brands around the world, and even the best tech companies are stunned, and the legacy brands are slack-jawed. The key is that the Gen Zers cannot have been on your site, platform, or app in the past. These "fresh eyes," particularly when observed by a generational researcher on our team, can expose numerous breakdowns, gaps, and workarounds that other generations do not see, particularly those familiar with how everything is supposed to work and where key navigation is located. Gen Z expects everything to be extremely easy and intuitive, and if not, they'll move on to another digital option.

Being mobile first is also important as search engines move to prioritize mobile experience over more traditional larger screen display experiences. By prioritizing mobile experiences search engines are trying to provide better results for their users who are trying to search from a phone. It is particularly frustrating to search for something on a search engine using your phone and then go to the site only to be unable to navigate it easily. The big search engines have figured this out and want to deliver search results that create a better user experience, because this is a win for their users, the content provider, and the consumer.

Videos and Visuals Are Advertising

Gen Z has been conditioned since a very young age, some since the first time they watched a YouTube video on their parents' iPhone, to be visual learners and buyers. They've been inundated with parents constantly taking pictures of them—and strangers constantly taking pictures all around them. They've been conditioned not to search for information on Google but rather to go to YouTube and search for the answer to their question—delivered in a video. All of these endless photos and videos, from those made by their parents and shared on Facebook to those teaching them on YouTube or entertaining them on TikTok, have made videos and visuals the channel for reaching Gen Z.

"Gen Z is the first generation that uses the Internet for entertainment first and information second," WP Engine CMO Mary Ellen Dugan shares. "And it's by a huge margin: 73% of Baby Boomers, 69% of Gen X, and 59% of Millennials go to the Internet for information first. But 72% of Gen Z say they go online for entertainment."

Dugan points out that Gen Z's "entertainment first" approach to the Internet means brands need to think about their EQ—that is, *entertainment quotient*—perhaps for the first time ever.

"Most brands think about whether their content is informative, and whether they're targeting the right audience, but they're not thinking about *entertaining* people. It's a huge factor with Gen Z," Dugan explains. "Is your brand funny? Is it serious? What is the component of entertainment that you're trying to hook this next generation with? Because if you don't understand how you're going to entertain and capture this next generation first, you could lose them very, very quickly."

Sprint went for entertainment and inspiration over information in their #LiveUnlimited campaign, and took it straight to YouTube and social media, where they knew Gen Z was watching. Adidas has had a huge resurgence with Gen Z, thanks in part to their collaboration with recording artist Stormzy. The British rapper partnered with Adidas to launch a new line of sportswear paired with original music videos featuring Stormzy decked out in Adidas from shirt to shoes—the embodiment of entertainment as advertising.

When it comes to advertising to Gen Z, relevant videos and visuals are critical ingredients—even more important than the channel used for the advertisement. Brands must make the first second a "wow" opening; otherwise Gen Z will skip as soon as they are able. The irony is that when Gen Z sees a video ad they like, they will forward, comment, and share, because to them ads that are relevant are another form of content with which to engage. Brands see this frequently with highly emotional ads, such as those about body image and dealing with emotional highs and lows that fit Gen Z's current life stage and experiences. Ads that particularly resonated in recent years include Kia's Great Unknowns commercial, where they commit to donating millions of dollars to education; Axe's #PraiseUp campaign, urging men to shun toxic masculinity and praise each other for what makes them special; and Microsoft's We All Win commercial, showing how their Xbox adaptive controller offers a more inclusive gaming experience. For brands seeking to attract and keep Gen Z as customers, crafting a video and visual ad strategy that can be used across platforms is absolutely critical. In particular, a strategy that is also highly targeted and easily measurable.

A key callout for brand leaders: be sure to showcase and celebrate the diversity that represents the generation, deliver the ads at the right time and location in Gen Z's purchasing journey (or spark one!), and visually reinforce the *why* behind the brand and why Gen Z should want to be a part of it.

To build credibility and drive interest faster, make your messaging highly visual, using less text and incorporating more video and images of Gen Z customers and influencers using your product. Advertisements must be immediately engaging and instantly entertaining to pull Gen Z right into the story line.

Convergence of Apparel, Sports, Music, Food, and Gen Z Culture

One interesting trend that continues to surface in our studies with Gen Z is the convergence of apparel, sports, music, and food with Gen Z culture. Now, celebrity endorsements of food and apparel are not entirely new—some of us old folks started wearing Air Jordans as early as 1984, and Michael Jackson first convinced us that drinking Pepsi was cool in 1983. But the phenomenon has come a long way, and when it comes to Gen Z you certainly don't need mega celebrity partnerships or a multimillion-dollar ad budget to build awareness. Sometimes creating a fun new experience or joining forces with a YouTuber who speaks to the same niche you serve is enough.

The convergence of apparel, sports, music, and food also opens doors to endless options for engaging and influencing Gen Z in fun ways.

Taco Bell took the concept to the extreme with the Taco Bell Hotel, a pop-up hotel in Palm Springs, California, only open from August 8 through August 12, 2019. The hotel was a fully immersive Taco Bell *experience,* and you'd better believe that everything, from the hot sauce packet–shaped throw pillows and pool floaties to the fiery-colored murals on the hotel room walls, was Instagram-ready. Music performances took place all weekend from artists including Wallows, FLETCHER, and Whethan (all of whom are members of Gen Z). Taco Bell also set up an on-site salon offering Cinnamon Twist Braids, Baja Manicures, and Fire Fades, and opened shops where guests could buy an entire wardrobe of Taco Bell–branded clothes.

Taco Bell made seventy rooms available to the public, which sold out in two minutes. It seems their bigger purpose was to get Gen Z influencers, especially YouTube stars, to stay at the hotel and share the experience with their audience. The desired outcome? Keep Taco Bell top of mind among young viewers. Makeup artist, influencer, and entrepreneur Jeffree Star stayed at the Taco Bell Hotel and documented every detail in a twenty-nine-minute video posted to his channel. Don't know who Star is? Well, his seventeen million YouTube subscribers sure do, and his Taco Bell Hotel video was viewed more than *ten million times* within six weeks of it being posted.

The website eHotelier has been recommending for years that hotels step up their social media potential. They recommend hoteliers outfit their accommodations with creative lighting, eclectic features, luxury items, theme rooms, and more in order to encourage photo taking and sharing. One unexpected entry into the hotel market, IKEA, seems to be taking eclectic to the max with its new business hotel in Sweden— rife with photo opportunities while also appealing to the budget-aware Gen Z. Though IKEA has been in the hotel business since 1964, as it turns out, the new version of the hotel features solar panels, LED lamps, and recycled materials.

Not every brand can offer such an immersive experience, and they certainly don't need to. But do think about how you might align your brand promises with another's to showcase a lifestyle, values, and a life philosophy that connect with Gen Z in an emotional and sensory way.

A Is for Amazon (Search)

Amazon is search for Gen Z. As Gen Z came of age, Amazon was working out many of its original inefficiencies to create a more seamless mobile experience, from Amazon Prime to 1-click purchasing to same-day delivery to Alexa placing orders by voice command—while Gen Z was still gaming. With each new innovation, Amazon has continually worked itself deeper into Gen Z's lives through simplicity, expanded search, product reviews, and now Fulfilled by Amazon businesses as well as the purchase of Whole Foods. As Amazon goes further and further to solve customer challenges, including expanding and improving engagement by voice command, the result is a better shopping experience for Gen Z—who does not remember a time before Amazon existed.

This makes Amazon a *must-win* for numerous brands and products if they want to be on the search radar for Gen Z. Gen Z will literally skip Google, open their preferred web browser, and go directly to Amazon to type in—or speak—what they want, and then find the product and recommended options. This has come up in many conversations we've led. Alexa makes this even easier by conditioning Gen Z at a very young age to place orders by voice—all without having to type (let alone learn how to spell).

At a bare minimum, every direct-to-consumer brand should have an Amazon strategy. This can be as simple as offering products on Amazon directly. If you're an individual or small service-based business, your Amazon strategy might include writing and offering e-books for fellow service providers, so you show up as experts on your topic, from plumbing to wedding cakes. And if your product is not available on Amazon because you sell direct-to-consumer or through another channel, recognize that your competition is Amazon itself and not just the brands it offers. By looking at how to compete and differentiate from Amazon in addition to your competitors, you better understand the marketplace and how you can stand out—such as customer service, company purpose, or building an online community of passionate fans.

Online Influencers

You have likely concluded by now that online influencers are the *currency of trust* for Gen Z. These include well-known celebrities and artists like the Kardashians, The Rock, and Post Malone, but also extend to a less well-known but potentially more influential group of product, service, and lifestyle influencers. Celebrities may grab headlines and drive sales from every Instagram post or YouTube video, but they also charge a tremendous amount for a product or service to be promoted to their social media or online following. This paradox creates an interesting challenge, whereby influencers are clearly paid to promote a product or service yet are also trusted and sought after by Gen Z to make recommendations on what to buy. But influencers keep selling—and in an increasingly transparent, measurable way—which means brands seeking to reach Gen Z should strongly consider an influencer strategy. In fact, an entire industry of "influencer agencies" exists to facilitate these commercial relationships.

For many brands, marketers, manufacturers, and service providers, a more affordable and higher-ROI solution is to work with the legions of smaller influencers who have built an engaged online following that consists of five thousand to fifty thousand of the right type of followers. Even Instagrammers with followers in the one thousand range—called nanoinfluencers—are now getting offered sponsorship deals. Nano-influencers promote everything from clothes and car parts to cookware, supplements, and the latest video game. Engaging the right influencers opens the door to instant awareness and trust with many in Gen Z as well as more cost-effective and ongoing access to members of the generation who have chosen to follow an influencer because they like their vibe, mission, or the types of challenges the influencer addresses.

As influencer marketing evolves, and as Gen Z gets older, we expect Gen Z to push for more transparency as they start looking for guidance on purchasing higher-ticket items. Gen Z will progress from purchasing makeup and clothes recommended by influencers to opening banking accounts, choosing insurance, and buying cars. Premier influencers are already lining up with companies offering these bigger-ticket items and high lifetime value services, such as Beyoncé becoming an investor in Acorns (an investment platform) and Snoop Dogg promoting Robinhood (another investment app).

When Gen Z Decide to Buy

When it comes to brand engagement, sales, and growth, the entire customer sales journey must eventually lead to a purchase. This first-time purchase or initial trial is the moment of truth when Gen Z consumers demonstrate they feel confident enough in the product or service offered that they tap the "buy" button, insert their debit card, pay with Apple Pay, or digitally sign on the dotted line. But what actually drives the all-important first-time trial? This was a question we explored in our 2018 State of Gen Z Study. We identified five key drivers that determine initial purchases.

The most important driver of an initial purchase was price. This aligns with Gen Z being fiscally conservative and practical along with their habit of comparing prices instantly for virtually every item—whether it's the same item sold in other places or recommendations for alternatives that may serve the same function.

The second most important factor is ease of purchase. This could include the ease with which you find the item online or in person, the checkout experience, or the ease of delivery or receiving the item. This is why we work so much with clients to make their purchase experience easy, obvious, and consistent. A huge blind spot we have seen is when online retailers require too many steps to complete the initial purchase. The more steps involved, the higher the risk Gen Z will not make it to the final checkout button. The same holds for physical stores. If they are hard to navigate, plagued by long checkout lines, or offer limited forms of payment, they are creating unnecessary barriers for Gen Z customers. One exception to this finding? Thrift stores, where the excitement of discovery and getting a great deal are part of the experience and offer their own kind of authenticity and value to Gen Z.

The third factor affecting initial trial is online ratings and reviews, which we'll discuss in the next section.

The fourth factor is ease of return. Gen Z has come of age being able to simply put whatever they bought online back in a box and return it—or have a mattress they bought online delivered to their home, try it out, not like it, and then donate it to a charity and get their money back. Even cars are now easily returnable, a la Carvana, which completely changes the expectations for ease of return on expensive and inexpensive products alike. Ease of returns is a key *hidden* driver because it affects the risk, both real and perceived, of making an initial purchase of a new product or service, choosing wrong, and then being stuck with that item—or not.

Rounding out the five drivers for a first-time purchase is knowing someone who has bought or used the product before. Getting that personal recommendation is similar to online reviews but has even more of an impact since it's coming from someone they personally trust. It also helps ease the stress of making a first-time purchase, especially as they age up and make many life stage–linked purchases, such as buying a couch, booking a hotel room, or selecting an apartment. A personal recommendation from someone who has bought it, rented it, or used it before makes a purchase feel less risky and increases buyer confidence.

Driving Positive Ratings and Reviews

> "If I discover a product through a YouTube review and that's the first time I hear about it, then I have to Google-Tube it and see if other people are saying the same thing."
>
> —Gen Z focus group participant

Ratings and reviews tip Gen Z over the edge when it comes to buying a product or service, both online and increasingly in-store. This is true not just for more expensive items, such as apparel, cars, credit cards, and consumer technology, but even everyday low-cost shopping decisions from picking a restaurant (Yelp) or deciding what movie to stream (Netflix) to renting a movie for twenty-four hours (Amazon Prime) or an apartment for a year (ApartmentRatings, Renter's Voice, etc.).

So how important are ratings and reviews to Gen Z?

In our 2018 State of Gen Z Study we found that 68% of Gen Z read or watch at least three reviews before buying something for the first time with their own money. This is a very large number considering how young they are, and yet they're already doing so much research before buying. In fact, 16% of Gen Z would read or watch nine(!) or more ratings and reviews before buying something for the first time with their own money. This number was even higher with Gen Z females, 21% of whom said they would read or watch at least nine reviews. The bottom line: ratings and reviews provide humanity, candor, validation, and a sense of community for those looking to purchase a product or service. These ratings and reviews can wipe out even the biggest ad spend, because once people actually go to check out ratings and reviews they can see what they perceive is real versus what the brand wants you to believe.

As Gen Z has made more purchases, they're also getting smarter about comparing ratings and review sources. One Gen Z focus group participant explains, "On YouTube, you have to cross-reference different product reviews for multiple products." Gen Z recognizes that ratings and reviews can be gamed, whether that is by paying an influencer to say great things, offering free stuff for a great rating or review, or even directly paying people or programmers to create a landslide of five-star reviews and great testimonials. To combat the realistic likelihood of gamed reviews, Gen Z wisely looks across platforms to figure out what is really true about the product or service. This is especially true with important or expensive purchases and includes looking at multiple videos by different people on YouTube, checking out Amazon reviews, and looking at Google search results for the product or service name and the words "reviews" or "ratings."

If you're going to sell to Gen Z, facilitating honest and recent reviews, ratings, videos, and testimonials is absolutely critical. This is true not just for daily purchasing decisions, such as a restaurant or food delivery options, but also for bigger purchasing, including finding your next apartment. Actively working on ratings and reviews is important for companies of any size seeking to drive initial trials and ongoing trust between their brand and Gen Z.

In fact, in our 2017 State of Gen Z Study, we found that 78% of Gen Z have used online ratings and reviews at least once in the past thirty days to purchase an item.

Gen Z is already spending *billions* of dollars per year, and their spending is only going to go up over the next many decades—and their impact on the spending of other generations will be exponentially greater. Understanding Gen Z's consumer mindset now will enable you to take the necessary actions right away to unlock the generation's potential while also being positioned for the influence they'll have on every other generation.

PART III

HOW GEN Z IS CHANGING THE WORLD OF WORK

10 GETTING THE RIGHT START WITH GEN Z EMPLOYEES

"Earning money, in my eyes, is really important just to save for the future. I'm really heavily invested in learning about finance and things like that. So personally, I want to have money so I can invest it, so that I can do more things in the future and not be tied down."

—Alessandro, sixteen

Ricky started looking for his first job when he turned sixteen so he could help his parents with rent. "I also wanted to just buy stuff to spoil them the way they spoil me," he tells us.

So he fired up his phone and googled companies that hired sixteen-year-olds. Immediately, job listings for a new In-N-Out Burger location came up. He applied through his phone and got a call right away inviting him in for an interview.

"At the interview they told me they thought I'd be great with customers, and they hired me on the spot."

Ricky's first reaction to working at In-N-Out: total overwhelm. "The main focus is the customer and the quality of our burgers and our fries. That makes it stressful. Have you seen the line of people? It's really stressful to be working on the drive-through, then working fries as well."

Despite the hectic setting, Ricky's managers created an environment that made him want to stay and excel. "If my boss comes up to me and says, 'By the way, you're doing a good job. I see that you kept calm and worked your best in a stressful situation,' that makes me feel I'm doing well. I can calm down and start focusing more on how I can do better.

"For a high school kid, getting paid is huge. I was their first hire and I was scared because my trainers were all higher levels. I thought, I'm a high school kid, they're grown-ups, are they going to be judging me?"

But Ricky didn't face any judgment. What he got was mentorship. "They told me, if you want to level up faster, learn to do this, and this, and this."

One of Ricky's favorite parts of working at In-N-Out is that he can grow as fast as he'd like. The more an employee is willing to learn, the sooner they can be promoted. Then the mentorship continues.

Ricky explains, "When you level up you first watch a video, but then they'll go with you and show you *how* to do everything. Then you do it by yourself. When you get it right you feel better, like, *okay, I can do this*. And then you start getting independent and feeling calm. You start to get automatic and your brain just triggers. You're like, *Oh, there you go!*

"My managers are like my moms. They treat you like family so you feel like home. My managers always welcome me and check in to see how I'm doing. We are all really close."

Ricky's experience touches on so many facets of what Gen Z tells us they are looking for in an employer: they want a rapid, mobile-friendly application process; they want opportunities for advancement, learning, and mentorship that leverage technology such as mobile phone–based training for each role; they want managers who care about them as individuals and are clear to show they don't judge them. All of these qualities would give an employer a defensible difference™ among others seeking to recruit Gen Z who have yet to adapt. But before we dig deeper into each of these points, we want to jump into key aspects of what our extensive research reveals about Gen Z and employment.

Gen Z wants to work. They want to work hard. They want to work for a stable company (it's true: they're not *all* ditching traditional work for the gig economy). They don't *all* want to be YouTube stars—many want actual jobs, and they want to grow within their company. Why do they want to work for a stable company? Our interviews show that they recall seeing and hearing about Millennials losing their jobs in the Great Recession. This leads them to place a priority on stability, and often they perceive stability to be linked to the size of the company. This leads Gen Z to say they want to work for bigger companies rather than smaller companies, which they perceive as higher risk—whether or not that is actually real.

As we took a deeper look, our research and that of others also showed that Gen Z wants to work in a place that offers a commitment to improving the environment locally and globally, delivers on social responsibility from equal pay to career pathways, and delivers employment benefits that typically are sought after by more experienced workers, such as retirement matching. In combination, the greater rate of communication Gen Z wants from their boss (even before they officially start); the work environment they want, from current technology to opportunities for mobile training; and the fact that they are so young yet have such a clear vision for what they want from an employer are all surprises we will explore in the pages ahead.

When we talk to Gen Z about work, the attitude we frequently hear from them is a variation of "I will take whatever job you have. Just give me a chance." This is already proving true among CGK's clients that employ a large number of teenagers and college-aged students. They are finding that retention is often higher among their Gen Z employees than their current Millennial employees.

Does this mean that all Gen Zers are going to show up on time and work hard? No. In fact, research by the recruitment firm Randstad USA shows that 43% of Gen Zers have accepted a job offer and then "ghosted" or disappeared on the company. (Don't worry—we will show you how to avoid having this happen to you in the pages ahead.) But Gen Z *does* have a zeal for work. It is an encouraging trend that we've seen and heard about from Gen Z as well as employers across the country, from quick-service restaurants to manufacturing and engineering. As one employer tells us, "I'll take a Gen Zer any chance I get. They are definitely proving to be a good fit and are hard workers."

However, engaging Gen Z as employees has its challenges. To start, fewer of them are actually working, or looking for work, compared to other generations at the same age. This is particularly true of teenage Gen Z. According to the U.S. Bureau of Labor Statistics, the workforce participation rate among sixteen- to twenty-four-year-olds was 55.2% in 2018, compared to 65.9% in 1998. Among sixteen- to nineteen-year-olds, that number dropped to 35.1% in 2018 compared to 52.8% in 1998! While the teenage unemployment rate may be low generally speaking, the unspoken larger trend is that fewer teenagers are actually working now than in past generations.

There is much speculation about why fewer members of Gen Z are working as teenagers, but we see that it generally comes down to a few key drivers, including: parents who don't want their teenage kids to work but instead want them to focus on school, enrichment, or other activities during the summer; difficulty in finding cost-effective transportation for low-income teenagers to get to where the summer or after-school jobs are located; lack of social, peer, or other pressure or stigma to work while a teenager; and a decrease in offerings of or participation in school vocational or career-technology programs that included part-time work for a local business. Whatever the reason for Gen Z's low workforce participation, it poses a major challenge for companies that are eager to hire younger workers yet are not seeing them as applicants or job seekers.

A smaller ratio of Gen Z participating in the workforce also points to an interesting change in the worker-employee relationship. Gone are the days when young workers would need to show up in person, fill out a paper application, and hope for a call back as the only pathway to earn income. Today, Gen Z has an endless suite of apps they can leverage to earn income through side gigs that offer flexibility and faster payment of earnings, from Care.com, Fiverr, and TaskRabbit to Lyft, Uber, DoorDash, and Grubhub. Making money as an online influencer or nanoinfluencer is even an option with the right strategy and hustle (that's another book entirely!). Our 2018 State of Gen Z Study found that 23% of Gen Z earn money with a side gig of some kind (such as odd jobs and short-term work) and 9% have their own business. And research from Instant Financial reveals that 76% of Gen Z would pick a job where they had the option to get paid daily over a traditional pay schedule.

With so many alternative income options that did not exist even just a few years ago, the Gen Zers who *are* looking for traditional jobs have specific expectations for any potential employer. Those expectations affect everything from the job application process all the way through to onboarding, training, scheduling, payroll, and ongoing professional development.

Another game changer for the employment world, especially as it relates to Gen Z, is today's always-connected culture of transparency, employee feedback, and online reviews. If your company does not treat its employees well, the world will know. *Fast.* Prospective employees won't even bother applying to your job openings after reading negative reviews online or hearing negative things about an employer from friends or family. Social media chatter and reviews matter as much in employment recruiting—if not more—as they do in the consumer marketplace. As we like to say in presentations, you check out a review for a restaurant to see if you want to eat there the first time, but you look at the restaurant's employment ratings to see if you want to spend a year working there.

74% of job seekers rate online employee reviews as being very important or somewhat important in helping them decide whether to apply for a specific job.

42% of college-aged Gen Z (and Millennial cuspers) say that a company absolutely must have ratings and reviews on its employment website in order for them to apply.

But there is a hidden bright side: the members of Gen Z who do seek employment are willing to give a job their all *for the right company*. We already touched on qualities that Gen Z is drawn to in an employer: fast application, customized onboarding and training programs, mentorship, opportunities for growth and learning as they progress, bosses who engage with them as high-potential individuals, and a commitment to social and environmental responsibility, among many others.

But how can a company get to the point of showing Gen Z what they have to offer? This chapter walks you through the "new normal" of what to expect when it comes to attracting, recruiting, and hiring Gen Z.

If anything here sounds overwhelming, excessive, or just not necessary, know that in the current labor market, employers of all sizes are looking for ways to get more applicants. Or, as Jason frequently says, "you can't hire people who don't apply." The key is to get the right people to apply. Looking ahead, attracting and adapting to Gen Z won't be optional, as Gen Z will make up an increasing percentage of the workforce every year for the next fifteen years.

Gen Z Job Search: Friends First, Then YouTube

Unlike Millennials, Gen Z starts their job search the same way they look for shopping recommendations: through friends and family. This makes sense given their age and life stage.

We saw this firsthand in our 2018 State of Gen Z Study. When we asked Millennials and Gen Z where they prefer to look when searching for a job, Gen Z's top two choices diverged from the Millennial generation. Gen Z's choices were: ask friends or family about job openings (60%), or ask someone they know who already works at the company (57%). Millennials, on the other hand, prefer to visit job search websites like Indeed or Monster (67%) or search company employment websites (65%).

But what happens after Gen Z goes to friends and family first when looking for a job? They go to YouTube for a deeper dive into the company's culture.

This is a big finding. Our research shows that YouTube is way more important to Gen Z in their job search than many employers and leaders believe. When it comes to checking out a potential employer, Gen Z does not typically go to the Millennial and Gen X information oasis of Glassdoor or LinkedIn. Only 24% of Gen Z say they would use Glassdoor to learn about a company before considering working there. Instead, they go to the same video platform where they watch Fail videos, dog tricks, viral lip-synching, and math tutoring videos.

But YouTube is not the only surprise that should catch the attention of executives, HR leaders, managers, and others involved in hiring and employee retention: 40% of Gen Z say they would use YouTube to determine if they want to work for a company, a close second of 37% would use Instagram, and 36% would use Snapchat. Snapchat?!?!

We love Snapchat, especially the great filters, but seeing it as a channel to have your company reviewed as a *potential employer* is likely a leap for many traditional mangers and recruiters. And yet, companies like Cisco, McDonald's, JPMorgan Chase, and Goldman Sachs are already using Snapchat to recruit Gen Z.

Goldman Sachs used Snapchat's College Campus Stories platform to run a series of ten-second recruitment videos that showed how a career with them could intersect with a student's diverse skills, educational background, and interests. The videos were only visible to people within sixty target campuses and ended with a call to action to visit their career page for more info on internships and entry-level opportunities. The Goldman Sachs Media Kitchen team reported that in the videos' nine-day run, they accrued over 2.1 million views and generated an 82% increase in visits to their Careers website from organic search.

Going even further, McDonald's has used what it calls "Snaplications" to recruit sixteen- to twenty-four-year-olds. They had employees post ten-second videos describing why they love their job and what it's like to work at McDonald's. Snapchat users were then prompted to swipe, which led them to the career page and a link to apply to McDonald's straight from their phone.

AT&T has realized that Gen Z recruits want to see—rather than be told—that "the old telephone company has become a modern media firm." They use text and Snapchat with job applicants, video interviews to connect with young hires, and virtual-reality goggles for walkthrough demonstrations of a day on the job.

To be clear, we're not saying you *must* get on Snapchat if you want to effectively recruit Gen Z. But understand that if you're seeking to hire Gen Z, it's critical to expand to online social platforms that you might historically think are outside the realm of recruiting. You don't have to be everywhere, jumping from YouTube to Snapchat to TikTok to Instagram, but do think about how you can leverage some of these platforms to attract younger workers. Word of mouth (and video!) is everything, whether it's coming from friends and family or coming from the social platforms through which Gen Z loves to scroll.

Get Your Referral Program, and Your Story, Straight

The parallels between how Gen Z shops and how they look for jobs might seem surprising at first. But it is a natural progression when you think about it: they grew up relying on friends, reviews, and videos to inform them. So when it comes time to look for a job, they will research companies in the same way they researched buying choices. In fact, many of the companies they research as potential employers may be the same ones they frequent as consumers, whether (especially as teens and college students) they're restaurants, retail outlets, or other local businesses offering part-time employment while they're in school.

But before you get Snap happy (or YouTube or Instagram happy), take a step back to consider the big picture of how Gen Z job searches, and see how you can adapt accordingly using one of the most powerful, often untapped, and effective resources you *already* have: your current employees.

Our research shows that Gen Z first turn to friends, family, and current employees at a company for job leads. With this in mind, make sure your employee referral system is the best it can be.

Ronald Kasner is president and COO of iCIMS, the world's largest recruiting technology platform. iCIMS provides software solutions for more than four thousand companies that are filling more than four million jobs around the world every year. The company is also deeply invested in creating a rich work experience for its own one thousand or so employees, with an emphasis on professional development, work-life balance, and giving back to their local New Jersey community.

Kasner shared with us that one of iCIMS's biggest forms of recruiting is employee referrals. The recruitment channel is so significant that the company developed features in its software that allow employees to share job openings with friends and connections on social media: one of the first places their Gen Z friends will be looking for job ideas and leads.

Similar stories ring true around the world. Salesforce is one of the most popular companies among Gen Zers looking for work—and not without reason. Salesforce has a special referral program based around Recruitment Happy Hours. Employees invite their referrals to the happy hour, which is more of an informal get-together than a corporate interview. Salesforce has reportedly paid out millions in referral bonuses, and according to their own website, it is their "#1 source of new hires." But they don't just recognize successful hires, they've also given out San Francisco Giants tickets to employees who submitted a referral who didn't ultimately get hired.

Referrals also take the lead in the hospitality industry. Kat Cole, the COO and president of Focus Brands in North America, shared with us that employee referrals are huge for hiring Gen Z within her company's brands, which include Auntie Anne's, Carvel, Cinnabon, Jamba Juice, and Moe's Southwest Grill. Cole explains, "Old-school theory applies here, times ten. The best recruiters for your next employees are your existing ones—and now they have social networks that amplify their ability to warn people about your business or recruit them into it."

Get creative with your employee referral program rewards. Also keep timing in mind. Many companies' referral rewards programs pay out a bonus after the referred employee has been with the company for a year. But to really incentivize Gen Z, consider offering smaller rewards over shorter periods of time. You can give a reward immediately when a referral starts a job, another one after six months on the job, and a third installment after the one-year anniversary. This not only provides instant gratification for the referring person but also aligns further incentives around tenure. This way everyone is aligned, from start to anniversary!

Alongside a robust referral program, make sure your company mission, values, culture, and story are very clear and accessible to job applicants.

What do you think Gen Z does once a friend piques their interest in applying for a job at their company?

No doubt: they will google (or as some say, "Google-Tube") the heck out of you.

78% of college-aged Gen Z and Millennials say that flexibility in their work schedule would convince them to accept a job immediately without bonuses.

Everything we said about what Gen Z consumers look for in a brand applies to what they're looking for in an employer. And they'll be looking on YouTube and social media for clues that you have what they want in a job and career. In addition to what we've mentioned so far, Gen Z also:

- Wants to work for a company that stands for something bigger than its product or service. They want to know that their work is contributing to something bigger than the task at hand.

- Wants to know that they won't be a cog in a machine. They seek companies and managers that care about them as individuals and want to help them excel, which means they need you to show them how their role—even the most entry-level—is important to the overall workings of the business.

- Values and demands diversity and inclusiveness, from the frontlines to the C-suite.

- Wants a fun workplace and flexible schedule. Our research shows that a flexible schedule is even more important to Gen Z than competitive pay!

Brent Pearson is the founder of Enboarder, an employee onboarding platform that helps companies create meaningful engagement with employees *before* their first day of work. Companies like Gap, Novartis, McDonald's, and Eventbrite are Enboarder clients, and Pearson's team regularly studies hiring and onboarding practices that are most effective with Gen Z.

"What we've discovered," Pearson shares with us, "is that Gen Z prioritizes working for a company that values its employees above anything else. They care about that much more than any dollar amount. They've realized that if they're going to spend a third of their life at work, they want to actually enjoy the work and find a company that shares their values."

Every leader and hiring manager we've spoken with shares similar stories. Tiffany Taylor, founder of Tiff's Treats, runs more than fifty bakeries throughout the United States, and a large segment of her employees are in Gen Z. Tiff's Treats has pioneered a business model of delivering fresh-baked, still-warm cookies (and milk!) to customers on demand. As Gen Z becomes a bigger part of their employee and customer base each year, Tiff's Treats is adapting their hiring process to better connect with young employees.

Taylor shares, "We have worked hard to create a more streamlined interview experience for candidates. One thing that stands out about Gen Z is a need for speed and to provide a unique work experience.

"We've created processes to speed up the interview process (HR reaches out to applicants and immediately asks them to set up an in-person interview at the office) while also enhancing the experience and selling them on our story and what we have to offer. We bring them in and explain to them all the things that set Tiff's apart from other jobs that are typically being sought by Gen Z applicants (such as typical quick-service restaurants) and, on the flip side, we want them to demonstrate to us what sets them apart from candidates for those types of jobs.

"We spend a lot of time emphasizing how we see our team members as not just drivers or bakers but as *ambassadors for the brand*. We want them to be all-in, at every level of job, and we have found that Gen Z is looking for something to believe in."

Taylor told us that Tiff's Treats is seeing a great response from Gen Z as the company puts more emphasis on how their work will help others.

"What really resonates with Gen Zers is our focus on creating *warm moments*, that while we are 'just delivering cookies,' the impact we make on people's lives can be substantial. Our purpose goes way beyond cookies, and we find that Gen Zers want to be part of something bigger than themselves and they want to work for a company that cares about more than just the bottom line," Taylor says.

"We're about small moments that make people's day. We talk about being part of a gratitude movement, of making it easy for people to reach out to the ones they love and express how they feel. There's a real emotion to what we do, and our people feel that every day."

Employers like Taylor who already hire Gen Z in droves know how important it is to weave their company mission and culture into every part of the hiring process.

When asked what has changed in hiring since she entered the workforce twenty years ago, Kat Cole of Focus Brands shares similar insight: "The content strategy is different and the channels are different. The content is more about the employee brand, affiliation, mission, and culture vs. the 'work.' The channels are more organic experience sharing—YouTube, TikTok, Snap—and shared by existing employees vs. 'corporate marketing messages.' We are early in this journey, but that is a noticeable difference between building awareness for job opportunities with the youngest demographic vs. older ones."

Cole has also witnessed a distinct change in Gen Z's expectations of employers compared to older generations. "There is more of an expectation to be aligned with their personal beliefs *and* position on things in the world (social, environmental, even political), and also the expectation to keep learning and doing something different quickly vs. just doing a job you were hired to do for a while."

These two core ingredients to recruiting Gen Z—employee referrals and a transparent story that reveals your company mission, value, culture, and story—will make up the foundation upon which to build your Gen Z hiring practice. Once you have these set you can start getting creative with outreach.

But please: do not try to appeal to Gen Z without consulting Gen Z on how they'd like to be reached. Just as the smartest consumer brands are asking Gen Z (or Gen Z researchers) how they'd like to be marketed to, it is wise to connect with them on best ways to reach them about job openings. If you already employ members of Gen Z, bring them into the conversation. Ideally they would deliver your content for you, either in video or other social media content, so the messaging is peer-to-peer. The key is to ask Gen Z what excites them about the job, where they would most want to hear about the job as an opportunity, and how to tell the story in a way they trust that also drives that initial application. Ask your Gen Zers and they will tell you!

Keep these key strategies in mind when generating content to recruit Gen Z:

1. Add videos on YouTube and other social media platforms showing what it is like to work at your company, detailing the types of training you offer, and showcasing your commitment to making a positive impact in your community and the world.

   SAP attracts and hires more than seven thousand Gen Z employees every year. Because SAP is a B2B company, prospective employees may not be aware of what the company does. They rebranded their employee value proposition (EVP) to "Bring everything you are. Become everything you want," which is featured on their employee brand channel called Life at SAP. The channel features employees in videos that share every facet of SAP's culture, from their employee adoption benefits and office accessibility features to videos focusing on individual employees' stories. Videos also give a glimpse of SAP's office spaces (including in-office swings, among other perks).

2. Make sure members of Gen Z are in the recruiting or employment-branding videos. Gen Z wants to see people who are about their same age and to whom they can relate when they talk on the video, reflecting ethnic and gender diversity as well as different educations, past jobs, and backgrounds. Search Starbucks College Achievement Plan for great examples of videos that show Gen Z sharing personal stories of how the company's commitment to covering tuition for employees to attend Arizona State University has changed their lives and community.

3. Use behind-the-scenes photos and candid photos showcasing your culture on your recruiting page and social media efforts. For Gen Z, social media is largely a visual connection. Don't talk about your culture, show them your culture in action!

4. Focus your recruiting on the hot buttons that we know will get Gen Z to apply, including a flexible schedule (when possible) and fun work environment, which was top on their "want" list in our research study. SAP's Life at SAP YouTube channel is an excellent example of how to do this well.

5. Emphasize how fast and easy it is to apply for a job with your company—and that they can do it right on their favorite mobile device. Hotel brand Marriott has a dedicated Marriott Careers YouTube channel, which includes a quick video on how to apply for a job with the company (complete with fun graphics and a Gen Zer in the video's opening frame).

Job Applications Applied to Gen Z

Remember the days of applying for a job on a paper application—or worse, a three-page paper application? Searching around for a pen or pencil if you didn't bring one and then trying to find a flat surface to complete the application in legible writing while sitting near the front door of the business? Gen Z does not know that experience. They don't carry a pen. They definitely didn't bring a pencil. In fact, they expect to complete a job application entirely online and preferably on their favorite mobile device—and to be able to save their application as they go.

Why is this important? Well, even with all the work you put into getting Gen Z to respond to your job listing, you can *very easily* lose them if your application is too complex. Being able to save the application as it is completed is particularly important, because so often young people don't have all the information they need handy. Being able to save as you go—and advertising this feature—not only gets more of them to start the application, but also gets more of them to finish over time. It also creates the opportunity to remarket to them to finish an application they started but didn't complete or submit (because you now have their contact information). You can send them an email or text that says, "Hi Sarah. Thanks for starting our job application! We'd love to see if you are a fit for us and we are a fit for you. Click here for a link to complete your application. We're excited to see if we're a fit!"

Without the right job application Gen Z won't start and definitely won't complete the application. Sometimes they'll look at the length of or detail involved in an application and not even start it—especially if they can't save as they go. In a tight labor market or in a company that is growing quickly and needs to hire the next generation of talent fast, driving completion of job applications—and often even job application *starts*—can make all the difference in getting or not getting the number of applicants needed to fill open positions.

But what type of job application does Gen Z expect? What factors will entice them to complete the application? We dove into this question because clients kept sharing that Gen Zers were on their career or job application page and didn't apply or would start an application but not finish.

What we found in our national study is that the *perceived and actual duration* of the job application process will have a big impact on whether Gen Z will start, complete, and submit the job application. Why is perception important? Because Gen Z will frequently scan a job application page and then decide if it is too much work or takes too long to complete. In our 2018 State of Gen Z Study, Gen Z reported that a fast, easy online application process was *more* important (58%) than listing the starting salary range for the job.

Some employers intentionally make their job applications long and complex because they want to weed out potential applicants who are "not committed" or lack the persistence to complete the application. However, for many companies, particularly those in retail, food service, service industries, and frontline sales, getting more applications is an urgent priority.

We found that 60% of Gen Z nationwide said that fifteen minutes is the maximum amount of time they would invest in completing a job application. However, 30% of Gen Z said ten minutes was the max and even 10% said five minutes or less! Tiffany Taylor and her HR team at Tiff's Treats understand this. She comments, "Speed and ease of access are crucially important to attracting and hiring Gen Z. Our application, interview scheduling, and onboarding process is all online and very quick and easy to complete. We don't want anything (like exchanged voice mails or paperwork) to get in the way of getting an interested candidate in the door and ready to work very quickly."

Before we criticize the generation and their lack of desire to complete a lengthy job application, it's important to step back and see the job application and even customer purchasing experiences they've been accustomed to up to this point in their life. Many in the generation have never completed a formal job application, so the process, no matter its complexity, can be intimidating. At the same time, everything in their world is about efficiency and the fewest number of steps possible, whether it's signing in to an online bank account or finding the video they want on YouTube. Indeed, they can make a major purchase online in less than five minutes and sometimes in only one click—especially if it is offering same-day delivery. Gen Z's behavior reflects what they've experienced and come to expect growing up. Frankly, this "get to the point" messaging is all they've ever known.

What works to get Gen Z to complete a job application? We've found six easy, low-cost solutions that drive completion:

1. Post a short video of someone walking through the process of how to complete and submit the job application. This video should be less than thirty seconds, high energy, and also reflective of your company culture and excitement for them to apply.

2. Allow people to save the application when it is partially complete. This is important because many in Gen Z are completing these applications not at the potential employer but in another location, where they could have something come up or they may not have all the information they need handy.

3. Collect their name and email or cell number up front to be able to re-market to them if they do not complete and submit the application. This simple nudge can help get them to complete the application. Sometimes people just get busy, but that doesn't mean they won't be a great employee or fit for a company. A gentle nudge via text or email—if they give you permission—works well. This also works well because often Gen Z tries to apply at companies familiar to them, so this is good for being on brand, too. If you have a choice, go with a text reminder over email. The same is true for confirming interview times and locations.

4. Make the initial job application shorter. Many hiring managers we've interviewed have shortened the initial job application in order to get more of them submitted. They then either do a phone, web, or in-person interview and provide a longer application with more of the details they need completed. They do this *after* they've been able to

talk to the applicant and determine if there is a fit and, in many cases, reinforce why the company is a great place to work. As one employer in the contracting industry tells us, "I make the application as short as possible because I want to be able to sell them on why they should work for me. A longer application means fewer chances to sell this generation on why we are such a great place for them to work."

5. Add marketing elements to the job application itself. Mention what's special about your culture. Cite awards and growth milestones that will separate your company from the rest. Send a message about what is important to you—your employees—and that both your company and future employees will have a bright future.

6. In addition to the usual details such as salary range and benefits, try adding content to your job description that shows the more human side of the job. Try quotes from employees or even a "Day in the Life" description of what it's like to work at your company, told in their own voice.

Ron Kasner at iCIMS notes an uptick in applications when companies offer the option to apply by text. The company found it works especially well in retail establishments and restaurants, where customers walking through a store or restaurant can see a "We're hiring! Text to apply" sign and immediately send in their contact information. From there, companies—either human recruiters or AI-powered chatbots—can answer questions, begin screening candidates, and walk them through the application process.

The bottom line: make your initial application *as easy as possible*. This will bring more applicants to the conversation, which will give you a chance to share your company story, mission, and vision for employees with more prospects. Each step in the hiring process can screen out applicants who are not the right fit. But don't inadvertently screen out potentially great hires by making your initial application too complex.

What would make Gen Z apply immediately?

- Job Salary: 85% of college-aged Gen Z and Millennials say the salary component of a job posting makes them want to apply immediately for the job.
- Benefits Description: 80% of college-aged Gen Z and Millennials say this information makes them want to apply for a job immediately.
- Day in the Life Description: 79% of college-aged Gen Z and Millennials say that a description of what a job would be like on a daily basis makes them want to apply immediately for the position.

Interviewing and Hiring

Interviews can be a stressful, time-consuming challenge for any generation, but especially for employers trying to hire Gen Z and for Gen Z trying to find the right employer. Employers often face a challenge hiring Gen Z because this generation is young and often has very little, and sometimes no, relevant work experience. At the same time the generation has very little experience conducting in-person, phone, or video-based job interviews. This presents a challenge when it comes to checking job references as well as looking for examples that the Gen Z applicant has an expertise, attitude, or experience that would lend them to be successful in the job.

Making this problem even more acute with Gen Z is the clamping down of unpaid internships. While many people debate the positives and negatives of unpaid internships, the reality is that unpaid internships—right or not—were a gateway for many first-time job candidates. Now that most internships are required to be paid, it has caused employers to place a higher value on the experience that a potential applicant brings to an internship, which, in turn, makes it harder for those without experience to get their proverbial foot in the door. This creates an even higher bar for Gen Zers.

At our research center in Austin, Texas, we offer paid internships through a program for rising first-generation college students. We are very proud of and highly engaged in our internship program and its larger initiative, Breakthrough Central Texas. We've found this to be a great way to help the next generation and our community. But not all companies can offer paid internships to a seventeen-year-old with little to no experience. This puts even more pressure on employers and managers to get the job interview "right" and find those members of Gen Z who can do a great job if hired, even with a lack of interviewing skills and experience.

The good news is that this gap will be bridged as the generation gets older and gets initial and future jobs under their belt, but right now, employers have to figure out how to interview a generation that may not have much work experience—and may not even know what to wear to a job interview.

We find a three-step approach works best to positioning both employers and Gen Z to find the right job match:

1. **Create and share clear expectations prior to the job interview.** We find sending an email or text message with key insights about the interview or interview process reduces Gen Z applicant stress, gives them the opportunity to show you what they can do, and makes interviews more effective for hiring managers. In this first step, an employer can message a potential applicant—and not just Gen Z, of course, but all applicants—some insights around the most stressful yet important parts of the job interview: what to wear, when to arrive, where to park, and what to bring. Our research has shown that terms such as "business casual" mean something very different by generation, gender, and geography. A simple example of what it means to you allows an interviewee to know how to dress appropriately and how early to arrive in order to be "on time." Right now, there is much debate about what is appropriate to wear to a job interview, and how closely that is linked to a company's workplace

culture and inclusion efforts, but we find it is good to give an example or selection and let candidates choose.

The second action to take is to let them know what they can or should bring, such as a list of references and their work history. If they haven't worked somewhere before, they might instead bring a list of personal references about them, their work ethic, and their character. Many young people today don't know to bring this to an interview because they haven't worked anywhere prior to the interview or been told what to do to get their first "real" job.

Third, let them know when to arrive, where to park, and where to sign in. These are all small details that make the entire process less stressful and more effective for everyone involved. In addition, providing these types of expectations creates the best chance for Gen Z to show you what they can do, which is a great frame of mind for them. It allows them to enter with confidence knowing that they're on time, prepared, and can show you they are the right person for this job.

Sometimes people think providing tips on how to be prepared for and deliver a good interview is coddling a generation. We disagree. Give people a chance to prepare and demonstrate the best they have to offer. There are so many cultural, generational, age, and other issues that separate us and can cause even experienced hiring managers to pass on a great potential hire. These pre-interview suggestions help to give every applicant an equal chance to show what they can do if hired, which, ultimately, is what hiring managers are trying to determine.

2. **Ask questions that allow them to show you their skills and determination.** When you don't have a lot of job experience, the typical line of questioning in an interview often reverts back to education performance or experience, volunteer activities, and other time-intensive pursuits. Rather than focusing on their education (they may have only just finished high school or are early into college), ask them about how they would solve certain challenges, scenarios, or problems. Allowing Gen Z to show you how they would think

about, approach, and attempt to solve a real business problem is not something that requires workplace experience, but rather is a chance for them to show their creativity and problem-solving skills. For example, you might ask them how they would make your website better or make your brand more engaging. Their suggestions or strategies are not the point of the question, but rather listening to how they go about approaching the problem will help you to get a sense of how they would approach problems in a workplace and, in a larger sense, whether they would be a good fit for your organization.

3. **Remember that an interview is still a mutual-marketing process.** An employer has to show they want the candidate and the candidate needs to indicate they want the job—and that there is a mutual fit. With Gen Z so intensely interested in on-the-job learning and professional growth, stability, and benefits, use the interview to talk about the types of learning and personal growth options you offer very early to new employees, such as on their first day and first week. Talking about the training provided, whether it is specific to the job or role or something broader, such as leadership, is a keen offer to this generation as they emerge. In addition, sharing about the stability of your business, the benefits you offer, and how you are employee-focused all align with hot buttons for Gen Z as they look for jobs and careers.

Also be mindful of how quickly you follow up with interviewees after the conversation, and what communication channels you're using. Ron Kasner and the iCIMS research team have mined fascinating insights about mobile communication and interviews. Studies conducted by iCIMS revealed that 45% of college seniors will begin to consider jobs at other companies if they don't hear back about their progress in the application and interview process *within one week or less.*

"Text communication is huge," Kasner shares. "The ability to rapidly communicate, not just to engage initially, but to engage with Gen Z throughout the hiring process, becomes so important."

iCIMS supported Hard Rock International and RPM Pizza, the largest Domino's Pizza franchisee, in their efforts to experience significant improvements in filling jobs quickly when they switched to text communication. The response rate from candidates grew from 50% to 75% when Hard Rock International switched from email and phone communication to texting. RPM Pizza similarly has a 99% open rate, 91% response rate, and one-minute response time when using text, compared to its 7.3% open rate and 2.1% response rate with email.

Video Interviews

We are often asked about video interviews and whether they are effective with Gen Z. The reality is that there are a lot of video interview platforms and techniques. The key benefit of a video interview for employers is that they can see and interact with the candidate, and provide more insights than a phone call, but without the travel hassle or time commitment involved for both parties. We hear repeatedly from job applicants that they don't like video interviews, yet companies continue to lean on this interview technique more and more. There is now even technology for candidates to video their answers to questions and send those recordings to the hiring manager rather than having an actual, live video interview.

Looking ahead, we see Gen Z as likely having more comfort with video interviews as they continue to get older. This generation grew up on video everything, from video chat and Houseparty to Google Hangouts and FaceTime. Being able to see someone while speaking might even be more comfortable and natural for some in Gen Z than talking on a phone. The key is, if a company is leaning on video interviews, take the same approach as the previous section but adapt it to the video experience. For example, let the applicants know that the best video interviews are conducted when they are in a quiet place with enough lighting where all parties can easily see each other. Again, provide a link of what to expect in a video interview, including the time to log on and the minimum technology required for them to be able to participate in the interview.

Making the Job Offer

Since most of Gen Z has never been employed before or has limited work experience, many of them do not understand all the details that come with taking on a new job. This includes expectations for training, professionalism, when they'll get paid, how much they'll earn, and other workplace benefits. For this reason, outlining these details when making the job offer has never been more important. Gen Z needs to understand both the significance and responsibility that go with taking a new job as well as the benefits to them for joining your team.

We find the best job offers are one page long and have a high-level snapshot of the key things that the new hire needs to know. This includes start date, compensation, benefits, and typical schedule. The scheduling part is particularly important as Gen Z may be in school or have other commitments, including other jobs. Letting Gen Z know that they will receive your company handbook that spells out all the details also lets them know that the job offer letter is not the only information resource they'll be receiving as they start their exciting new journey working at your company.

Here are three best practices for making the job offer:

- Make key points using bullet points. This makes them easier to read.

- When listing the start date, be sure to list the start time and the schedule for the first week of employment.

- Include a key contact to confirm acceptance and any other elements required prior to or due on the first day, including a drug test, valid driver's license, etc.

Once an offer is received, we then recommend sending a welcome message. This is often a quick video (ideally) or text message and is different from a formal offer letter you might have sent to full-time employees, because if they're receiving this welcome message they've already accepted the job and now you can go into the actions that will prepare them for their first day. In the welcome message, there are four things to emphasize:

1. Reinforce your excitement about them joining the team. They should hear they've made a great decision, and this is going to open new doors for an exciting career and learning.

2. Remind them of anything they need to bring or do before arriving for their first day.

3. Let them know where to park or the best public transportation options. This is a big one for new hires on their first day.

4. Tell them who to ask for when they arrive and what to expect on the first day. Many times, the person who did the interviewing and hiring is not the person with whom they'll directly work or who will be their boss or first-day trainer. We recommend providing this person's phone and email in case they have questions in advance, but that is a company culture decision.

This is your chance to show them the culture of your organization and to truly make them feel welcome.

The key to a good welcome video is for Gen Z new hires to feel warmly greeted and to increase their excitement for their first day at a new job. This helps put them on a path for success early and reduces the questions and frustration that managers often face when a new hire arrives and isn't prepared. They may also immediately forward the message or tell their friends, which leads to more applicants—which is really important in a tight labor market.

If you're unsure about how much detail to include in your welcome message, another option is to create a password-protected FAQ page for new hires. This page can include all the most commonly asked questions that new hires have before they start a job with the company.

Gen Z has come of age with everything online being self-serve, and this is an easy way to offer that experience and reduce questions directed to HR and managers before the first day.

While these are all great baseline actions to take, if you truly want to wow Gen Z and welcome them into your company culture, you can easily take a next-level approach to greeting and onboarding your new hires. And it can start *well* before their first day of work. More on that in the next chapter.

11 UNLOCKING THE GEN Z EMPLOYEE'S LONG-TERM POTENTIAL

"I'm really difficult on myself, always telling myself, 'You can do better, you can do more, you can just be more,' so having a supervisor who takes time out of their day to not send me an email, to not send me a Skype message, but be present in person and say, 'Hey, you're doing well. We're really proud of you,' or, 'We're really glad that you're here. We value you,' is a big deal."

—Gen Z employee

Isabella is so excited. She's been attending career fairs and applying to design assistant jobs since the spring. In between, she's taken on more than thirty-five freelance gigs to build her design portfolio. She graduated from Temple University in May, and in August accepted a position at a digital marketing agency in Philadelphia. She starts in two weeks.

She's excited, but terrified. This will be her first job, and she's never worked in an office before. What should she wear? In her interview she'd been told the dress code was "creative casual," and she has no idea what that means. But she remembers from googling the company before applying that every team member has a short video about him or herself on the company website. So she revisits the videos to study outfits: some people are in jeans, some are in funky shirts and ties, one woman is wearing a killer dress that looks like a '90s vintage thrift store find. It seems anything goes as long as it's clean and put together—with room to get creative. Isabella feels she'll fit right in.

But she's anxious about her boss, Casey. They'd talked in the interview about how Isabella would have the chance to learn new design software and offer creative input on their projects, but Casey also seemed overwhelmed. She mentioned she's juggling nine client accounts and needs Isabella to manage calendars and logistics for all of them. Would there really be room for anything beyond admin work?

Then there's the red tape. Since Isabella built her design experience as a freelancer, she's never actually been employed. She has no idea how to select the right health insurance plan or set up a 401(k).

Lost in a trance of enthusiasm and anxiety, Isabella jumps when a text buzzes in on her phone. Hmm. It's not from anyone in her contacts. She opens the message and notices it's a video. She taps to watch.

"Hey, Isabella! This is Casey. I'm so excited we'll be working together! Let me know if you're free for breakfast this week. I'd love to chat before our first day. Do you have a favorite coffee shop in Center City?"

Isabella is shocked and so relieved. Her first day is weeks away, but she will get to speak with Casey again much sooner. And she is touched that Casey asked her to suggest a favorite spot.

In the days following her job offer, Isabella's phone buzzes some more. She receives texts from the creative director asking some unexpected questions: What are her hobbies? Favorite food? Favorite 3 p.m. pick-me-up snack? These were not the intake questions Isabella had anticipated, but she complies: hiking, tacos, black licorice.

She also receives texts covering essential homework: she taps through a questionnaire that populates her W-4 form and is e-introduced to a financial advisor who sends her a quick guide to understanding her 401(k) options. HR texts a video explaining her health insurance elections and the differences between each plan.

Wow, Isabella thinks. She can feel the anxiety melting away.

In the two weeks leading up to her first day Isabella feels completely ready to make her insurance and 401(k) elections, and has even sketched out a plan with Casey over breakfast for her to start learning Adobe Illustrator in the next six months.

The last surprise text buzzes in one week before her start date: it's a video from four people at the company (she recognizes them from the Team Bios web page).

"Hey, Isabella! This is Nikki. This is Celia. This is Ian. This is Joe." Ian is holding the phone in selfie mode while everyone squeezes together to fit into the frame.

They take turns talking. "We're the other design assistants and just wanted to say hi before you start next week. Also, we hope you're free Thursday after work. There is a margarita happy hour at a great place down the street. We heard you like Mexican, so hopefully you can join us?"

Then Celia chimes in: "I signed up to be your welcome buddy, so I'll find you on your first day and show you around. You can ask me anything at all about working here. Our contracts system kind of sucks, but I'll show you how to get past the glitches. Do not get the Caesar salad in the cafeteria unless you like soggy croutons. Of course there's more to it all. We'll talk next week!"

Wow. Wow. Wow. Isabella thinks. *They seem so nice, and we have happy hour plans before even meeting!* She flips her phone to selfie mode to send a quick video response.

"Hi, guys! That's so nice, thank you! I'd love to do margarita happy hour. Can't wait to meet you in person. Thanks again—I'm excited for next week! Also, soggy croutons are a no-go for me. Noted."

When Isabella gets to work on her first day, Casey greets her in the lobby and walks her to her desk.

Woah. She did not expect what she saw.

Sitting on Isabella's desk is a bucket of every black licorice variation she can imagine: laces, nuggets, wheels, straws. A note taped to the bucket says, "Hope this will cover your 3 p.m. pick-me-up for a while! ☺"

On her keyboard is an REI gift card with a Post-it Note that reads "Spruce up your hiking gear, on us! Welcome!"

Before Casey leaves, she asks Isabella if she'd like to join the team for lunch. They'd made reservations at a taco bar in the neighborhood for a first-day gathering.

As Isabella settles into her new digs, she's feeling *great*. The gifts are nice and all, but beyond the things themselves, she's so relieved to be working at a company that clearly seems to care about its people. They didn't have to do any of this. But they did, and she's so grateful. She feels *included*.

If you're reading this and rolling your eyes, we get it. Most of us who are Gen X or older never experienced anything close to an onboarding process like Isabella's when starting a new job. Her story may seem so unfamiliar that it's laughable. When we were starting out, we got our onboarding info in a big folder at HR orientation—if we had an orientation at all. Having an overwhelmed boss meant we put our heads down and got the job done. Gifts on our desk? Cheery welcome videos? Welcome buddies? Breakfast with the boss focused on what *we* want to learn? Talk about coddling.

Here's the thing: none of these things actually require much time, effort, or money, but they have a huge impact on how an employee approaches their job. Research published in *Harvard Business Review* shows employee retention increases by 33% within the first six months on the job when employers use an onboarding approach that is focused around the individual's personal identity rather than on the organization's identity and needs.

Also, it's not coddling. We don't think *any* employer should coddle their employees. You're simply being mindful of how you can make the employee feel welcome, valued, and appreciated and connect with them, human to human. When you show employees that you care about them, they will, in turn, care more about the company, coworkers, and even their boss.

Brent Pearson and his team at Enboarder design onboarding experiences to help companies thrive with Gen Z employees. He puts it best when he says, "Just because you had to suck it up if you had a less-than-warm onboarding experience, it doesn't mean that's the right way to do it. Don't treat your experience as normal."

Pearson also points out that many companies don't think about how their employees' experience translates to their customers' experience. "You cannot deliver a great customer experience unless you deliver a great employee experience," he explains.

"We've all been there," Pearson says. "You walk up to an airline counter and get a grumpy representative sitting behind the desk. They're so disengaged that the best you're going to get is a mediocre customer experience. But compare that to walking up to, say, the Southwest Airlines counter, a company that is all about employee engagement and experience. You're usually greeted by an amazing employee who loves their job, and that's reflected in your customer experience with that person."

This couldn't be more relevant for Gen Z, who have told us, again and again, that they want to work for a company that cares about their employees, is willing to mentor them, and offers them opportunities for talent development. The trade-off to this human-centric approach is better employee retention *and* better customer experience. And, ultimately, that means a more robust bottom line. Research by Gallop reveals that companies with highly engaged employees outperform their competitors by 147%. When employees are engaged, everyone wins.

But to truly unlock Gen Z's potential as long-term employees, you need to live out these promises beyond the first day. Based on our work with companies large and small, it often costs way less to engage employees given the ROI you'll receive by way of employee retention, performance, and customer satisfaction. You will also stand out as an employer Gen Z would be eager to work with, since, according to our 2019 national study, 64% of Gen Z feel employers do not understand their generation.

Ultimately, almost any employee of any generation would appreciate the approach to hiring, onboarding, training, and recognition that we recommend for Gen Z. It's why so many people in older generations react with, "Gee, that would be nice!" when they hear this advice. But our sentiment is the same as Pearson's: just because nobody offered this to you when you would have appreciated it doesn't mean you shouldn't offer it to those you hire! In fact, the upside of taking these actions is so great that you as a leader still end up directly benefitting.

As we've mentioned, historically low unemployment, alternative income options via the gig economy, and workplace transparency via social media are just a few reasons it's a good time to adopt this more human-centric approach to working with Gen Z if you haven't already. You'll also be investing in your company's future as Gen Z ages up and comprises more of the workforce, including becoming the new generation of managers, supervisors, and leaders.

We're about to take a deeper look at the factors that matter to Gen Z when it comes to staying at a job and giving it their all. As you think about applying these insights, consider adopting similar practices for employees of all ages, as every generation appreciates being valued and appreciated—even if some generations are more comfortable with selfie videos than others.

Making the Offer

Before Gen Z can thrive at your company, they need to accept your job offer. So how you package your offer is a big deal. For Gen Z, think beyond the standard listing of salary and health benefits. Both are important to Gen Z, but they're not everything. Research across several studies shows that when considering a job offer, Gen Z values:

- **On-the-job learning and talent development.** Gen Z is eager to learn and develop their talent: 62% of Gen Z participants in our 2018 national study said that paid, on-the-job training was a top factor in their decision to *apply* for a job. Others confirm this as well. The job search platform RippleMatch, which is designed to help Gen Z connect with employers, surveyed more than 1,100 college graduates from the class of 2019, and 59% of respondents said that the opportunity for professional development was the number one most influential factor in deciding to *accept* a job offer. When making your offer, emphasize how your company is invested in helping its employees grow, starting from their very first day on the job. This can range from full-scale, in-house training programs to mentorship programs or reimbursement for professional development courses taken outside of work or online.

- **Flexible schedules.** Research from Glassdoor shows that flexible work hours are a top driver in Gen Z's decision to apply for a job, second only to a great work environment. Some companies are leveraging software like HotSchedules to allow workers to select and change their own schedules directly through a mobile device. Flexible schedules are especially important to employees who are still in school and juggling classes, homework, and extracurricular activities alongside work—as well as possibly working more than one job at a time.

Top five things that directly impact whether an older member of Gen Z (18–24) will accept a job:

- 82%: Good pay for the work you do
- 65%: Flexible scheduling
- 49%: Easy to get to work
- 45%: Good benefits, such as insurance and retirement matching
- 41%: Acquiring new skills you can use for future jobs

* % of Gen Z ages 18–24 who noted an item as a top-five job requirement, based on our 2019 State of Gen Z Study.

- **Potential for a pay increase in less than a year.** Our research studies reveal that 62% of Gen Z expect to receive their first salary increase at a new job in nine months or less. Outline potential for raises in your offer letter or communication, with a clear explanation of what is expected from the employee in order to reach those milestones. Connecting performance to future raises is key for aligning expectations and creating the shared accountability that leads to trust, loyalty, and retention.

- **Opportunities for advancement.** Mention in your offer where the job can take the employee within six months, a year, and two years, if they meet clear learning and performance goals. This goes beyond our previous point about pay increases to include possible promotions or chances to work in other departments or on different types of projects and challenges within the company. Like any relationship, nobody wants to be the one to ask, "Where is this going?" Be clear about the potential if they put in the requisite effort. When you do, you'll be best positioned to benefit from the talent the employee has developed and the career path they now see.

- **Lifestyle benefits.** A client once shared that when they asked a Gen Z candidate why they preferred another similar job offer, the candidate said the competitor had included a gym membership with their offer. But my client had offered an additional $3,000 in pay! This anecdote confirms what our research shows, which is that Gen Z values an employer that offers lifestyle perks even more than higher pay. This can include gym, spin, or yoga memberships; free or discounted tickets to concerts or fun events; pet insurance; free car washing service; pre-negotiated discounts with local stores, restaurants, or retailers (which is always a win-win); or even paying for a Netflix account or discounted high-speed Internet. We've even seen some companies offer lifestyle rewards tied to tenure or performance. At our research center, when you complete three years of employment, you receive a "make a wish" gift. We give you $3,000 to spend on anything you want and have had team members use the money on everything from weddings and dream vacations to family trips.

- **Retirement matching.** As we mentioned in chapter 5, many in Gen Z are already saving for retirement. They value employers who want to help them reach their goals. Having a short video about how their money can grow can be very valuable for these new employees, especially a video that shows how even very small contributions made consistently at a young age can grow to an extraordinary amount through compound interest. While Gen Z often tells us they expect they will not get Social Security or other government-funded retirement benefits, they also often are not aware of the impact saving for retirement can have right away. They just know it is something they need to do. Show them how to take the right steps now and you'll not only be increasing their appreciation of you but also improving their future.

- **Paid time off.** Make it personal by giving them their birthday off in addition to whatever paid time off you are able to offer. We found that many young people like to take their birthday off from work—they see it as a holiday, so giving them this as a benefit also allows for their colleagues to know they won't be working that day well in advance. Surprisingly, older generations really like the birthday holiday, too, as we offer this to everyone at our research center.

- **Snacks at work.** Snacks and similar in-office perks make for a fun, inviting work environment, which is at the top of many Gen Zers' priorities when deciding to work for a company. Our work has shown that you don't have to have fancy or expensive snacks, but rather to ask employees—including Gen Z—what snack they would most like to have. By providing the snacks they actually want, it both saves money and reduces waste. Plus, employees feel heard and valued.

- **Access to pay every day.** A huge perk to gig work is accessing pay on the same day you work. Many employers are meeting the competition of gig work head-on by offering access to earned wages and tips every day through platforms like Instant Financial, which enable your employees to receive up to 50% of their earned income on the same day they work for no fees. This will be the norm with Gen Z as they get older, as companies from retail, hospitality, and restaurants already offer this pay option, and soon we expect the same in healthcare, professional services, and technology. In fact, in our research on access to pay, we found that having access to pay on the same day you worked is such a big driver that younger generations will take worse shifts, work on holidays, and stay at an employer longer for this benefit.

"The explosion of gig economy platforms has introduced a massive burden for the traditional employer," explains Steve Barha, founder of Instant Financial. "Companies now have to compete with gig jobs that don't have required scheduling and that offer immediate access to pay. But typically they're charging a fee to access pay instantly, and Gen Z has a huge sensitivity to fees. Employers that offer no-fee, instant access to pay are discovering they can highlight this benefit in their recruiting. It shows they care about their employees and that they're aligned with their needs and expectations."

Remember, Gen Z wants to work for a company that shows it cares about its employees. Offering benefits such as those we've mentioned proves your commitment to helping your employees thrive in and outside the workplace. Incidentally, the factors that attract Gen Z to accept a job offer are also what will build their trust and loyalty as long-term employees. So offering a robust set of benefits up-front that is tailored to what Gen Z values creates the ideal foundation for you to deliver on those promises in building their loyalty to you every day.

Orientation and Onboarding

Isabella's first day of work wasn't all tacos and candy. Her day kicked off with SAP training to learn the contracts system she would use for all of Casey's accounts. A few days earlier she'd received an email from HR linking to a video library organized by every task she'd need to master in SAP. She started by watching each one, then going to a one-hour training session on her first day where a colleague from IT walked her through each part of the software. Later, her welcome buddy Celia spent fifteen minutes helping Isabella input a new contract into the system.

Celia also took charge of introducing Isabella to everyone in the office. By the time lunch rolled around, Isabella had met each person there and was excited to keep chatting. In the afternoon, Casey invited Isabella into her office so she could brief her on each account and any client quirks she should look out for. It was a packed day, but Celia, Casey, and HR all made plans with Isabella for weekly checks-ins during her first month on the job and an open-door policy for her to ask questions without worry.

Isabella's onboarding experience may not sound earth-shattering, but it includes a blend of personal and technical elements that is important to keep in mind. Great orientation and onboarding goes beyond training to create connections with new coworkers, supervisors, and company culture. In fact, in a national study we led with the Distribution Contractors Association (DCA), we found that the number one most important thing to a new hire was to meet their team and team leader. The second most important thing to a new hire was to learn about training programs for skill and leadership development.

When a Gen Z new hire completes orientation and onboarding, they should have a core understanding of what they need to do to succeed in their new role. This includes knowing how to approach solving challenges, including whom and when to ask for help, and understanding any tools or technology they'll need to do their job.

There is often a lot to cover, with huge potential for overwhelm. So try to break things up. Some parts of orientation and onboarding, like meeting colleagues and touring the workplace, need to be done in person and are great opportunities to keep things warm and engaging. Team breakfasts, buddy programs, and having a few team members reach out before an employee's first day are excellent options for Gen Z.

We find that the best practices for orientation and onboarding with Gen Z work well at companies of all sizes, whether an employer has five employees or fifty thousand. Here are six key practices we've seen in our frontline consulting work helping organizations and leaders bridge generations with Gen Z:

1. **Introduce them to their coworkers.** In our national study with DCA we found this to be the most important step a supervisor can take to immediately make Gen Z feel part of the team. The second-best

action was for the supervisor to provide personal contact information, such as a cell phone number.

2. **Make small gestures to show you're happy they're there and that you care about the employee as an individual.** A modest welcome gift linked to one of the employee's personal interests—such as a favorite snack or memorabilia from a favorite sports team—shows you care about them as a human outside the parameters of their job. A little goes a long way, because what you're trying to show is that you listened to them and took action to make them feel welcome. You can even decorate their desk or announce your excitement that they're joining the team on social media.

3. **Explain the values and culture that are the North Star (mission or purpose) for the company and how the employee's work helps contribute to that larger mission.** Gen Z wants to know how their role contributes to the company and overall vision, even if they are in the most entry-level position within the company. Rather than just stating the values and having a culture statement, we find Gen Z best responds to being *shown* what those values and culture look like in action. Have current employees share how the company culture has helped them thrive or how they've seen their work touch the world at large, or let customers film a video that talks about how the company, product, or service affected them.

4. **Offer a blend of short, video-based training and person-to-person reinforcement.** Gen Z has come of age with on-demand how-to answers and training 24/7, 365 thanks to YouTube. Can you imagine how strange it must be to show up to work and be handed a printed binder for training? Yikes! This is a generation that hasn't turned in handwritten homework their entire college experience, yet now they are supposed to read a binder written in 1994? They weren't even born then. . . .

Yes, this is an exaggeration, but sometimes it's not off by much.

Depending on a company's commitment and approach to training and onboarding, the experience can run from printed three-ring binders or "just shadow Tim" to classroom-style learning or mobile-driven training. Remember, Gen Z grew up learning how to do everything from making slime to doing long division by watching YouTube. But they also value human-to-human mentorship. Combine these preferences by providing them with videos they can watch on demand on their phone to learn skills required for their job. Then pair them with a colleague to help practice what they've learned. The best method we see is showing a short video, discussing or demonstrating in person, and then showing the video again. This creates both consistency and scalability in training but also allows for in-person testing with immediate feedback.

5. **Start by teaching a new hire the minimum they need to know to be successful for the first one to three months.** They will learn more as they go and through additional training. Right now, the goal is to get them up to speed to start adding value quickly and not slow down coworkers too much as the new hire is ramping up. In the beginning, they just need to know how to succeed for the first few months, not all the skills they need for the next several years. Teaching longer-term skills and perspective will be easier and more meaningful once they have the context of a few months on the job. Up front, focus on what they need to be successful out of the gate.

6. **Try to gamify the onboarding experience.** If you can do this, it works particularly well with Gen Z. Gamification can be online badges for learning or course mastery or something as simple as creating a scavenger hunt around the office or workplace to find out where all the key areas, technology, and offices are located. Gamifying onboarding—whether that is for competition if in a cohort or completion if they are the solo new hire—provides a sense of achievement and progress that also makes it easier to consistently deliver initial learning.

Ruth Ann Weiss is the owner of Eagle's Landing Day Camp in New Jersey. She shared with us that she has completely revamped her counselor orientation program to adapt to Gen Z's learning preferences. Training sessions have gone from large groups to very small groups, with no more than five counselors per session so that orientation is close to a one-on-one experience. She also includes entertaining video clips. A video that Weiss has found clicks with trainees is a scene from the movie *Coach Carter*. "It talks about teamwork and how important it is for the team to come together and help one another when one member is down. That always resonates with them," Weiss shares.

Orientation has also become more of an ongoing experience than a onetime session. Counselors meet with senior staff weekly to ask questions and even just vent. "We can't solve every one of their problems, like when they're frustrated with how often the five-year-old campers stop activities to go to the bathroom, but we've realized it's important for the counselors to feel heard. Even if we can't make the problem go away, having a safe space to talk about it helps them through it."

Remember, orientation and onboarding is as much about helping an employee adapt to the company culture and understand your expectations of them on the job as it is about teaching technical skills. Make it personal. Help them spark a connection with colleagues. Help them know that they belong and that you're there to help them. But also deliver the key learning they need up front so they can get to work and start delivering value quickly.

Investing a little time into a strong, repeatable orientation and onboarding system is one of the highest ROI activities a company can undertake in any industry. Not only does orientation and onboarding drive performance and create connection and trust, but it can also increase retention, which is so important as Gen Z's skill set becomes more valuable and they begin to make up a larger segment of our workforce—including moving into management roles.

First-Week Mentor

"I work at a bank, so I deal with money. I don't play around with that. I'm scared most of the time. I find myself reaching out to (my mentor) all the time."

—Gen Z employee

In our national studies with young employees, CGK and DCA found that having a first-week mentor, or welcome buddy, is often the best activity for new hires to feel like they are a valued part of the company. While the mentor may not provide the detailed training or instruction of an orientation or onboarding program, the first-week mentor does provide a human contact that the new hire can trust and rely on for questions and information *without* asking their boss. The first-week mentor is usually introduced to the new Gen Z hire on their first day of work. They might have coffee or lunch together, or maybe a fifteen-minute kickoff meeting in the mentor's office.

At some companies, the mentor provides the shadowing that a new hire needs, and at other companies the mentor is simply a text, phone call, IM, or short walk away to answer a question. A first-week mentor provides both camaraderie and safety for a new hire who may complete the orientation or onboarding process but still be unsure about the unwritten rules or other norms within the company (such as the unassigned, assigned parking spots!). The first-week mentor can help a new hire feel more welcome by being both a company advocate and a culture ambassador.

Exactly how important is a first-week mentor? In our national study, we found that having a first-week mentor was more important to a new hire than detailed pre–first day job information, having the equipment needed to start on a first day, being taken on a tour of the company facilities, or being given a welcome gift! So, give your company and the new hire a gift that actually matters and benefits everyone involved: a first-week mentor.

Fast Communication

"This past summer I had an internship at a fairly large company. A lot of the supervisors were not on-site but located in other cities. Sometimes they would fly into town and were able to check in with us. They would pull the interns aside and tell us, 'Hey, we're really grateful for all that you're doing. You're helping us a lot.' Just knowing that we're actually helping impact whatever projects they were working on was really valuable."

—Gen Z college student

Much has been written about generations having different communication styles. You call, they text back. You email, they jump on Google Hangouts. All these different communication preferences are colliding within a single workforce, which creates communication challenges, frustrations, and opportunities for even the most experienced managers and leaders.

Having seen Gen Z at restaurants, in your community, or even your home, you know they are almost constantly on their phones and connected to social media. They operate on a very short feedback loop—whether that is getting instant likes on an Instagram selfie or a question posed in a Snapchat streak—and those short communication loops carry over to work. Gen Z wants more communication *frequency* than any other generation in today's workforce. Not only do they want more frequent and rapid communication, but they view it as necessary to staying at a company!

How strongly? In our 2018 State of Gen Z Study, we uncovered that two thirds of Gen Z say they need feedback from their supervisor at least every few weeks in order to *stay* at their job. In comparison, less than half of Millennials need the same amount of communication to stay with an employer. Going further into the data: one in five members of Gen Z need feedback daily or several times each day(!) in order to stay with an employer. This could be a challenge for Millennials as they will be the most likely generation managing Gen Z, as Gen Z enters the workforce already expecting more frequent communication than even Millennials are accustomed to giving or receiving. And if you recall, it wasn't that long ago that other generations said Millennials wanted way more feedback than they were accustomed to giving. Gen Z takes this to a whole new level, and that ongoing, fast feedback is all they've ever known.

This frequency of communication could be performance feedback or input, a simple hello while they're on the job, a short text to say "great work" when it is deserved, or a sticky note on their workspace. The key is that Gen Z wants more frequency of communication, and there are two big positives hidden in this heightened desire for communication and feedback on the job.

The first big positive is that a desire for more frequent communication creates more opportunity to provide feedback, input, training, and quick course corrections to develop Gen Z's talent faster. This creates a tremendous opportunity to help the generation develop their workplace skills, mindset, and attitude so they can deliver the best job performance possible for you and your team as well as advance their own careers.

In addition, through our qualitative work with Gen Z employees, one insight we've uncovered is that just because Gen Z wants more *frequency* of feedback doesn't mean they want more *total feedback*. Gen Z shares that they want to know how they are doing, where they could be improving, and areas to focus on at work, but those interactions with managers and colleagues could be extremely short—even less than a minute and potentially all via technology. The key is that the interactions and communications need to occur *consistently* so Gen Z knows how to deliver the most value to you.

The result is that Gen Z's desire for frequent communication can actually end up saving managers *significant* time and frustration by helping Gen Z do a better job faster and more consistently with potentially less overall communication. A two-minute conversation every week could be more beneficial than an hour meeting every month, which would save both the manager and the Gen Z employee significant time, especially when you're likely to not have just one Gen Z employee but many.

Plan to give Gen Z quick-interaction feedback at least once a week. This might only be a one-minute conversation, quick text, or even a deserved "nice presentation" comment, and the result will not only be their getting better faster but also their staying with you longer. Both of those are huge wins for Gen Z, their managers, and their employers.

Aligning Motivation

Our research with Gen Z reveals there are several motivators that managers and leaders can tap into right away to begin to unlock this generation's tremendous potential. This is true whether a Gen Z employee is in an entry-level job working at a restaurant, a career-starting position with a consulting company, or a part-time position as they explore different career paths within a company or industry.

The key actions our research shows most motivate Gen Z are alignment, company impact, and ongoing progress.

When it comes to alignment and Gen Z, our research shows that they are highly motivated by working in a career or job they are passionate about. In our 2017 State of Gen Z Study, 44% said that their biggest sign of success was having a career they are passionate about. Meanwhile, 36% said their biggest indicator of success is knowing they are making a difference.

Now, it's understandable that not every job will align with an employee's personal passions. Sometimes the link *is* easy enough: someone who loves to bake works in a cupcake shop, or someone with a devotion to mentoring kids finds a job at a summer camp.

Other times, alignment goes hand-in-hand with company impact. This theme has popped up in nearly every chapter of this book: Gen Z wants to align themselves with companies that aim to make a difference in the world. Every company can and should get clear on how their work helps others. While this should already be on your radar, as we've mentioned it as an important part of attracting customers and job applicants, the same approach keeps Gen Z motivated to stay with your company and do great work.

Sometimes a company's impact is obvious, such as a nonprofit that provides drinking water to people in developing nations (Charity: Water) or a company that donates shoes to communities that don't have them (TOMS). Other times, the impact is not so clear—but it may still be there. For instance, you can show how working in your retail store creates jobs, helps families, and improves the local community; or how working at an accounting firm helps local small businesses thrive so they can employ even more people. You can also point to charity work completed by colleagues or how your company empowers employees to volunteer in the community or some other way your company makes the world a better place.

Company impact also ties into everything from product development and supply chain management to delivery methods. If you're a restaurant, do you source ingredients that are sustainably grown or provide food for those in need? Do you support local suppliers or have a commitment to donating a percentage of profits to the community? If you're in manufacturing, do you stand by equal pay and safe work conditions for factory workers? How your company impact plays out can vary greatly from industry to industry and geography to geography, but just like in the consumer world, your employees will care about how your business affects the world—for better or worse. This commitment to a cause besides profit can be a great motivator for employees to see how their day-to-day work has a positive influence on the world.

One best practice we've seen work well is to map out how a Gen Zer's actions—or a specific position—touches every other position in the company and, in turn, the company's larger mission. Often entry-level or early career employees don't see how they are part of a larger picture that creates value and affects people and communities. Even the most junior person affects customers, culture, processes, and experience, and showing them that they do so is often empowering and motivating—and helps to tee up accountability for their actions and outcomes.

Money Works to Motivate, in the Right Circumstances

"One of the main reasons I left was because I received no recognition for my hard work. I put a lot into the job and I worked in several different departments—rock climbing, party hosting, service expo—and I was always there when they needed me. But there were no pay raises."

—Gen Z female

The classic approach of seeking to motivate through money, whether it's by offering bonuses, incentives, gift cards, or other financial rewards to drive effort, is effective but should not be seen as the only approach to motivating Gen Z. Money-driven incentives can come to be expected, and employees may no longer do their best unless additional rewards are offered, especially if the monetary incentives are not tied to specific, measurable outcomes. The incentives may not even motivate if the goals feel unreachable or it's assumed that a higher-performing employee will win them. These challenges are relevant to all generations, but knowing that Gen Z can be motivated by non-monetary rewards positions your incentives for the greatest, lasting impact.

In fact, when it comes to motivating Gen Z, they feel doing something they love far outpaces doing something just for money. How strongly? In our 2017 State of Gen Z Study, 63% of Gen Z said "doing something you love" is the most important aspect of choosing a career compared to 16% who chose "do something to make money." Sure, Gen Z's view about living their passion and making an impact vs. making money will evolve over the years as they incur more personal and financial responsibilities, but for now, Gen Z seems inspired by the nonfinancial aspects of a job. With this insight, consider offering rewards and incentives that are not tied to money but rather tied to experiences or impact, such as free tickets to a concert, winning a ride in a helicopter, or getting to pick which charity receives an extra donation. While this takes a bit more effort than handing out yet another Amazon gift card, it does seem to drive both the connection and emotional response that employers want from Gen Z long term.

That said, when it comes to entry-level and minimum-wage jobs, frequent raises can help with long-term employee retention. Our 2018 State of Gen Z Study showed that 69% of Gen Z expects a raise within the first nine months of working at a job. Interestingly, half of Gen Z males expect a raise within just six months compared to 40% of Gen Z females.

This brings us to the third biggest motivator for Gen Z: ongoing progress. Gen Z appreciates a step-by-step process of feeling like they are moving forward at their job. Let Gen Z know if or when a promotion may be on the horizon for them and what they need to achieve to ensure it will happen, even if it is a small raise or new responsibility. Having promotion requirements spelled out as much as possible in an easily accessible place is a win with this generation. Remember, Gen Z appreciates lots of ongoing, incremental feedback. Keep them posted on how they're doing, if they need to correct or improve in any way, and how they're progressing in their job. Sometimes even stopping to point out how much they have learned and grown can deliver the perception of progress they need to see to know they are not spinning their wheels but making a smart investment in their future by staying in their current job. If you don't, you could risk having a great Gen Z employee quit solely because they feel they are in the dark about how they are making progress in their job.

Training and Talent Development

You already know that Gen Z is eager to learn. Remember, one of the main reasons Gen Z decides to take a job is the promise of talent development and on-the-job training. But it's also why Gen Z stays in a job. So don't stop with orientation and onboarding but look at talent development as something you strategically provide every year of employment. This not only increases the value of the employee but also increases their value to you.

Ideally, you'd have a program in place that fosters ongoing learning among your employees, whether it is a full-scale "university," as companies like Deloitte have created, or a more intimate mentorship program where employees can learn one-on-one. If you don't have a talent development program in place, this is a *great place* to start as you invest in adapting to Gen Z employees. The program doesn't have to be fancy or detailed, but can simply provide training and resources that employees can use at key steps or stages within their job and career—whether that is via online videos, quarterly lunches with a senior leader to discuss a business problem and potential solutions, or watching a TED Talk and then exploring how the insights could be used in their career.

Gen Z and Email

Christian, our twenty-year-old intern, shared with us his uncertainty on how to write an email. He asked:

- Can I open the email with Hey Mar?
- Can you use emojis like on social media?
- Can you say "hahaha"?

People who work in an office and email all day long may find this shocking. *How can you not know how to write an email?!* But remember that Gen Z did not grow up with email as a primary form of communication. Many rarely use it, opting for text instead. A training program that includes email etiquette would go a long way with many new hires if it is a key communication channel in your industry.

Interestingly, what Gen Z wants to learn and develop for their job performance may not be all that obvious to older generations. When we asked them which skills they feel are most important to be successful in the workforce, these were their top three answers:

Communication (57%)

Problem solving (49%)

Learning (32%)*

However, when we asked the same group of Gen Z a different version of the question, we received a slightly different result. We asked them, "Which of the following skills do you wish you were stronger in so that it would be easier for you to be more successful at work or school?" Here were the top three answers:

Public speaking (50%)

Communication (45%)

Problem solving (29%)

The good news is that employers consistently say they want their employees to be better at problem solving and communication, so there is *great* alignment between what Gen Z wants and the skills employers most want to see from employees.

Gen Z knows they need help to be successful in the workforce, and they really want this help. They also have a strong sense of where they think they need to improve. In both cases, the skills they prioritized can be summed up as communication and problem solving—both of which are solvable through onboarding, training, and talent development.

While communication is often core to most training programs, for entry-level employees, both in professional and more hands-on jobs, problem solving is frequently overlooked. Ironically, in our qualitative work, when we ask employers a similar question, they almost always report problem solving as the top complaint they have with Gen Z,

---

* Total exceeds 100 because each Gen Z participant selected their top two.

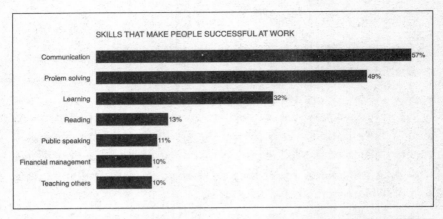

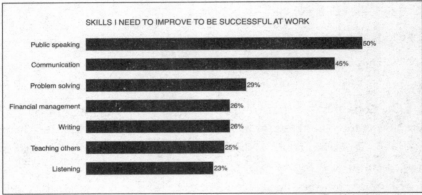

and communication, internal and external, as the next one. Both of these challenges can be solved—developing Gen Z employee talent and addressing a key workforce challenge—by tackling these head-on through employee development, which creates a win-win for everyone involved (including customers!).

To further bring this point to life, during a discussion with a hiring director for a popular fast-food restaurant chain in Austin, Texas, it became clear that Gen Z has its own unique contributions and challenges as a growing presence in the workforce. Cheryl, who has been hiring for two popular local chains for over nine years, described some of the experiences and trends she has noticed within this emerging generation. She described how they tend to be very technologically savvy, fast

Gen Z and Problem Solving:
Handling Customer Service Conflicts at Work

Brittany, a nineteen-year-old and the newest manager at a quick-service restaurant, told us about a time when an upset customer called to complain about expired soy sauce. As the customer was venting their frustration, Brittany became nervous and *hung up on the customer*! Why did this happen? All of these reasons, it turns out:

- She didn't know what to say
- She wasn't sure what her options were (no customer service training)
- She didn't know how to apologize appropriately
- She grew up handling most of her own peer groups' complaints via text message

Role-play common problems employees may face at your company. The solutions may seem intuitive to you, but remember that for many in Gen Z, they simply don't have the real-life or professional experience required to respond appropriately.

learners, and sociable. Additionally, they often thrive in competitive environments where they are measured and given consistent feedback. She explained, however, that they tend to follow task structure very literally, which limits their ability to anticipate new tasks or to problem solve. If they aren't specifically told to do something, then they often won't. She also said that they can be less resilient in general. If they aren't quickly improving, grasping concepts, or meeting expectations, they tend to get frustrated and give up quicker than older generations.

Putting all of this together, a good training and talent development program will help with both communication and problem solving as core offerings. We find that problem solving works best in terms of scenarios where one right answer is not obvious, but that thinking through the options and picking the best one or creating potential solutions works well with Gen Z. This teaches them not only how to solve problems but also how to look for constraints and barriers as well as recognize that they can solve many more problems—or bring potential solutions to managers rather than just bringing problems. Taking this approach unlocks the value of Gen Z employees faster and also makes them more valuable and nimble as team members.

In addition to communication and problem solving, many Gen Zers don't have a lot of work experience. This is largely a function of their youthful age and lower workforce participation for their age group. This means that training on core workplace activities should be included in your onboarding and overall talent development approach, with the basics, such as how to use your company's preferred communication system (yes, even email), how to sign up for or check payroll, and how to use the most common technology involved in their position. Most of these skill-based training outcomes can be covered in a single day with modest or spot reinforcement during the first thirty days. The key is to provide the training so they learn faster, it saves you a ton of time, and you can hold them accountable in the future. You can't hold them accountable if you haven't trained them because it's likely no one else has either.

Problem solving and communication can be covered in quarterly training or other ongoing learning sessions that are provided. For larger employers, assessing current skill levels is often core to their ability to scale as well as manage both onboarding and talent development. For smaller employers, we see that a monthly one-hour meeting where a new skill is taught to a department is a good, cost- and time-effective approach. This could be as simple as watching a TED Talk and then discussing the key message or going through some exercises individually or as a group. Often trade associations offer some type of recommended online training for their industry and so do numerous third-party training companies, such as Schoox, which now offers training on demand, by mobile, and with clear tracking and metrics.

In terms of *approach*, what we suggested for orientation and onboarding applies to ongoing training as well. Our research across several studies shows that Gen Z expects learning and quick how-to instructions to be a combination of in-person training and YouTube-style videos that are available self-service and as part of a structured talent or career development pathway. The trade-off is that while Gen Z wants a hybrid, in-person approach for training—such as learning a new skill—they want to be able to watch a video to get a quick question answered if it fits their work environment and company culture. For example, in a financial services sales environment, video-based training is often the best, followed by role-plays and practice. Meanwhile, someone working at a coffee shop, hotel, or sporting event—what we call a non–desk employee—likely does not have the time or the ability to look at a traditional laptop or other screen to learn a new skill or technique, especially since their job requires them to be mobile and always on. In those situations, in-person on-the-spot training works well, as does providing direct links to videos they can watch when they are between customers or tasks.

However, when the situation is right, Gen Z is fine to simply watch a video on a screen (whether in a classroom, at their desk, or on their phone) to get a question answered and keep going with their job. In fact, in our national study, we found that 85% of Gen Z goes online to watch a video to learn something new at least once each week! Wow. Once a week!

When it comes to integrating training videos into the workplace, the best training or how-to videos are short, say up front the skill that will be taught or learned, show the steps clearly, recap the instruction at the end—and are at least somewhat entertaining to watch. We also find that on-screen text can help with retention and ease of learning, especially if in a loud work environment or a situation where listening can be difficult and getting a question answered via quick training is important.

VidREACH is a sales, customer, and employee engagement platform built around personalized automation via video, email, and/or mobile. Their CEO, Sean Gordon, shared with us that they've had tremendous success training sales reps, including Gen Z, using a library of twenty- to thirty-second drip learning videos (micro-videos viewed in succession) that trainees can watch at their own pace on their preferred mobile device. Gordon shared that they recently onboarded a group of Gen Z sales reps, and within one week of video training, those reps developed a level of sales skills that would normally require three weeks to six months of traditional training to achieve.

VidREACH achieves this by having their top sales reps create brief videos that demonstrate their sales approach. Trainees can sort through a series of micro-videos on different topics and questions, and also get to see a variety of personalities and successful sales strategies—so they can watch the one that most connects with them. Gordon points out that this approach has so many benefits for everyone involved, from saving time in training and learning to building morale and community among new reps who are trying to find their own voice and approach to selling within a larger organization.

"By having access to a variety of twenty- or thirty-second videos," Gordon explains, "not only does it cut down on onboarding and training time by almost 70% in some instances, but it is so much more effective than the old way of handing a big binder to the trainee and giving them a test after a couple weeks.

"Because once they get in the field and start shadowing other reps, it's so common for a young person to immediately doubt themselves. If the rep they're shadowing has a different personality from their own, they may think, 'I can't be like that person. If they expect me to be like this, maybe I'm the wrong fit here.' And that person quits. Compare that to having a library of videos of all different types of people and personalities that have done well after being on the frontline of sales. The trainee can click through thirty-second videos and pretty quickly find approaches and personalities that they're comfortable with."

Part of VidREACH's training also has new hires create sales videos as they're learning new techniques. This allows for an instant feedback loop where trainers, managers, or mentors can watch the videos and immediately offer advice for improvements.

Even if you're not in the business of hiring and training sales reps, think about how you can leverage video beyond the onboarding phase of employment. Not only does video save time and money since you can share the same video series with each new hire, but it also empowers employees to learn in the format they prefer, at their own place, and with the option to revisit learning as needed. You not only create the ability to scale learning and accountability but also use the collective experience, wisdom, and best practices of your organization.

Training Beyond the Basics

Many companies are making substantial investments in their employees' training, talent, and professional development. Deloitte invested $300 million into Deloitte University, a learning facility in Westlake, Texas, dedicated to offering employees an immersive experience while they develop their leadership, professional, industry, and technical skills. DU, as it is known, is a full-scale university-style campus, complete with living quarters, fitness facilities, and thirty classrooms. While at DU, employees enjoy wellness breaks, biking trails, free Starbucks drinks, and outdoor gathering areas complete with fire pits and musical entertainment.

Adobe, which was identified by *Forbes* as one of the top companies for new graduates to work in 2019, stands out among Gen Z for their ongoing commitment to employee professional development. "It's all about learning, exposure, and the opportunity to be part of something that's bigger than themselves," Donna Morris told *Forbes*. Morris is executive vice president of customer and employee experience at Adobe—a position that shows just how much Adobe believes that a great employee experience translates to a great customer experience. When it comes to hiring new graduates, Morris explained, "If someone early on in their career knows there's a path for growth and career progression, that's super important."

Adobe has developed Accelerate Adobe Life, a two-year program designed by Adobe's University Talent team to launch new employees' paths to success. The program includes private Q&As with the CEO, live virtual discussions, on-demand leadership development courses, and $10,000 in educational reimbursement each year.

As we've said, you certainly don't need to develop such full-scale training programs if it's not in your budget or responsibility. But think about how you can offer lifelong learning to your Gen Z employees—which benefits every employee, including those who work alongside them that have decades of experience. Gen Z values this investment in their career tremendously, and it is a key to employee motivation and retention. Small-budget options can include reimbursements for online courses, interdepartmental mentoring programs, or getting an industry or other certification that is relevant to their career, responsibilities, and goals.

Retaining

"In my first job, I got out of there in less than a month. I realized that they didn't see me as an individual and the potential that I had. Also just the kind of people I worked with. They were there for themselves. Not as a team."

—Shawn, Gen Zer

"If I needed a new job I would definitely look for flexibility. Probably room to grow, too. That's why I left my other jobs, because it felt like I worked there for two years and I was still getting paid the same. I was training people. I was leading little workshops and I wasn't getting anything more. So yeah, just somewhere that has room to grow, and flexibility."

—Gen Z employee

As we look at retention and Gen Z, it is clear that regular, ongoing communication is key to their workplace experience and for driving employee retention. They want to know they are making progress, learning new skills, and having "small wins" along the way to show that they are increasing their contribution and creating momentum. This is particularly important as Gen Z often realizes that they will not be receiving pay raises as frequently as they would like or expect once they are in the workforce.

As we noted earlier, our studies show that Gen Z expects raises after nine months working at a job, where Millennials now expect their first raise after twelve months in a new job. We would expect these to eventually show more alignment once Gen Z has more years of work experience, and once they enter the full-time workforce, but as of right now this is their current expectation for an initial pay raise. But as Gen Z awaits their *deserved* pay raises, let them know how they're doing and if they're on the right track or what they can do differently to get on the track you collectively envision.

Outside of more frequent communication and providing well-deserved pay raises, the behavioral drivers that lead to Gen Z employee retention include recognizing them for learning new skills and celebrating small wins both one-on-one and with their team. Those wins can be as straightforward as meeting individual customer service, quality, or sales benchmarks, or fun team goals like beating your store's record for the quickest time between when a customer order is placed and (accurately!) fulfilled.

When it comes to giving recognition, our research found that Gen Z most appreciates and values recognition in person rather than online or through a technology platform. They also prefer this one-on-one rather than in front of their team. But if a supervisor was to recognize them in front of their team the value of that recognition is about the same as recognizing them in front of the company, which is often much harder to do and less frequent. The bottom line: one-on-one recognition and recognition in front of a team are the most efficient types of recognition with Gen Z.

Another way to look at retention is through the lens of employee happiness, and in this case we find the same general result. In our 2018 State of Gen Z Study, 55% of Gen Z said they want positive encouragement or reinforcement at least once per week from their boss in order to be happy at work, and 30% of Gen Z said they wanted some sort of positive encouragement at least daily to be happy at work! While this might be driven by life stage, their desire for fast feedback loops and knowing they are doing the right things—or not—does significantly influence their happiness at work.

Another cornerstone to Gen Z employee retention is offering flexible scheduling. We mentioned it as a hiring perk, and it's just as valuable—if not more so—for their employment retention.

Offering flexible schedules can be difficult for some companies due to their type of work, industry, or job role requirements, but whenever possible flexibility in scheduling is a major retention booster for Gen Z. Scheduling flexibility can range from being able to quickly earn or start with a block of personal days that can be used as either paid or unpaid days off from work, or offering quick vesting of personal days so they accumulate days off within a couple months rather than by pay period or taking a year to build up a meaningful block of days that they can take off from work. For part-time Gen Z workers who likely don't receive paid time off from work, scheduling flexibility is *absolutely* a motivator for accepting and staying with an employer. Since most working age Gen Zers are in high school or college—or at least approximately in that age group—and are balancing work with education or transitioning to more adult responsibilities, flexibility is being able to work around these commitments and experiences.

Alternatively, if your company doesn't offer personal days off work or vacation days upon starting, then consider making it easy for employees to change shifts with other team members. There are now numerous payroll and scheduling apps that allow team members to request shifts or days off from work via a mobile phone, which allow other team members to accept the extra shift or days and then immediately get approval (or not) from a manager for the scheduling change. This takes all the unnecessary back and forth emails, texts (pinning a Post-it Note to a wall in the employee break room!), or conversations of trying to get someone to pick up your shift or day and replaces it with automation, mobility, and approvals—all of which also create a record of what actions were requested, taken, and approved, and by whom.

For many small companies, providing a full day off from work or easy shift changes may not be possible. In those situations, Gen Z who are full-time employees could either earn or receive the ability to get off work early on Friday afternoons. This scheduling bonus is a big deal for younger people who are very lifestyle driven or are still in high school or college. It's also a time of week when clients' or others' work pace may lessen so there is less disruption to the overall company. Alternatively, we've met with employers who hire one extra person in order to give employees scheduling flexibility throughout a week. This ends up costing about the same amount of money, or not much more, yet that one extra person can pick up shifts and provide coverage for sick days, personal days, and help on busy days, which is a huge, high ROI value add.

Gen Z Can Make Great Employees

There is no doubt that Gen Z has proven to be promising, high potential employees when handled with the right employment approach. Every company and manager will have to choose how and in what ways to adapt to unlock the potential of this exciting generation, but their benefit to an employer is clear and immediate—and will only grow over time. Whoever adapts first will make the fastest gains in each step of the employment lifecycle, from recruiting and training to performance and retention.

THE DISRUPTIVE 10

With the pace of change and breakthroughs accelerating, the future in which Gen Z will navigate adulthood for the next fifty-plus years will be unlike any that previous generations experienced. Gen Z will eventually think flying cars are normal, custom-made organs are part of aging, and space travel is not science fiction but just takes financial planning.

Technology advancements and breakthroughs will create opportunities, risks, and interactions that other generations cannot imagine.

Demographic and population changes and risks to the health of the planet will create new pressures on daily living, movement, and resources. And, who knows? Space travel for tourists could become as common as spring break (if they still have colleges, that is . . .). What a time to be young and coming of age!

Gen Z is growing up surrounded by breakthroughs in everything from personalized medicine and autonomous transportation to workplace automation and AI virtual assistants. Looking ahead twenty- and thirty-plus years, we can spot a number of trends, breakthroughs, challenges, and innovations that will likely influence the generation in decades to come.

We Call These the Disruptive 10 . . .

1. Car and Transportation Evolution

In the last twenty-plus years, new technology has infused cars, from GPS and streaming your favorite podcast to semiautonomous cars and electric vehicles with long driving range. At the same time, Uber, Lyft, and the ride-share economy—not to mention social media and new laws—have decreased the urgency for Gen Z to get their driver's license. What was once a moment eagerly anticipated, complete with an anxiety-filled trip to the local department of motor vehicles, is now something frequently postponed by Gen Z.

In fact, in the next twenty years, Gen Z may not even need a driver's license because they won't drive. Truly autonomous vehicles will be at the ready to drive people if they physically need to go somewhere, flying cars may finally take off (and land!), and autonomous or semiautonomous trucks will change a tremendous amount of the congestion and risk on the road. If Gen Z changes their driving behaviors, to the point where they're not driving or driving very limited miles, that will directly transform everything from car insurance, motor vehicle accident rates, and the need for garages to overall demand for the entire auto industry. Gen Z will be in the driver's seat for all of this automotive and transportation change, but they may actually end up in the passenger seat and let technology do all the work.

A 2016 study by Morgan Stanley and BCG illustrates that young consumers already use ride-share and new mobility options more frequently, with eighteen- to twenty-four-year-olds using these services monthly or several times a month. Moreover, 28% of them are using ride share daily or weekly! These numbers will only grow as driverless technology and cheaper, more reliable transportation (electric vehicles) become more accessible on a mass transit level. So long, gas stations and convenience stores.

Gen Z will likely drive the carless revolution.

2. Virtual Reality and Augmented Reality

While much has been written about Gen Z and the future of cars for travel, the truth is Gen Z may not need to get in the car if virtual reality and augmented reality (VR/AR) reach mass adoption. VR and AR allow you to experience a world as if you're there, from flying over fields and mountains to being alongside a teacher showing you a new skill. While VR can be fully immersive, including adding smells, breezes, and much more to stimulate the senses, future VR will likely be fully immersive, including touch. This could eliminate the need for plane travel because you can visit a location and experience the sights and sounds—even smells—without getting on a plane and avoid all the cost, discomfort, and risk that might be associated with travel. On the flip side, Gen Z might prefer VR for the experiences they can't actually have, such as flying a spaceship in a fantasy realm or being inside a volcano.

The impact of virtual reality might be felt in everything from business travel, where virtual meetings could be as effective as in-person meetings, to leisure travel and education. Not to mention the impact virtual reality could have on entertainment, content creation, relationships (virtual ones that seem real!), and so much more. You could attend a concert with fifty thousand cheering people—all from the comfort of your home without the overpriced sodas.

Over half (52%) of Gen Z expect to use virtual reality as their primary device to play video or online games or watch others play video or online games in the near future.

And 60% of Gen Z (of this, 63% eighteen and under) are likely to play and watch virtual reality games, shows, and movies in the near future.

Augmented reality is also fast becoming real and could play a fascinating role in making every day more interesting, entertaining, and unexpected. Augmented reality takes the world you are seeing and adds images and more to it in a way that allows you to see things that are not actually there but appear completely real. For example, if you looked at a book in augmented reality, and the book was partially blocked by a vase on a table, you could move to the other side of the table and see the full book—just like in real life. Augmented reality opens a world of new immersion that could also affect marketing, sales, and training, along with education. Messages, visuals, and experiences would come to life in ways that don't currently exist—from product placement and billboards in your home to paying for experiences that only the AR participant can experience.

VR could be particularly useful in the workforce, such as creating a whole new level of training on how to perform tasks under stress, like landing a plane or solving complicated problems.

The combination of VR and AR, along with the pathways for augmenting people with technologies, means more and deeper integration of technology into our world and how we view and experience the world. Want to walk with the dinosaurs? Done. Want to sit in the front row of a class at Harvard? Done. Want to role-play asking someone to marry you? They'll have that, too.

Obviously, there could be downsides to this new world, too. Already Gen Z feels anxiety about not having their phone close or not getting an instant response. They also feel anxiety about having to conduct face-to-face communication, especially in the workplace. How will they feel in twenty years with a fully immersive technology experience? Gen Z will find out.

3. Aging Population and Generational Transition

Baby Boomers are living longer than they expected, including often outliving their savings, retirement, ability to work, and government programs to provide financial and healthcare support. The aging of the Baby Boomer population will continue to be a challenge for many in the generation, and at the same time it will put pressure on governments and families around the world to work out solutions to help them age more comfortably. Baby Boomers often don't want to retire, and many times are unable to retire for financial reasons, so they will continue to stay in the workforce as long as they are physically able.

In many ways, the world is not prepared for a rapidly aging large percentage of the population. Not only will this affect those aging, but those younger than them will frequently bear the financial and physical responsibility for helping this aging generation, whether family member, neighbor, or fellow citizen.

At the same time, Gen X will be moving into a later stage of adulthood where they are not just parenting their own Gen Z kids but also helping their parents and eventually their grandkids as well. Gen X will be saddled with tremendous responsibility helping all of these generations while also being the elder statesman in the workforce, yet being a significantly smaller generation than those who precede them. Gen X will move into a pivotal time in their role as senior company leaders, as political leaders and voters, and as an actively working and influencing generation that also happens to have the most experience in both areas. Gen X will be the generation that Gen Z looks up to, much more than Millennials, as Gen X will be grappling with helping their parents, communities, families, and employers.

Over the next twenty years, Millennials will move further and further away from being the "it generation" to becoming another generation of middle-aged adults. Millennials will take on more traditional responsibilities as employees and continue to be the largest generation in the workforce and as consumers, but the reality of one day wanting to possibly retire or work less will also start to take hold as Millennials—and their Gen Z kids—age up.

The impact of an aging world brimming with generational transition will shift power from the Baby Boomers to Gen X and, ultimately, Millennials. Gen Z will see all of this happening and want to know how the change and new political vision and government regulations will affect them—and, gasp, their own kids! Initially, Gen Z will simply be along for the ride as other generations drive voter turnout, policies, and population-based decisions. However, Gen Z will eventually emerge as a force and will move conversations in a way that aligns with their social causes and generational priorities.

4. AI, IoT, Connected Devices, and Consumer Tech

AI is already changing our world, habits, news, content, and even investing. This is only the beginning of the AI revolution that Gen Z will be affected by throughout their life. AI will likely become embedded throughout everything we do, have, and engage with—whether that is dieting and physical fitness, dating, shopping, advertising, or endless and more accurate recommendations. Adding to the power of AI is the IoT and connected devices. As more and more devices connect to the web and the cloud, more data will be collected and analyzed, and better recommendations will be made as a result. This will change everything from Gen Z's homes operating dramatically more efficiently and healthcare breakthroughs that are tracked directly in your body to every imaginable device suddenly being connected to your phone—or whatever future communication devices are developed. There is much debate about whether AI will herald in the end of the world and human dominance or a breakthrough for a time of more and better food, quality of life, and peace. Whatever the outcome, Gen Z will be the first generation that will think it's normal to have every device in your home (washer, dryer, microwave, coffee maker, bed, TV, refrigerator, lights, sprinklers, etc.), car, work, and life connected, tracked, optimized, analyzed, and fully integrated.

When it comes to AI:

- 61% of Gen Z think AI is a positive influence for society.
- 43% of Gen Z think that AI is a positive influence in their personal life.

How Gen Z feels about smart devices:

- 80% of Gen Z think they will own and use more smart devices, products, or services in the near future than they do now.
- 80% of Gen Z think that smart devices, products, or services will make their lives significantly easier in the near future.
- 55% of Gen Z would be willing to pay a higher price for a smart device, product, or service that would make their lives significantly easier in the near future.

Going even further, new breakthroughs such as quantum computing will dramatically increase computing power and decision-making, leading to outcomes many of us can't imagine (and some don't want to). Gen Z is the generation that will truly be at the convergence of data, algorithms, hardware, and life. This will also create new and tremendous pressures on data privacy and security—for everyone from individuals and manufacturers to tech companies and governments.

In addition to the broad stroke technology advancements driven by software and code such as AI, IoT, and connected devices, enormous change is also in store for Gen Z in key areas such as 3D printers making everything from houses to sneakers on demand, robots being relied upon in the household, mind-to-machine interface (yikes!), nano-technology reaching its potential and being embedded in consumer products, and potentially less ownership of assets (who needs a car when you have Uber, VR/AR, and everything comes to you). Consumer technology is only beginning to show what is possible, and that will ramp up rapidly as more technology is integrated into even the most basic childhood toy or pair of adult sunglasses.

5. Workforce Automation

There is much conversation about the potential jobs that could be eliminated through ongoing workforce automation, including from AI integration, advanced robotics, and IoT. Many people assume that the jobs most likely to be lost are those that are low skill and repetitive, but that is not the case. With rapidly advancing technology, white-collar jobs such as accounting and finance are also at risk. This could have a significant impact not only on careers, but on the colleges, degrees, and learning pathways that feed into those careers, or it could spur the retraining (if possible) of the people already in those accomplished fields.

Even middle managers may go the way of the dinosaur if better tracking of workforce performance, needs, and strengths leads to just-in-time training, coaching, and promotions—all unique to the employee and their individual strengths, areas for development, track record, and goals. *Gen Z will likely be the first generation that is managed by software rather than people,* which could be a huge breakthrough in unlocking their performance and the performance of all generations but also yield massive change to corporate structures, planning, and existing careers.

In one philosophical camp are the workforce automation thinkers who believe workforce automation will lead to significant, sustained job losses that will not return, and governments will have to help people find new things to do with their time, which may not include work. In the other camp are those pointing out that workforce automation and technology advancements within the workplace do cause job loss and job transition but also create a huge number of jobs that do not exist in the present and must be filled, leading to a better standard of work for many involved.

A total of 48% of Gen Z think that AI would be a positive influence for them at work. And 49% of Gen Z agree that using AI in the workplace will make their job better by doing things like helping them find the right job more quickly and helping their employer better understand their feelings and needs regarding their career and work.

More than half (59%) of Gen Z's main concern about the use of AI in the workplace is that they are nervous about AI replacing their job.

Either way, for Gen Z, workforce automation, the cloud, AI software, and so much more are going to change the nature of work and the workforce education and skills needed to be successful. Gen Z will likely be at the forefront of this change given their current age and the pace at which workforce automation is being tested. In other words, many in Gen Z will end up working in jobs and careers that may not exist today and see the careers of their parents as no longer viable.

6. Medical Breakthroughs

Gen Z will likely be the first generation to fully benefit from the rapid advancements in medical care over the last thirty years. In particular, Gen Z is young enough to benefit from recent biotechnology advancements like genome editing (commonly called CRISPR) and the extraordinary benefits of personalized medicine. This could include being able to grow organs specific to an individual, medicines designed specifically to eradicate a disease (such as cancer), and numerous forms of health, wellness, and medicine that could extend life spans significantly (which creates a whole new set of issues).

The promise of personalized medicine is incredibly exciting, as is the ability to combat horrible diseases such as cancer and Alzheimer's. However, personalized medicine, particularly genome editing, also creates ethical and philosophical challenges that Gen Z will confront as they themselves become parents. Going further, many in Gen Z will not have to physically drive or travel for medical attention, as telemedicine and other devices and testing—including in-home—will play an increasing role in diagnosing and providing medical services on demand, wherever Gen Z is at that moment.

The result of these many medical breakthroughs, including designer medicine and disease eradication, could lead to much longer lives, which would put pressure on everything from healthcare and families to government structures. Gen Z is truly the beneficiary of the modern medical breakthroughs that could lead to a time in the not-too-distant future when most if not all major medical issues are treated—potentially even before their children are born.

7. Consumer Space Travel

Yes. It's coming. Elon Musk, Richard Branson, Jeff Bezos, and many more are working night and day to commercialize space travel so anyone can feel zero gravity. The prospect of cost-effective space travel, initially as entertainment but eventually as commerce (such as mining, etc.), creates a universe of possibilities including that Gen Z's own children or grandchildren might be able to live on or visit another planet. Fifty years ago people huddled around black-and-white TVs to watch a man land on the moon. For Gen Z's kids and grandkids, they may be able to experience that firsthand.

8. Global Challenges

While this is a hugely sensitive and divisive topic, for Gen Z it will be something they're messaging about weekly if not daily. Global population growth will most likely continue, putting increased pressure on governments, geographies, resources, and services—from housing and food to water and transportation. At the same time, climate change is likely to shape Gen Z more than any other current generation, as they are now the youngest generation and the one with the most time ahead. This could mean everything from changing sea levels affecting major cities to more natural disasters. Gen Z is positioned to be the generation to drive change to combat the threats to the world, as they are likely the generation to most profoundly experience many of these changes throughout their life.

9. Blockchain

Gen Z will come of age with integration of blockchain and distributed ledgers in many aspects of their lives, from personal finances and legal contracts to healthcare innovation and real-estate record keeping.

Money is not cash anymore. It is not plastic anymore. Instead, for Gen Z money is a concept stored in a cloud. Money may soon be a digital signature only, a singular series of digits that unlocks value on a distributed worldwide network.

Already teens can skip the bank by using apps like Venmo and have adopted digital wallets without needing bank accounts or credit cards. Blockchain has the potential to make banks (in their current form) obsolete, because instead of having the bank handle your money, the blockchain can do it more cheaply and more securely—in a split second, anywhere on the globe.

As blockchain scales to handle retail and investment dollars, potential implications for Gen Z could be numerous. Gen Z could opt out of banks entirely, if banks don't evolve quickly enough with their own versions of blockchain. Stocks could be useless to Gen Z because of their enormous volatility and lack of transparency. Gen Z might want more secure, transparent ways to deal with money than the stock market. Instead, they may become investors by purchasing tokens like Bitcoin (digital assets based on blockchain technology), to directly invest in companies instead of using stock exchanges.

The youngest members of Gen Z will not remember a time when cryptocurrencies were not just a normal part of life. Just like many of us don't remember a time before ATMs, Gen Z won't remember a time when they couldn't buy Bitcoin. Crypto assets and crypto-economics might be courses they take in an MBA program. Block-chain technology will fundamentally shape how they view money, banks, legal agreements, healthcare records, and investing.

10. College Transformation

For over two hundred years, colleges have been the source of learning, personal development, and transition into the real world for many. With the rise of AR/VR, mobile learning, and changes in workforce skill needs, college could become much less relevant or be replaced with cloud-based learning and other measures of skill besides grades and standardized testing. The youngest members of Gen Z will see some of this change, but the children of Gen Z will be the likely group of disruptors that put pressure on higher education to rethink their offerings, education platforms, and how to deliver learning while increasing the benefit to cost ratio.

This is just the tip of the generational iceberg. We also believe that COVID-19 and its aftermath could have a pronounced impact on the generation, including how they learn, work, and think about their futures. While it is too early to determine the long-term effects, the impact will clearly be significant on Gen Z.

All of these trends, breakthroughs, challenges, and innovations— and many more that will be transformative but are not yet known or named—will dramatically shape and alter the beliefs and expectations of Gen Z. This will happen in a much deeper, faster, and more integrated way than when personal computers altered Gen X or smart-phones connected Millennials or the web bridged continents instantly (and on social media). The collisions of these trends with Gen Z will shape everything from the generation's work pathway to life expectancy, relationships, travel, health, beliefs, and view of other generations before and after.

GEN Z IS JUST GETTING STARTED

When we started to write this book, we did not know what we would uncover and how it would shape lives. We hope as you've joined us on this journey that you've been moved by the excitement, surprise, and humanity that Gen Z brings—along with the solutions and strategies we've discovered for unlocking their potential as employees, team members, innovators, consumers, and future leaders.

As researchers, speakers, students, and parents of this generation, we are incredibly excited for what Gen Z means for us and you. This generation will bring a new normal that will create change, uncertainty, discomfort, confidence, and breakthroughs. We know that diving into a generation at such a critical time in their emergence is inspiring and sometimes dizzying, but so is the future they bring with them.

One thing is clear from our conversations with Gen Z: this generation is bringing a new worldview, talent, and energy that can bring out the best in each of us. Yes, they are different. But in that difference is *tremendous possibility* if we take the time to understand them. The better we get to know Gen Z, the more we will know how to unlock their talent—and how they can help us reach our own full potential as forward-thinking leaders.

Our belief is that the insights, stories, stats, and extensive research shared in this book will help you create a customizable pathway that works for you and your organization as well as the impact and legacy you want to leave.

Gen Z is counting on you to rise to the challenge *and opportunity* they present by helping them, starting with where they are today—and by using everything that we have learned in our own generational journey. As much as we need them for their future, they will also benefit from us now and in the future.

It is undeniable that Gen Z will play a massive role in shaping not only the next many decades but likely the next century and beyond. This generation's potential, hope, dreams, fears, ideas, and resilience are directly connected to the actions that leaders like you take today to develop their skills and mindset. This is true in everything from creating meaningful customer experiences to implementing actions from this book that tap into Gen Z's talent as employees, colleagues, and future entrepreneurs.

In short: Gen Z needs us as much as we need them—and we have as much (if not more!) to benefit from as they do.

The key is for us to act now to reach out to them, using the strategies in this book along with your own unique strengths and expertise, to tap into the potential we create when we come together. Together *we can build the Zconomy* and unlock new ideas and potential that will change the world.

What You Can Do Today

If you have not yet taken steps to adapt to Gen Z, you haven't missed your opportunity! Gen Z is right now at the very life, education, and career stage where you are ideally positioned to help them and fine tune your own skills in the process. Yes, Gen Z is already starting to upend industries, from technology and hospitality to cosmetics. But they are evolving every day. Gen Z's consumer spending is rapidly accelerating. Their segment of the workforce is growing dramatically. Their worldview and trendsetting abilities are just now taking hold and spreading like a viral video. They are not too old and it is not too late to engage with them, as long as you start taking action *now*.

One thing our research shows without question: the sooner you start taking action, the sooner you'll start seeing results. The opposite is also true: delaying adapting to this generation will only make engaging with them later much more difficult. Now is the time to reach out to them.

If you're not sure where to start, keep the following insights in mind as you put to use the tools, examples, and ideas in this book.

If You're Looking to Engage with Gen Z as Consumers or Employees

- **Consider how the world looks through Gen Z's eyes.** Taking this step helps to create all-important *generational context*, which creates room for understanding, empathy, trust, and influence. Remember that Gen Z wants to align themselves with leaders and companies that are committed to making a positive impact on the world. It's okay if a higher cause is not baked into your company's DNA. Gen Z just wants to see that you're working to make a difference, whether it's in your local community, on your team, or in your day-to-day actions. Show them that you want to have a positive impact on the world—and on them.

- **Ask Gen Z about their experience in your workforce or as your customer.** If you're not sure how you're doing with Gen Z or where you could improve, just ask them. This generation wants to be asked and wants to share—and it's always better to do that in person than hearing about it on Twitter (and then on Instagram, Snapchat, and more). If you're looking to connect with Gen Z as consumers, consider hiring members of the generation to be on your marketing or innovation team—or let them serve on panels at events where they can share their firsthand perspective with leadership. On the employment side, ask your Gen Z employees what they'd like to see you do differently. They will be happy to tell you if you're willing to listen. Often what will most impact their employment experiences—and make your leadership experience easier—are interactions and resources that cost very little money and work over and over, a win-win for everyone.

- **Reach Gen Z where they are.** Forget traditional ad campaigns that aim to speak to everyone and potentially influence no one in the process. Find niche influencers on the digital platforms Gen Z loves, such as YouTube, TikTok, and Instagram, and see how you can collaborate with them to spread the word about your product, brand, or service. These platforms and influencers can drive exactly the measurable engagement and ROI that brands and budgets need now.

  At the same time, think of creative ways to engage with Gen Z as customers. Remember, Ally Financial skipped spending millions on a Super Bowl ad and instead created an interactive virtual reality game that only worked during Super Bowl commercials. They closed out the campaign by donating hundreds of thousands of dollars to people who played the game. In the process, they got to know their customers by asking them to share their savings goals.

  Baylor University is another example of this nontraditional approach. They took a risk to collaborate with YouTube influencers and the result not only exponentially increased popularity about and excitement for the school, but it also introduced the school to members of Gen Z who did not know about Baylor. The same students likely would not have considered applying to Baylor in the past, but now they plan to attend!

To Win Gen Z as Consumers and Advocates

- **Prioritize meaningful value and engagement.** Gen Z wants to get the maximum value from their spending. They want to know they got a "good deal" and that the buying process was easy. At the same time, they want to get the best quality possible and then share their purchase with friends on social media. Remember, this is the generation that will receive money as a gift for their birthday, put the money away, and then ask their parents for money to go buy something. As adults, they do this by seeking out brands they know deliver quality and will last a long time, whether it's jeans or a set of headphones.

- **Connect your brand and team's humanity to Gen Z.** Gen Z wants to know that the people behind your brand care about *them* as individuals. Billie razors connects with customers not by promising a flawlessly shaved body, but by acknowledging every person's shaving needs are different, and Billie is there for all of them. Aerie does not sway teens to buy their apparel by promising they'll look like the slim models of last decade's glossy magazines. Instead, they encourage women to be themselves and love their body as it is.

- **Tap into their love for learning.** And their love of videos. Cosmetics brands teach young customers how to manage their skin and apply their products through YouTube videos. If you manufacture sports gear, become the go-to authority for learning how to throw a curveball, or swim an official breaststroke through your own YouTube channel. If you're a plumber, teach people how to unclog their toilet, clear a tub drain, or locate where the leak in their basement is coming from. You won't lose customers by doing this. You will become the first person they call. This is true whether they're opening their first retirement account online or looking for driver's education resources, such as Blake Garrett shared about Aceable.

To Unlock Gen Z's Talent as Employees

- **Fire up the referral engine.** Unlike Millennials before them, Gen Z does not immediately turn to job boards when looking for employment. Instead, they turn to friends and family. Engage with current employees and make it easy for them to spread the word about job openings through social media. Give them appealing incentives to refer trusted friends, such as experiences (concert tickets, travel, or tickets to sporting events) or cash bonuses that they don't need to wait months or a year to receive.

- **Make it easy to connect, and then stay in touch.** Make it easy to start and save your job application on a mobile device. If they don't finish completing the application, send a follow-up reminder with a direct link to their job application—and reinforce your interest in learning more about them. When they see that you're interested in learning more about them, they'll be much more interested in learning more about you and your company. This is especially important in a very tight labor market, and we've seen this action drive many more applications.

- **Offer talent development—from day one.** Whether Gen Z is working with you part-time after school or you're hiring for full-time, career-path positions, you will have a better time attracting, hiring, and retaining Gen Z if you show them you care about their talent development. Several studies show that Gen Z will choose a job that offers mentorship and opportunities for learning transferrable skills over similar jobs that pay more but do not offer that kind of mentorship. Make it clear in your job postings, hiring process, and onboarding steps that you are committed to developing their talent and they'll be much more committed to you.

- **Keep training ongoing and on demand.** Gen Z will roll their eyes if you drop a two-pound, three-ring binder in front of them during orientation. Make training short, engaging, and interactive—whether that is for the most routine role or advanced safety, sales, or technology training. Empower them to get started as soon as possible by delivering training that provides a solid foundation during onboarding or orientation. Then build on that with access to training videos, FAQ videos, and other on-demand resources that enable them to learn as needed. This frees you up by scaling the learning and empowers them to dive into the areas that are most urgent for them. Our research shows that Gen Z is eager to contribute and motivated to make a difference at work, but they also need the ability to learn on demand, including from their mistakes.

Looking Ahead: What We See

When we look across all our Gen Z research, conversations, focus groups, and data analysis, one thing is clear: what we see ahead with

Gen Z is incredibly exciting. It's exciting for us, for them, and we hope for you, too.

Gen Z offers a *huge* opportunity for leaders and organizations to grow, strengthen, innovate, and outperform—if leaders like you are willing to adapt to the generation.

Are you ready to unlock all this generation has to offer? We are, and we're excited to be on this journey with you.

Discover Our Latest Findings

Life is always changing, sometimes faster than expected. In 2020, COVID-19 and racial justice protests changed our world. For our latest research please visit GenHQ.com.

ACKNOWLEDGMENTS

We would like to acknowledge and recognize the talented, passionate people who helped us to make *Zconomy* the book it is today. First, we'd like to thank our stellar research team at The Center for Generational Kinetics, specifically Elli, Heather, and Jared. Without them, their creativity, and their dedication, this book would not have been possible. Thank you!

We'd like to recognize our great literary agent, Nena Madonia. Nena has believed in this book since the first email we sent with the idea. We'd also like to thank the outstanding editorial and publishing teams at HarperCollins for making this book a reality. You are amazing.

We'd like to thank our writing partner, Maria Gagliano. Maria, thank you for shepherding the manuscript through the revision process and helping us to showcase Gen Z as well as our research and insights.

We'd also like to thank our families, who have been there for us no matter the challenge or breakthrough. They've been generous with their time to allow us to invest ours in this book. In particular, we'd like to thank Robin Shirley, Elida Gonzales, Dan Dorsey, Mariano Gonzales, and Rob Shirley.

In addition to our families, we'd like to thank our mentors and friends who have supported us on this journey. They have helped us not only bridge generations but also bridge the distance between the vision for the book and the book you're holding now.

Jason would like to thank his speaking and author group for their unwavering support and encouragement with the book: Jay Baer, David

Horsager, and Rory Vaden. He'd also like to thank his entrepreneur group, Q2, for their belief in CGK and *Zconomy* from the very beginning. Thank you!

Denise would like to thank her mentors and friends, including her EO Austin Forum, F2, and all the brave women she has known for giving her strength and lots of laughter when she needed it.

We'd like to thank our amazing clients. Whether you're in technology, retail, automotive, apparel, healthcare, banking, insurance, or one of the other industries we work with, we thank you for partnering with us to solve your generational challenge. You've enabled us to build a firm that we believe brings out the best in every generation.

Last, we'd like to thank all the members of Gen Z who boldly contributed their stories, words, and perspectives to help bridge generations, including our daughter, Rya. Thank you! We are so excited about the energy, perspective, talent, and change you will bring to the world.

NOTES

INTRODUCTION: GEN Z IS HERE

6   our 2019 State of Gen Z: The Center for Generational Kinetics, "The State of Gen Z 2019," 2019, GenHQ.com.

1: WELCOME TO THE NEW NORMAL

25   Carter decided pretty quickly: Carter Wilkerson, https://nuggsforcarter .com/making-a-difference, accessed November 25, 2019.

26   Marketing analysts at the Ayzenberg Group: H. B. Duran, "#NuggsFor Carter Means over $7 Million Earned Media Value for Wendy's," *AList Daily*, May 11, 2017, https://www.alistdaily.com/social/how-nuggsforcarter-became-an -emv-win-for-wendys/.

27   Odyssey's president, Brent Blonkvist, and his team: Brent Blonkvist, interview with the authors, August 2019.

2: REDEFINING THE TERM "GENERATION"

37   Gen Z has an unprecedented dependence: The Center for Generational Kinetics, "The State of Gen Z 2018," 2018, GenHQ.com.

37   According to research by Common Sense Media: Common Sense Media, "Social Media, Social Life: Teens Reveal Their Experiences, 2018," https://www .commonsensemedia.org/sites/default/files/uploads/research/2018_cs_socialmedia sociallife_fullreport-final-release_2_lowres.pdf.

3: THE EVENTS THAT SHAPED GEN Z

44   As of September 2019, fifteen million Millennials: U.S. Office of Federal Student Aid, "Federal Student Loan Portfolio by Borrower Age and Debt Size," September 30, 2019, https://studentaid.ed.gov/sa/sites/default/files/fsawg /datacenter/library/Portfolio-by-Age-Debt-Size.xls.

45 We discovered that 86% of high school–aged: The Center for Generational Kinetics, "The State of Gen Z 2018," 2018, GenHQ.com.

46 According to the Pew Research Center: Richard Fry and Kim Parker, "Early Benchmarks Show 'Post-Millennials' on Track to Be Most Diverse, Best-Educated Generation Yet," Pew Research Center, November 15, 2018, https://www.pewsocialtrends.org/wp-content/uploads/sites/3/2018/11/Post-Millennials-Report_final-11.13pm.pdf.

46 2016 State of Gen Z Study found: The Center for Generational Kinetics, "The State of Gen Z 2016," 2016, GenHQ.com.

50 According to a 2018 We are Flint study: We are Flint, "Social Media Demographics 2018, USA & UK, February 2018," https://costfromclay.co.uk/main-findings-social-media-demographics-uk-usa-2018.

50 The average viewing session: Salman Aslam, "YouTube by the Numbers: Stats, Demographics & Fun Facts," Omnicore, January 13, 2020, https://www.omnicoreagency.com/youtube-statistics/.

50 Our 2019 national study revealed: The Center for Generational Kinetics, "The State of Gen Z 2019," 2019, GenHQ.com.

51 One YouTuber, Ryan: Madeline Berg, "How This 7-Year-Old Made $22 Million Playing with Toys," *Forbes,* December 3, 2018, https://www.forbes.com/sites/maddieberg/2018/12/03/how-this-seven-year-old-made-22-million-playing-with-toys-2/#128a34e94459.

52 42% of Gen Z say social media affects: The Center for Generational Kinetics, "iGen Tech Disruption," 2016.

52 55% of Gen Z: The Center for Generational Kinetics, "The State of Gen Z 2019," 2019, GenHQ.com.

52 A 2019 report published in the *Journal of Abnormal Psychology*: Jean M. Twenge, et al.,"Age, Period, and Cohort Trends in Mood Disorder Indicators and Suicide-Related Outcomes in a Nationally Representative Dataset, 2005–2017," *Journal of Abnormal Psychology*, 2019, vol. 128, no. 3, 185–99, https://doi.org/10.1037/abn0000410.

53 In our 2019 national study: The Center for Generational Kinetics, "The State of Gen Z 2019," 2019, GenHQ.com.

4: LIFE THROUGH A 6.1-INCH SCREEN

57 our 2019 national study showed: The Center for Generational Kinetics, "The State of Gen Z 2019," 2019, GenHQ.com.

59 In our 2018 State of Gen Z Study: The Center for Generational Kinetics, "The State of Gen Z 2018," 2018, GenHQ.com.

61 Our 2016 national study: The Center for Generational Kinetics, "The State of Gen Z 2016," 2016, GenHQ.com.

61   in our 2018 Gen Z study: The Center for Generational Kinetics, "The State of Gen Z 2018," 2018, GenHQ.com.

61   Our research shows that: The Center for Generational Kinetics, "The State of Gen Z 2018," 2018, GenHQ.com.

66   our 2019 national study showed: The Center for Generational Kinetics, "The State of Gen Z 2019," 2019, GenHQ.com.

71   Blake Garrett is the founder and CEO of Aceable: Blake Garrett, interview with the authors, August 2019.

5: MONEY, SAVING, AND SPENDING

75   Kylie Jenner and Sofia Richie: Ariana Marsh, "This 19-Year-Old's Designs Have Been Worn by Kylie Jenner and Sofia Richie," *Teen Vogue*, December 1, 2016, https://www.teenvogue.com/gallery/this-19-year-olds-designs-have-been-worn-by-kylie-jenner-and-sofia-richie.

Shelby Le Duc, "Local Fashion Designer in with Celebs," *Green Bay Press Gazette,* June 28, 2016, https://www.greenbaypressgazette.com/story/life/2016/06/28/de-pere-fashion-designer-celebs/86245256/.

77   our 2019 national study: The Center for Generational Kinetics, "The State of Gen Z 2019," 2019, GenHQ.com.

78   study of Gen Z ages fourteen to twenty-two: The Center for Generational Kinetics, "The State of Gen Z 2018," 2018, GenHQ.com.

79   Research out of the University of Applied Sciences: Mathias Bärtl, "YouTube Channels, Uploads and Views: A Statistical Analysis of the Past 10 Years," *Convergence: The International Journal of Research into New Media Technologies*, 2018, vol. 24, no. 1, 16–32, https://doi.org/10.1177/1354856517736979.

79   According to data from Online Schools Center: "Doing It Their Way: Gen Z and Entrepreneurship," Online Schools Center, accessed November 23, 2019, https://www.onlineschoolscenter.com/gen-z-entrepreneurship/.

80   more than twenty-four *billion* US dollars were transferred on Venmo: J. Clement, "Venmo's Total Payment Volume from 1st Quarter 2017 to 4th quarter 2019 (in billion U.S. dollars)," *Statista*, January 30, 2020, https://www.statista.com/statistics/763617/venmo-total-payment-volume/.

80   cash than older generations: Global Cash Card and The Center for Generational Kinetics, "Paycards: Generational Trends Shaping the Future of Worker Pay," 2017, The Center for Generational Kinetics.

81   our 2019 national study reveals: The Center for Generational Kinetics, "The State of Gen Z 2019," 2019, GenHQ.com.

81   Scott Gordon, CEO and cofounder of Kard: Scott Gordon, interview with the authors, August 2019.

81   Meanwhile, Larry Talley and his team: Larry Talley, interview with the authors, August 2019.

84   plan to go to college: The Center for Generational Kinetics, "The State of Gen Z 2018," 2018, GenHQ.com.

84   50% of all private colleges and universities: Marjorie Valbrun, "Discount Rates Hit Record Highs," *Inside Higher Ed*, May 10, 2019, https://www.inside highered.com/news/2019/05/10/nacubo-report-shows-tuition-discounting -trend-continuing-unabated.

84   on any student loan debt at all: The Center for Generational Kinetics, "The State of Gen Z 2018," 2018, GenHQ.com.

85   In our 2017 State of Gen Z Study: The Center for Generational Kinetics, "The State of Gen Z 2017," 2017, GenHQ.com.

86   23% of Gen Z believe: The Center for Generational Kinetics, "The State of Gen Z 2017," 2017, GenHQ.com.

86   Early data from TransUnion: Matt Komos, "Consumer Credit Origination, Balance and Delinquency Trends: Q2 2019," Transunion, August 23, 2019, https:// www.transunion.com/blog/iir-consumer-credit-origination-q2-2019.

86   36% of Gen Z ages eighteen to twenty-four told us: The Center for Generational Kinetics, "The State of Gen Z 2019," 2019, GenHQ.com.

88   12% of Gen Z: The Center for Generational Kinetics, "The State of Gen Z 2017," 2017, GenHQ.com.

88   69% believe that: The Center for Generational Kinetics, "The State of Gen Z 2019," 2019, GenHQ.com.

89   Over one third (35%) of Gen Z: The Center for Generational Kinetics, "The State of Gen Z 2017," 2017, GenHQ.com.

6: WHAT GEN Z WANTS FROM A BRAND

93   Nike's stock price surged: Bloomberg, "Nike's Big Bet on Colin Kaepernick Campaign Continues to Pay Off," *Fortune,* December 21, 2018, https://fortune .com/2018/12/21/nike-stock-colin-kaepernick/.

93   according to Apex Marketing Group: Angelica LaVito, "Nike's Colin Kaepernick Ads Created $163.5 Million in Buzz Since It Began—and It's Not All Bad," CNBC, September 6, 2018, https://www.cnbc.com/2018/09/06/nikes -colin-kaepernick-ad-created-163point5-million-in-media-exposure.html.

94   *Ad Age* said it was: E. J. Schultz and Adrianne Pasquarelli, "Assessing the Fallout—Good and Bad—from Nike's Kaepernick Ad," *Ad Age*, September 4, 2018, https://adage.com/article/cmo-strategy/assessing-fallout-good-bad-nike-s-kaepernick -ad/314809.

94   YPulse polled Gen Z and Millennials: YPulse, "How Do Gen Z & Millennials Really Feel About Nike's Kaepernick Ad?" September 12, 2018, https:// www.ypulse.com/article/2018/09/12/how-gen-z-millennials-really-feel-about -nikes-kaepernick-ad/.

94   Brent Blonkvist, president of: Brent Blonkvist, interview with the authors, August 2019.

97   Gen Z showed the biggest jump: thredUP, "2019 Resale Report," 2019, https://www.thredup.com/resale.

98   24% of Gen Z ages thirteen to seventeen: The Center for Generational Kinetics, "The State of Gen Z 2019," 2019, GenHQ.com.

99   44% of Gen Z say: WP Engine and The Center for Generational Kinetics, "Reality Bytes: The digital experience is the human experience," 2018, https://wpengine.com/blog/reality-bytes-second-annual-generational-study-reveals-how-gen-z-behaves-buys-builds-online.

99   Dugan shares: Mary Ellen Dugan, interview with the authors, September 2019.

99   Lisa Utzschneider is CEO at Integral Ad Science: Lisa Utzschneider, interview with the authors, September 2019.

100 as the Business Roundtable: Maggie Fitzgerald, "The CEOs of Nearly 200 Companies Just Said Shareholder Value Is No Longer Their Main Objective," CNBC, August 19, 2019, https://www.cnbc.com/2019/08/19/the-ceos-of-nearly-two-hundred-companies-say-shareholder-value-is-no-longer-their-main-objective.html.

101 Lisa Utzschneider at IAS sees: Lisa Utzschneider, interview with the authors, September 2019.

103 Arlo Gilbert is the founder of Osano: Arlo Gilbert, interview with the authors, August 2019.

7: WHAT GEN Z IS BUYING

109 The lingerie frontrunner reported: Sophie Alexander, et al.,"Victoria's Secret Has More Than a Jeffrey Epstein Problem," Bloomberg, July 29, 2019, https://www.bloomberg.com/news/articles/2019-07-29/victoria-s-secret-has-more-than-a-jeffrey-epstein-problem.

112 according to a study by consumer research firm Whistle: Whistle, "From Nerdy to Norm: Gen-Z Connects Via Gaming," 2018, https://www.whistlesports.com/report-from-nerdy-to-normal.

112 Our own research studies found: The Center for Generational Kinetics, "The State of Gen Z 2018," 2018, GenHQ.com.

112 According to a study by Nielsen: Nielsen, "Millennials on Millennials: Gaming Media Consumption," 2019, https://www.nielsen.com/wp-content/uploads/sites/3/2019/06/millennials-on-millennials-gaming-media-consumption-report.pdf.

112 Andrea Brimmer, chief marketing and PR officer at Ally Financial: Andrea Brimmer, interview with the authors, September 2019.

113 Unify Square and Osterman Research: Eileen Brown, "Millennials Are

Twice as Likely to Use Unapproved Collaboration Apps in the Workplace," ZDNet, August 14, 2019, https://www.zdnet.com/article/millennials-are-twice-as-likely-to -use-unapproved-collaboration-apps-in-the-workplace.

115 popular musician Marshmello: Martin Barnes, "The Past, Present & Future of Advertising Within Video Games," *Trendjackers,* February 25, 2019, https://trendjackers.com/the-past-present-future-of-advertising-within-video -games/.

118 a study by research firm Packaged Facts: Packaged Facts, "Gen Z and Millennials as Pet Market Consumers: Dogs, Cats, Other Pets," February 16, 2018, https://www.packagedfacts.com/Millennials-Gen-Pet-Consumers-Dogs-Cats -Pets-11268949/.

120 Andrea Brimmer recalls: Andrea Brimmer, interview with the authors, September 2019.

122 The *Wall Street Journal* reported: Adrienne Roberts, "Driving? The Kids Are So Over It," *Wall Street Journal*, April 20, 2019, https://www.wsj.com/articles /driving-the-kids-are-so-over-it-11555732810.

123 choosing sedans over SUVs: "Decoding Gen Z the Car Buyer," *Automotive News*, June 17, 2019, https://www.autonews.com/sponsored/decoding -gen-z-car-buyer.

123 John Fitzpatrick is the CEO of Force Marketing: John Fitzpatrick, interview with the authors, December 2019.

125 91% of Gen Z tell us: The Center for Generational Kinetics, "The State of Gen Z 2019," 2019, GenHQ.com.

125 according to data from TransUnion: Ben Lane, "Forget Waiting on Millennials, Gen Z Is Starting to Buy Homes," *Housing Wire*, August 15, 2019, https://www.housingwire.com/articles/49863-forget-waiting-on-millennials-gen-z -is-starting-to-buy-homes.

126 The *New York Times* reported: Lisa Prevost, "Forget Tanning Beds. College Students Today Want Uber Parking," June 25, 2019, https://www.nytimes .com/2019/06/25/business/college-dorm-uber-amenities.html?.

126 household items connected to the Internet: WP Engine and The Center for Generational Kinetics, "Future of the Internet," 2018.

127 alert them before they need it: WP Engine and The Center for Generational Kinetics, "The Future of Digital Experiences: How Gen Z Is Changing Everything," 2017, WPengine.com.

127 In our 2017 State of Gen Z Study: The Center for Generational Kinetics, "The State of Gen Z 2017," 2017, GenHQ.com.

8: EARNING BRAND LOYALTY WITH GEN Z

133 with a net loss of $1.2 billion: Sprint, "Sprint Returns to Net Operating Revenue Growth, Near-Record Operating Income, and Positive Adjusted Free Cash

Flow with Fiscal Year 2016 Results," May 3, 2017, https://s21.q4cdn.com/487940
486/files/doc_financials/quarterly/2016/Q4/1-Fiscal-4Q16-Earnings-Release
-FINAL.pdf.

134 one person on Reddit gave Sprint the thumbs-up: miversen33, "How Sprint
Leveraged Gen Z to Pivot Their Brand," Reddit, August 25, 2017, https://www
.reddit.com/r/Sprint/comments/6vz22l/how_sprint_leveraged_gen_z_to_pivot
_their_brand/.

135 from $1.2 billion in *net losses* to a *net income* of $7.4 billion: Sprint, "Sprint
Delivers Best Financial Results in Company History with Highest Ever Net Income
and Operating Income in Fiscal Year 2017," May 2, 2018, https://s21.q4cdn.com
/487940486/files/doc_financials/quarterly/2017/q4/Fiscal-4Q17-Earnings-Release
-FINAL.pdf.

135 As Mary Ellen Dugan from WP Engine says: Mary Ellen Dugan, interview with
the authors, September 2019.

138 and more than 185,000 beanies: Love Your Melon, accessed November 25,
2019, https://loveyourmelon.com/pages/giving.

   Leigh Buchanan, "How These 2 Millennial Founders Rallied 13,000 College
Students to Help Kids Battling Cancer," October 8, 2018, https://www.inc.com
/leigh-buchanan/2018-inc5000-love-your-melon.html.

140 Consumer research by Narvar reveals: Narvar, "The State of Returns: What
Today's Shoppers Expect," 2018, https://see.narvar.com/rs/249-TEC-877/images
/Consumer-Report-Returns-2018-4.3.pdf.

9: CUSTOMER ENGAGEMENT AND AWARENESS

145 In 2018, Jason Cook and his marketing team: Jason Cook, interview with the
authors, August 2019.

148 In our 2018 State of Gen Z Study: The Center for Generational Kinetics,
"The State of Gen Z 2018," 2018, GenHQ.com.

149 our 2019 national study revealed: The Center for Generational Kinetics,
"The State of Gen Z 2019," 2019, GenHQ.com.

152 Gen Z is the first generation: Mary Ellen Dugan, interview with the authors,
September 2019.

155 encourage photo taking and sharing: eHotelier Editor, "Make Your Hotel
Instagram-Friendly with These Redesign Tips," *eHotelier*, June 24, 2015, https://
insights.ehotelier.com/insights/2015/06/24/make-your-hotel-instagram-friendly
-with-these-redesign-tips/.

   IKEA Hotell, accessed November 25, 2019, https://ikeahotell.se/en/story/.

160 In our 2018 State of Gen Z Study: The Center for Generational Kinetics, "The
State of Gen Z 2018," 2018, GenHQ.com.

160 in our 2017 State of Gen Z Study: The Center for Generational Kinetics, "The
State of Gen Z 2017," 2017, GenHQ.com.

10: GETTING THE RIGHT START WITH GEN Z EMPLOYEES

167 and then "ghosted" or disappeared on the company: Karen Gilchrist, "Employees Keep 'Ghosting' Their Job Offers—and Gen Zs Are Leading the Charge," CNBC, April 24, 2019, https://www.cnbc.com/2019/04/24/employees -are-ghosting-their-job-offers-gen-z-is-leading-the-charge.html.

168 According to the U.S. Bureau of Labor Statistics: "Civilian Labor Force Participation Rate by Age, Sex, Race, and Ethnicity," U.S. Bureau of Labor Statistics, accessed November 25, 2019, https://www.bls.gov/emp/tables/civilian -labor-force-participation-rate.htm.

169 Our 2018 State of Gen Z Study found: The Center for Generational Kinetics, "The State of Gen Z 2018," 2018, GenHQ.com.

169 research from Instant Financial reveals that 76%: Instant, national study on generational work behaviors, 2017, https://www.instant.co/.

169 spend a year working there: Convergys and The Center for Generational Kinetics, "Attracting and Retaining Millennials in Contact Center Careers," 2017, https://genhq.com/wp-content/uploads/2018/12/Convergys_White-Paper2.pdf.

169 42% of college-aged Gen Z: PLRB and The Center for Generational Kinetics, "Insurance Claims as a Millennial Career: An Unexpectedly Great Fit for the Next Generation of Employees," 2016, https://www.plrb.org/distlearn/plrb /webinars_tutorials/handouts/PLRBMillennialWhitePaper.pdf.

170 in our 2018 State of Gen Z Study: The Center for Generational Kinetics, "The State of Gen Z 2018," 2018, GenHQ.com.

171 Only 24% of Gen Z: The Center for Generational Kinetics, "Gen Z and Work," 2018, GenHQ.com.

171 Goldman Sachs Media Kitchen team reported that: "From the 8th Annual Shorty Awards: Goldman Sachs & Snapchat," Shorty Awards, accessed November 25, 2019, https://shortyawards.com/8th/goldman-sachs-snapchat.

171 McDonald's has used what it calls "Snaplications": Jennifer Calfas, "McDonald's Is Using a New Method to Recruit Young Employees—Snapchat," *Fortune*, June 13, 2017, https://fortune.com/2017/06/13/mcdonalds-snapchat-jobs-2/.

172 AT&T has realized: Lorraine Mirabella, "Get Ready for Gen Z, Employers. First Hint: They're Not Millennials," *Seattle Times*, June 4, 2019, https://www.seattletimes.com/explore/careers/get-ready-for-gen-z-employers-first -hint-theyre-not-millennials/.

172 Gen Z first turn to friends: The Center for Generational Kinetics, "Gen Z and Work," 2018, GenHQ.com.

173 Ronald Kasner is president and COO of iCIMS: Ronald Kasner, interview with the authors, September 2019.

173 Salesforce has a special referral program: Neelie Verlinden, "7 Brilliant Employee Referral Programs Examples," Academy to Innovate HR (AIHR), accessed November 25, 2019, https://www.digitalhrtech.com/employee-referral

-programs-examples/. Sarah Boutin, "Behind the Scenes at Salesforce: Our #1 Recruiting Secret," *Salesforce blog*, January 14, 2015, https://www.salesforce.com /blog/2015/01/behind-scenes-salesforce-our-1-recruiting-secret.html.

173   Cole explains: Kat Cole, interview with the authors, September 2019.

174   78% of college-aged Gen Z: PLRB and The Center for Generational Kinetics, "Turning Millennial and Gen Z Job Seekers Into Job Applicants," 2016.

175   Brent Pearson is the founder of Enboarder: Brent Pearson, interview with the authors, August 2019.

175   Taylor shares: Tiffany Taylor, interview with the authors, September 2019.

176   shares similar insight: Kat Cole, interview with the authors, September 2019.

180   In our 2018 State of Gen Z Study: The Center for Generational Kinetics, "The State of Gen Z 2018," 2018, GenHQ.com.

180   Tiffany Taylor and her HR team: Tiffany Taylor, interview with the authors, September 2019.

182   Ron Kasner at iCIMS notes: Ronald Kasner, interview with the authors, September 2019.

183   What would make Gen Z apply immediately?: PLRB and The Center for Generational Kinetics, "Turning Millennial and Gen Z Job Seekers Into Job Applicants," 2016.

186   Ron Kasner and the iCIMS research team: Ronald Kasner, interview with the authors, September 2019.

11: UNLOCKING THE GEN Z EMPLOYEE'S LONG-TERM POTENTIAL

194   Research published in *Harvard Business Review*: Dan Cable, Francesca Gino, and Bradley Staats, "The Powerful Way Onboarding Can Encourage Authenticity," *Harvard Business Review,* November 26, 2015, https://hbr.org /2015/11/the-powerful-way-onboarding-can-encourage-authenticity.

194   Brent Pearson and his team at Enboarder: Brent Pearson, interview with the authors, August 2019.

195   Research by Gallop reveals: Susan Sorenson, "How Employee Engagement Drives Growth," Gallup, June 20, 2013, https://www.gallup.com /workplace/236927/employee-engagement-drives-growth.aspx.

195   according to our 2019 national study: The Center for Generational Kinetics, "The State of Gen Z 2019," 2019, GenHQ.com.

196   62% of Gen Z participants: The Center for Generational Kinetics, "The State of Gen Z 2018," 2018, GenHQ.com.

196   college graduates from the class of 2019: Ripplematch, "The State of the Gen Z Job Search," 2019, https://info.ripplematch.com/the-state-of-the-gen-z-job -search/.

197   Research from Glassdoor shows: Amanda Stansell, "The Next Generation

of Talent: Where Gen Z Wants to Work," Gallup, February 20, 2019, https://www .glassdoor.com/research/studies/gen-z-workers/.

197 in nine months or less: The Center for Generational Kinetics, "The State of Gen Z 2018," 2018, GenHQ.com.

200 explains Steve Barha, founder of Instant Financial: Steve Barha, interview with the authors, August 2019.

201 with the Distribution Contractors Association: Distribution Contractors Association and The Center for Generational Kinetics, "Gen Z and Millennial Employee Take-Action Playbook," 2019, dcaweb.org.

201 In our national study with DCA we found: Distribution Contractors Association and The Center for Generational Kinetics, "Gen Z and Millennial Employee Take-Action Playbook," 2019, dcaweb.org.

204 Ruth Ann Weiss is the owner of Eagle's Landing Day Camp: Ruth Ann Weiss, interview with the authors, August 2019.

205 national studies with young employees: Distribution Contractors Association and The Center for Generational Kinetics, "Gen Z and Millennial Employee Take-Action Playbook," 2019, dcaweb.org.

206 In our 2018 State of Gen Z Study: The Center for Generational Kinetics, "The State of Gen Z 2018," 2018, GenHQ.com.

208 In our 2017 State of Gen Z Study: The Center for Generational Kinetics, "The State of Gen Z 2017," 2017, GenHQ.com.

210 In our 2017 State of Gen Z Study: The Center for Generational Kinetics, "The State of Gen Z 2017," 2017, GenHQ.com.

211 Our 2018 State of Gen Z Study showed: The Center for Generational Kinetics, "The State of Gen Z 2018," 2018, GenHQ.com.

217 we found that 85%: The Center for Generational Kinetics, "The State of Gen Z 2018," 2018, GenHQ.com.

217 Their CEO, Sean Gordon, shared with us: Sean Gordon, interview with the authors, August 2019.

219 Deloitte invested $300 million into Deloitte University: Dan Gingiss, "How Deloitte's $300 Million Investment in Employee Experience Is Paying Off," *Forbes*, April 30, 2019, https://www.forbes.com/sites/dangingiss/2019/04/30/how-deloittes -300-million-investment-in-employee-experience-is-paying-off/#174e1ce6ecc1.

219 one of the top companies for new graduates to work in 2019: Vicky Valet, "America's Best Employers for New Graduates 2018," *Forbes,* September 5, 2018, https://www.forbes.com/sites/vickyvalet/2018/09/05/americas-best-employers -for-new-graduates-2018/#4554a7cc2894.

   Adobe Sales Academy, accessed November 25, 2019, https://blogs.adobe.com /adobelife/adobe-sales-academy/asa-learning-experience/.

221 In our 2018 State of Gen Z Study: The Center for Generational Kinetics, "The State of Gen Z 2018," 2018, GenHQ.com.

LOOKING AHEAD: THE DISRUPTIVE 10

226 Morgan Stanley and BCG: "Shared Mobility on the Road of the Future," Morgan Stanley Research, 2016, www.morganstanley.com/ideas/car-of-future-is -autonomous-electric-shared-mobility.

227 Over half (52%) of Gen Z: Cognizant and The Center for Generational Kinetics, "Gen Z: The World by the Thumbs," 2019, https://www.cognizant.com/gen-z.

227 60% of Gen Z: Cognizant and The Center for Generational Kinetics, "Gen Z: The World by the Thumbs," 2019, https://www.cognizant.com/gen-z.

230 When it comes to AI: Ultimate Software and The Center for Generational Kinetics, "National Research Study," 2018.

230 How Gen Z feels about smart devices: Cognizant and The Center for Generational Kinetics, "Gen Z: The World by the Thumbs," 2019, https://www .cognizant.com/gen-z.

232 48% of Gen Z think that AI: Ultimate Software and The Center for Generational Kinetics, "National Research Study," 2018.

INDEX

ABOUT THE AUTHORS

About Jason Dorsey

Jason Dorsey is the leading Gen Z, Millennial, and generations key-note speaker and researcher. He has received more than a thousand standing ovations for his keynote presentations around the world, for audiences of sixteen to sixteen thousand.

As cofounder and president of The Center for Generational Kinetics (CGK), Jason and his research team have led numerous generational research studies and consulting projects to solve challenges for many of the biggest global brands in industries ranging from technology and healthcare to retail and financial services.

Jason's passion is separating generational myth from truth so leaders can drive faster results. His specialty is uncovering hidden drivers to rapidly increase sales, strengthen workforces, and lead innovation *across generations. Adweek* called Jason a "research guru."

A bestselling author at age eighteen, Jason has appeared in more than three hundred media interviews, including on *60 Minutes, Today, The Early Show,* CNN, and CNBC, and in a *New York Times* cover story. He is known for discovering that Millennials are not tech-dependent but tech-savvy and that Millennials are breaking into two generations, Mega-llennials and Me-llennials. Jason's most famous quote is "Technology is only new if you remember it the way it was before."

Jason serves on public and private company boards, and actively advises CEOs, corporate boards, venture capital, startup founders, and private equity. To contact Jason Dorsey for a customized keynote or executive presentation, board or advisory role, or custom research, please visit JasonDorsey.com.

Twitter: @JasonDorsey
Instagram: @Jason_Dorsey
LinkedIn: Jason Dorsey

About Denise Villa, PhD

Denise Villa, PhD, is the CEO, cofounder, and visionary behind The Center for Generational Kinetics (CGK). Dr. Villa had the original idea to lead research that would separate generational myth from truth so leaders could make better decisions across generations.

Dr. Villa leads the research and insights team at CGK. She has led custom research for senior leadership in global brands from entertainment and insurance to healthcare and consumer technology. She has delivered research-based presentations to leaders from New York City to Miami, Dallas, and Las Vegas.

Dr. Villa has been featured as a generational expert in numerous media outlets, including a feature story in the *Washington Post* about her work with Gen Z, as well publications including the *Wall Street Journal*.

Dr. Villa completed her undergraduate work at the University of Texas at Austin and her master's and doctorate at Texas State University. She was a finalist in Profiles in Power and the Woman's Way Business Awards.

In addition to leading CGK, Dr. Villa runs a real estate development company and serves as a board member or advisor on several Austin nonprofit boards. She is an avid runner, and loves the outdoors and homemade Mexican food.

To contact Dr. Villa for a customized research presentation, board

of directors or advisory role, or custom research by CGK, please visit
GenHQ.com or DeniseVilla.com.

Twitter: @DrDeniseVilla
LinkedIn: Denise Villa Phd

About The Center for Generational Kinetics

The Center for Generational Kinetics (CGK) is the leading Gen Z, Millennial, and generations research, consulting, and keynote-speaking firm. CGK's expert team has served over seven hundred clients around the world, representing many of the biggest brands and almost every major industry, including B2B technology, financial services, consumer technology, banking, insurance, hoteliers, manufacturing, retail, restaurants, apparel, governments, associations, healthcare, private equity, and many more.

CGK's talent is uncovering new ways to solve generational challenges—from recruiting to sales—while bringing a positive, actionable perspective about generations. Our PhD-led team includes researchers, strategists, graphic designers, consultants, and acclaimed keynote speakers. CGK's keynote speakers have headlined events around the world, for audiences from sixteen to sixteen thousand—and over one hundred thousand participants at a single event. Recent speaking event locations range from Singapore and Paris to Amsterdam, London, and Mexico City.

CGK has led numerous original research studies on four continents in multiple languages. Each study and consulting project CGK leads is unique to the client, because every client has a unique generational challenge: from recruiting Gen Z and developing Millennial management talent to driving product innovation and selling across five generations. CGK uses a frontline approach, combining quantitative and qualitative research with deep generational expertise to uncover new insights, hidden trends, and specific actions that solve urgent challenges for clients.

CGK believes *every* generation brings value. We also believe that generations are not a box but powerful clues to drive greater connection, trust, influence, and results.

CGK's research team invented generational context™, a unique approach to understanding and solving generational challenges. This approach leverages the research strengths and expertise of CGK, including quantitative and qualitative research, along with the research and data provided by clients.

CGK is a majority female and minority-owned business. We are passionate about driving results for leaders of every generation. To contact CGK for custom generational speaking, research, or a media interview, please visit GenHQ.com.